NARRATIVE OF JAMES WILLIAMS
AN AMERICAN SLAVE

NARRATIVE OF JAMES WILLIAMS
AN AMERICAN SLAVE

ANNOTATED EDITION

Edited by Hank Trent

Louisiana State University Press Baton Rouge

Published by Louisiana State University Press

Manufactured in the United States of America
FIRST PRINTING

DESIGNER: Mandy McDonald Scallan
TYPEFACE: Whitman
PRINTER AND BINDER: Maple Press

Frontispiece: Engraving of James Williams by Patrick Reason, originally published in 1838 edition of *Narrative of James Williams*

Library of Congress Cataloging-in-Publication Data

Williams, James, 1805–
Narrative of James Williams, an American slave / edited by Hank Trent.
— Annotated edition.
pages cm
Includes bibliographical references and index.
ISBN 978-0-8071-5102-0 (cloth : alkaline paper) — ISBN 978-0-8071-5103-7 (pdf) — ISBN 978-0-8071-5104-4 (epub) — ISBN 978-0-8071-5105-1 (mobi) 1. Williams, James, 1805– 2. Slaves—Alabama—Biography. 3. Slavery—Alabama—History—19th century. 4. Slaves—Virginia—Powhatan County—Biography. 5. Fugitive slaves—United States—Biography. 6. Underground railroad—Pennsylvania—Philadelphia Region. I. Trent, Hank, 1959– II. Title.
E444.W74 2014
306.3'62092—dc23
[B]

2012048441

The paper in this book meets the guidelines for permanence and durability of the Committee on Production Guidelines for Book Longevity of the Council on Library Resources. ♾

A special thank-you to my wife, Linda Tope Trent, for her assistance in research, and to Silvana Siddali at Saint Louis University for her assistance on the way to publication

CONTENTS

INTRODUCTION

The fugitive who arrived at Emmor Kimber's home on Christmas Day 1837 seemed different from the numerous enslaved people the wealthy old Quaker had helped along the Underground Railroad over the years. Like many, James Williams arrived alone, tired, poorly clothed, and afraid of capture. But as he rested and talked about his years in slavery, he impressed Kimber not only with the story of his adventures but also with his forthright manner, his impressive memory, and, as other abolitionists described him, his "expressive countenance shadowing forth 'sorrow rather than anger'—a symmetrical figure, graceful in its movements—an intelligence that seemed to be the result of acquaintance with the style and usages of the best society in the South."[1] Close to thirty, he stood about five foot ten, slightly taller than average, with a complexion that showed the influence of the wealthy white man he claimed as his grandfather. Even his Alabama owner had grudgingly called him a "likely fellow" in a runaway notice.[2]

Williams described his life as a body servant to a kind master in Virginia, the horrors of slavery he had witnessed in Alabama, and finally his escape alone on foot a thousand miles, to Carlisle, Pennsylvania. Quaker families had passed him eastward from there, until now he had arrived here at Emmor Kimber's in Kimberton, outside of Philadelphia. Kimber was the richest of the Quakers who had aided him as well as the most educated. Besides owning substantial property in the town that bore his name, Kimber and his family ran a respectable boarding school, training girls to become teachers. He had written a few books on educational and religious topics, so he could recognize a natural-born narrator when he met one, and Williams intrigued him.[3]

The immediate problem, however, was securing Williams's safety. Some fugitives ended their journey in the Quaker communities around Philadelphia, but Williams's horror at the prospect of being recaptured made clear he would need to be transported farther. The ports of New York City opened up numerous directions for flight—Boston, Canada, England—but sending Williams to New York also suggested another possibility to Kimber.

Earlier in the year he had attended the Pennsylvania Anti-Slavery Convention in Harrisburg, where Lewis Tappan, representing the New York–based American Anti-Slavery Society, spoke about the efforts of his organization. The quantity of antislavery publications emanating from the New York offices was impressive: seventy agents were hawking four different papers, resulting in twenty-eight thousand copies going out each month, publicizing the evils of slavery and recruiting for the cause of abolition. Tappan had ended with a plea for donations and support to continue the publishing campaign.[4] Kimber decided to write him in New York, explaining that he had a fugitive he needed to send there for safety. But he also must have realized the power that Williams's eyewitness testimony could have in one of Tappan's publications—if it proved to be true.

The reality behind memoirs of enslaved people has intrigued scholars to this day, but until now most have considered the authenticity of Williams's story resolved. Basing their opinions mainly on an investigation in 1838 by an Alabama newspaper editor, historians have generally concluded it to be the fanciful tale of an imposter who perhaps was never even a slave or, if he was, not under the circumstances he described.

This annotated edition provides independent evidence for the first time that confirms Williams was an actual enslaved man in Virginia and Alabama and that most of the slaveholders he mentioned existed, with the names he used or close phonetic variations. It also identifies his owners in both states, explains how he altered his story to throw investigators off the track, points out where he inserted fictional elements, and includes other extensive details of his life not in the narrative, including some adventures as exciting as anything he told but which he chose not to reveal. Rather than being a free conman or a puppet of the abolitionists, as many have suspected, Williams was a genuine freedom seeker and a skilled narrator, able to shape his own real life into a cohesive, romanticized story.

REJECTED AS A FRAUD

When John W. Blassingame, Gilbert Osofsky, and other historians began to look anew at slave narratives in the late twentieth century, they discarded Williams's without further investigation. Blassingame explained, "Alabama whites proved [it] was an out-right fraud."[5] In 2001 K. K. Ruthven noted it as an example of a fake slave narrative, stating it was written by "a free and opportunistic African American called James Williams."[6] Opportunistic he may have been, but free he was not.

Because the narrative had supposedly already been proven to be a fraud, other historians could feel safe in pouncing on inaccuracies that were not in fact its weak points. Laura Browder, writing on ethnic impersonators, found it "hard to believe that an abolitionist [who apparently wrote the narrative] did not know that slave marriages were not legally recognized, that slave women were the sexual property of their masters, and that it was far more common for slaves to be separated from those they considered their spouses than it was for them to be sent on honeymoons by their masters." Yet we now know that both Williams's Virginia and Alabama owners acknowledged that Harriet was his wife and tried even harder to keep them together, selling them as a family to Alabama rather than separating them, as Williams claimed.

Browder also scoffed at the "interracial congregation" where Williams's brother preached, not noticing the clear reference to the interracial First Baptist Church of Richmond, and chided Williams for turning his flight to freedom into "a tour through a fantasy of the American Wild West, transposed onto a Deep South landscape," apparently not recognizing his description of the Federal Road through Alabama's Creek Indian territory. Ironically, she concluded, "had 'James Williams' done a little more research into the names and places of the South, his narrative might never have been exposed as false."[7] Yet he had actually experienced slavery firsthand in the states he wrote about and traveled at least four times between the upper and lower South.

Lara Langer Cohen, writing in 2012 on the "fabrication of American literature," attempted to research the narrative anew but was stymied by the same incorrect assumptions as investigators in 1838 had been. Abolitionist Lydia Maria Child, like others over the years, had suspected that Williams had told the truth but "had resorted to the common artfulness of a slave, with regard to *names*."[8] In fact, he had generally done just the opposite, using real names of white people, even if he fictionalized their activities or locations. Cohen therefore came up empty-handed, producing only more negative evidence. She reported that none of the "names of any of the neighboring planters in Alabama appear in the 1840 census for Greene County," missing the fact that they appeared in the census for Dallas County. She tried relying on dates, "if names were too dangerous to reveal," and looked for the obituary of Williams's master in 1832. His owner, Joseph Janey, did die in 1832, but Janey was one of the few white men's names that Williams *had* omitted by readjusting the story.

She checked for plantations with the large quantity of slaves he had reported, not knowing he had exaggerated the number.

In a final attempt to trace him, Cohen surmised that "common practice would have dictated that his owner advertise for him when he ran away," noting that Jean Fagan Yellin had discovered a runaway ad to help authenticate Harriet Jacobs as the author of *Incidents in the Life of a Slave Girl.* But she found "no advertisements for a runaway from Alabama resembling Williams . . . from the summer of 1837 to the end of the year in any of the major newspapers of the South" that she examined, not realizing that Williams had changed the date and that she needed to look in newspapers from 1835, when his owner published ads in five papers for over three months. She concluded: "Of course, it is difficult to understand what Williams's book *does* without understanding what it *is*. Did he write a true history, altering minor details for self-protection? A wholesale fabrication? A fictionalized frame relating true incidents, lived or reported?"[9]

Now readers can have answers to those questions and gain a better understanding of what the book is, to help them interpret what it does. Yet for those wanting insight into the past, the greater question is not whether any name or date is accurate but whether Williams honestly depicted his unique view of life as an enslaved man. Many incidents that he related would have occurred in the loneliness of plantation fields, witnessed only by him, other slaves, or a few white men who apparently left no record. His words captured events and facets of people that might otherwise never have been preserved, and yet their very rarity allows for no corroboration.

Some of the people who appear in the book were asked about it at the time and denied the incidents: "I have not only no recollection of any such occurrence, but am satisfied that none such ever did take place."[10] Other contemporaries substantiated the descriptions: "the lady knew the wife of George Larrimore, Jr. . . . and declared that such was the accuracy of the delineation of her character, that she would have recognized it without her name being mentioned."[11]

In many instances the annotation provided here can only offer context to suggest whether something would be plausible or implausible, without providing definite answers. In those cases the reader can be no more satisfied than the abolitionists who heard what *seemed* like a true story yet could not verify it. But with names and places tied to real people, the narrative at least now can be examined for the first time as the work of a genuine enslaved man, who had a surprising and complex life story even beyond the book he left.

TO NEW YORK CITY

Emmor Kimber's concern, however, was more immediate. Pennsylvania Quakers knew that slave catchers sometimes sent imposters to discover safe houses and routes.[12] This intelligent, humble, forthright man with the heartrending story was either someone who deserved all the help that abolitionists could give him or a sly, rehearsed pretender. In his letter Kimber included an outline of what Williams had described about his past. Perhaps the New Yorkers could question him and find holes in the story because Kimber and his abolitionist friends nearby could not. Keeping secret the trap he had set to test Williams's tale, Kimber looked for a conductor to convey him to Philadelphia and then on to New York.

Approaching the problem with a binary mind-set—that Williams was either a genuine runaway or a liar—might have prevented the abolitionists from suspecting a more complex truth. Only months later, after a puzzling and frustrating series of events, they realized "it may have been that James could not feel confidence in his new friends sufficiently strong to persuade him to trust them with the *whole* secret of his life."[13]

If Underground Railroad conductors needed to worry about slave catchers' decoys, slaves needed to worry about criminals disguised as Underground Railroad conductors.[14] Williams already felt he had wasted two years of his life as a victim of one such individual, but he knew white men expected black men to be humble, grateful, and show no suspicion, so he played the role necessary to succeed at this second chance for freedom. Despite giving a detailed account, full of specific names and places, he tailored his story to omit several important pieces of information: the names of his owners in Virginia and Alabama, their exact locations, and his recapture during his first escape from Alabama. He apparently changed the names of most enslaved people, except his wife and brother, and also failed to mention his own birth name, Shadrach Wilkins, by which all his former masters knew him.

These abolitionists, whose help he so desperately needed, seemed to respond best to sincerity and honesty, so he recollected all the other accurate names, places, and facts he could muster, spinning them into a cohesive narrative that smoothed over the gaps left by the information he chose to withhold. Rather than make up fictional names, he claimed to have grown up in the home of real-life George Larimer in Virginia and to have been sent to work on Larimer's nonexistent absentee-owned plantation in Alabama. This allowed him to leave out the name of Larimer's mother-in-law, Mrs. Joseph Janey, who was his actual Virginia owner, as well as the name of Caleb Tate, the Alabama planter to whom she sold him.

As far as Emmor Kimber knew, Williams had arrived in Carlisle, Pennsylvania, on December 9, 1837, directly after a four-month journey alone on foot from Alabama. After that the facts were in no dispute: abolitionists in Carlisle helped him to the home of shrewd old Quaker Daniel Gibbons, whose long experience as an Underground Railroad stationmaster gave him a talent for identifying slave catchers' decoys. Gibbons accepted him as genuine and let him rest his sore feet, probably commiserating because Gibbons himself suffered from chronic lameness.[15]

A few days later Gibbons asked his nineteen-year-old son, Joseph, to convey Williams to Lindley Coates's home in Lancaster County. Heading east toward Philadelphia, he arrived at Coates's on December 20 and stayed for two days. Coates was yet another Quaker long experienced in helping runaways, and "few had more skill than he in detecting and exposing the fallacies of error," but he was also convinced of Williams's honesty.[16] Coates forwarded him to the home of John Vickers, a Quaker potter and another experienced conductor. He rested there until Christmas Day, when Vickers sent him on to Emmor Kimber's.[17]

What Kimber did not know, and what the honest-sounding runaway did not tell, was that Williams had actually arrived in Carlisle from New Orleans, by way of Cincinnati, Ohio. His life over the past two years had been at least as interesting as any story he told, but for whatever reason—perhaps because it included his own betrayal of an abolitionist—he covered it over by adding two years to his time in slavery, then simplifying his escape into a straight trip from Alabama to Pennsylvania. Now close to freedom once again, Williams pretended to trust these Quakers as they pretended to trust him. He acted as one who "had suffered much from the 'slings and arrows of outrageous fortune'—who had courageously buffetted its waves, and had found, unexpectedly, when nearly spent, a rock on which he might temporarily rest," as if he had full confidence in these Underground Railroad conductors.[18]

He mentioned that his wife and children were enslaved in Virginia, only about two hundred miles away. Apparently, no one offered to help liberate them—fortunately for the integrity of his story, given that they were actually still in Alabama—but the Quakers were enthusiastic about aiding him personally. After writing ahead to Tappan, Kimber found a conductor to convey Williams to New York City. Williams pretended to be the white man's servant as they traveled unnoticed on the steamboat and railroad cars, probably up the Delaware River to Bordenton, then by rail to Amboy and by boat again, arriving in New York City on New Year's Day 1838.[19]

The abolitionists installed him there in the home of John W. Hill at 604 Water Street, a block back from the East River. Hill, a woodturner sympathetic to the antislavery cause, also took in boarders, and he currently had an international gathering of abolitionists and refugees. Staying with him were Massachusetts poet John Greenleaf Whittier, German-born Rev. Charles Follen, and a friend of Follen's, an Italian political refugee from the ill-fated attempts to unite Italy, who had some talent as an artist.[20] Whittier was working temporarily as a secretary for the American Anti-Slavery Society for eighty dollars a month, after a newspaper position in Maine had fallen through. The antislavery work suited his Quaker abolitionist nature. Although he hated the expensive, dirty city, he enjoyed the pleasant view of City Hall Park across from the society's Nassau Street offices.[21] Follen had lost professorships in both Europe and at Harvard University due to his outspoken liberal views, so he had given up teaching to become a Unitarian minister and also now served on the American Anti-Slavery Society's executive committee.

Both the runaway slave and the Anti-Slavery Society members must have felt they had stumbled upon circumstances almost too good to be true. The group embraced their new boarder, who impressed them as much as he had Kimber. His life became a whirlwind of activity. Abolitionists peppered him with questions, then huddled secretly to compare their notes with Kimber's letter and to pore over maps of the South, checking towns and distances. They observed the scars on his back. Since he claimed to come from Alabama, they brought in James Birney, a former Alabama slave owner–turned–abolitionist, who was now living in New York and serving as an executive secretary of the society, to judge whether Williams's descriptions of that state sounded believable.

Later, Birney and Tappan recalled, "not withstanding all there was about James to command confidence, no means were left unessayed by those who conversed with him to test the truth of what he had related. He was examined and re-examined by different individuals. Difficulties did present themselves, yet they were found, on closer scrutiny, not to be irreconcileable with the probabilities of the case." They concluded, "The appearance, narration, &c., of James, seemed to carry conviction to the mind of every person who conversed with him, that his story was true in all the principal particulars."[22]

Williams asked for little, borrowed nothing, wanted no money, but "the fear of being retaken had fastened itself upon his mind with an agonizing hold. To escape it, he was willing to do anything—to go to the most secluded spot in the Union States—to Canada—any where, only that he might once feel safe from the pursuer." A few days after he arrived, his fear materialized. "Information was received that two white men were in pursuit of him, accompanied by a colored man, who knew James, and would be able at once to recognise him. The informant stated that they had been as far as Boston, and had just returned to this city."[23] This news "seemed to strike new dread into his soul; his slumbers became unquiet, and in his sleep he would cry out in alarm of the man-hunter."[24]

But rather than sending him safely out of the country immediately, the abolitionists sought to milk their unexpected find, even if it exposed him to additional risk. His story was too valuable for just an article. The executive committee wanted it as a book, the first full-length narrative by an escaped slave that the American Anti-Slavery Society would publish. They made their offer, implicitly if not explicitly: after he had dictated all the information to John Greenleaf Whittier, they would conduct him to safety by providing him passage to Liverpool, England. Williams agreed.

At Hill's house he sat down to his partnership with Whittier and began retelling his oft-repeated history, interrupted by curious visits from other abolitionists. The Italian refugee at the boardinghouse drew his portrait, which a local African American engraver, Patrick Reason, prepared as an illustration for the upcoming book.[25] Williams watched the abolitionists' reactions, concentrating on the parts that seemed to interest them most, such as descriptions of his overseer's brutality, and omitting the parts that reflected badly on him or on abolitionists in general. Nevertheless, it surely was not all an act. His natural gratitude and humility, his excellent memory and eye for detail, and his fairness to all involved consistently showed through. Although he was giving real names and choosing which incidents to exaggerate, make up, include, or omit so he could praise or condemn real people at will, "he gave way to no denunciatory language—no resentful expressions against his master who had deceived, nor against the monster Huckstep who had degraded and abused him. His story he must have known, needed no exaggeration—but rather a reduction from its realities, to secure for it the fullest confidence of those who were not fully conversant with the horrors of southern slavery."[26]

Williams portrayed himself as unable to read or write, but in the midst of the excitement he managed to send a letter to his sister, who belonged to the Hundley family of Essex County, Virginia, a few miles from his own former Virginia owner.[27] Unlike the crafted story he told the abolitionists, in the written letter he shared the full secret truth of how he had spent the last two years. Either he found a trustworthy person in New York, who would neither betray him to the abolitionists nor turn him in as a runaway slave, or else he was able to write the letter himself. In the narrative he mentioned that his brother was literate but that "the whites do not know that he can write, and have often wondered that he could preach so well without learning."[28] The same may have been true for himself.

The dictation went swiftly. Theodore Weld wrote to James Birney on the evening of January 12 that Whittier's book "will be out this week," though that date turned out to be somewhat optimistic. Whittier dated his introduction to the finished book on January 24, and on February 5 Weld revised his earlier announcement: "Whittier's book, 'James Williams' will be sent this week probably day after tomorrow."[29]

As promised, Lewis Tappan wrote Williams a glowing letter of introduction to British philanthropist and antislavery supporter John Cropper, and Williams boarded a ship for Liverpool. Again, on the other side of the ocean, he impressed those who met him. Joseph Sturge, Cropper's brother-in-law, wrote back to Tappan on April 30 that Cropper's "acquaintance with [Williams] fully confirmed your favorable account."[30] Finally safe from recapture, Williams disappeared into anonymity. Tappan and Birney reported that they heard no more after the April letter, "except that he was soon to sail from England for some one of the British colonies."[31]

His absentee fame in the United States, however, had just begun. Jubilant to have secured such a firsthand account of the horrors of slavery, the American Anti-Slavery Society mailed the newly published book free to every member of Congress, printed excerpts, and advertised it for sale in its publications.[32]

A CHALLENGER

The cruelties in Williams's narrative resembled what abolitionists had already gleaned from southern newspaper ads, which detailed the scars, brands, and injuries of slaves. Whittier had even included a handful of unrelated examples in his introduction, to bolster the believability of Williams's account. But the bulk of the narrative claimed to describe brutality performed in Greene County specifically, naming the plantation owner, overseer, and several neighbors. Word of the book soon reached John Beverly Rittenhouse, the young editor of the weekly *Alabama Beacon*. His newspaper was located in Greensborough, in the county that Williams had substituted for the real location of the Alabama plantation where he had lived.

Incensed at this libel, Rittenhouse jumped to protect his county's reputation with the fervor of a native son, although he had arrived there only a few years earlier. Born in the District of Columbia, he would abandon Alabama and the newspaper business two years later to accept the position of purser in the U.S. Navy. That career seemed to suit him better, for he followed it the rest of his long life, residing up and down the East Coast as far north as Boston in between shipboard service and serving on the Union side during the Civil War, though he still visited his adopted hometown occasionally. He never married, and he died in the Philadelphia Naval Asylum in 1874.[33]

But for now J. B. Rittenhouse rose to the task of indignantly representing Greene County. Unbeknownst to both him and the abolitionists, the actual location in Alabama where Williams had been enslaved was about fifty miles to the southeast, in Dallas County. Both counties were in the fertile Black Belt cotton-growing region, so the substitution sounded reasonable, except that Williams had also claimed the plantation belonged to his Virginia master's wife, rather than give the real owner's name. To make matters worse, he had exaggerated the number of slaves on it.

The sum of the details created a situation that would have made a splash even among the big cotton plantations in the area: a Virginia family named Larrimore moving down more than two hundred slaves to Alabama in the fall of 1833 and opening up fifteen hundred acres to cultivation. In fact, his Virginia owner had sold him and his family to Alabama resident Caleb Tate, who did own over a thousand acres in Dallas County, but there was no big splash of arrival. Tate, originally from Georgia, had lived in the county and managed his plantation with well under a hundred slaves for a decade, as he would continue to do until his death in 1841. Although he was influential in his own community, he had no particular connection to Greene County, and nothing about his situation matched the circumstances that Williams described, other than the names of several wealthy neighbors and perhaps his overseer as well.

On March 29, 1838, just a few weeks after the book left the press, Rittenhouse published the first attack in his newspaper: "We have been politely favored by our correspondent with the lying abolition pamphlet entitled the 'Narrative of James Williams,' copious extracts from which we find in the papers of that sect. We have not had leisure to give it that perusal which we design doing, but we are assured by some of the oldest residents of this county that it is a foul fester of falsehood, a miserably 'weak invention of the enemy.'"[34] The American Anti-Slavery Society gently returned fire in their newspaper, the *Emancipator:* "We hope the editor of the Beacon will make a thorough investigation . . . The story of James Williams made a strong impression of truthfulness on the minds of all in this city who heard it from his lips. If it is a 'foul fester of falsehood,' we shall be glad to be undeceived, for we know as well as they can tell us, that falsehood can not help our cause."

Rittenhouse began his investigation. He first asked some former residents of Powhatan County, Virginia, who happened to be living nearby, if they knew of any plantation up there named Mount Pleasant, owned by "the family Larrimore or Larrimer," where Williams claimed to have been born in 1805. By coincidence one of them had a grandfather who at the time owned an estate by that name, and he reported that no Larrimores had owned it then or since.

Rittenhouse crowed in the April 5 edition of his paper, "Thus we see that these Larrimores, a family described to be of immense wealth, magnificent style and highest connexions, are not only utterly unknown to all the Virginians, & they are many, with whom we have conversed, but that old residents of Powhatan, natives of the county, and living but a few miles from this plantation, are entirely ignorant of their name!!"[35] Unfortunately for Rittenhouse's efforts, just as Williams had changed Dallas to Greene County, he had changed Essex to Powhatan County. The plantation in Virginia from where he had been sold to Alabama was actually Monte Verde, near Bowler's Wharf, Essex County. Virginia State Delegate George Larimer (or Lorimer) still lived there with his wife and Williams's former owner, Adelaide Janey, who was Larimer's mother-in-law.[36] For a while, however, no one realized the real George Larimer's connection to "George Larrimore" in the narrative.

Although Rittenhouse was certain that no one named Larrimore owned so many acres and slaves in Greene County, Alabama, he checked the local county tax records to be sure, and "they contain no mention of such an individual or any one having the remotest resemblence [*sic*] to his name. The same also is the fact with regard to the names of Flincher & Goldsby, said to be neighboring planters [in Alabama], and Huckstep and Crop, two conspicuous dramatis personae."[37]

So intent was Rittenhouse on looking for Larrimore's plantation in Greene County, he missed the fact that he had now shifted into the real Alabamans in Williams's story. Armel Fincher, not Flincher, and Thornton Goldsby lived within a few miles of each other and also near Williams's actual owner, Caleb Tate, at Valley Creek (now Summerfield), Dallas County, Alabama. Fincher had a modest farm and a dozen or so slaves, but Goldsby's holdings had grown to over a hundred slaves and more than a thousand acres. Illiterate James W. Huckstep of Dallas County was the only man with that last name in any of the surrounding counties. Williams had claimed Huckstep was his master's overseer. *Crop* may have been a typesetter's misreading of *Cross* handwritten with a long *s* followed by a regular *s*, and several Cross families lived in the area. Two other neighbors mentioned in the book, Sturtivant and Ludlow, were also identifiable. Robert Sturdivant of Valley Creek was a friend and neighbor of Tate and Goldsby. Adam Ledlow interacted with Tate's family and Huckstep but resided in the western part of the county, matching Williams's report that Ludlow lived farther away.[38]

The editor of the *Beacon* and the abolitionists argued back and forth, focusing on the alleged Larrimore plantation of Greene County. Lewis Tappan wrote the *Beacon* on April 20, suggesting if there was no plantation in Greene County, "is there not one thus owned and managed in Perry, or Marengo county," edging closer to Dallas County, and offering alternate spellings: "George Larrimore, Lorimer, or some similar name." *Lorimer* was in fact one common spelling that the Virginia family used, more so even than *Larimer*.[39] But by focusing on Larrimore rather than the neighbors whom Williams named, and keeping the search close to Greene County, both sides missed the Tate plantation of Dallas County.

Yet Tappan and the other abolitionists could not bring themselves to believe Williams was lying entirely: "Persons of the first respectably [*sic*] in Pennsylvania and this city conversed with James at length; he was interrogated by gentlemen who have lived in Alabama, and who had traveled on the route he took to the free states; his travels were traced on the maps, and remarkable accuracy was found to exist between his statements, and the names of towns and rivers; and he stood 'confessed' an unassuming, intelligent, and upright man so far as we could determine."

Rittenhouse "kept up a running fire," as the abolitionists described it, by pointing out tidbits such as the fact that George Larrimore could not have attended the University of Virginia at age fourteen because it had not been founded yet—a mistake consequent on Williams having concealed the name of his real owner at that age. But Rittenhouse promised even more, declaring on May 10, "We have set on foot inquiries . . . by which we shall be enabled to set forth the manner in which these fictitious romances are usually contrived." Indeed, Rittenhouse would be the only investigator to uncover the real George Larimer.

GEORGE LARIMER OF VIRGINIA

The abolitionists, continuing to focus on the wrong counties in both Alabama and Virginia, became frustrated at finding nothing, while Rittenhouse struck gold. He managed to discover George Thacker Fauntleroy Larimer "residing in Essex county, Virginia, full 100 miles off" from Powhatan, who actually recognized Williams from the narrative. Rittenhouse printed a long letter from Larimer, which laid bare an accurate account of Williams's activities before, during, and after his time in Alabama. (The letter is reprinted in appendix A.)

With a touch of sarcasm, Larimer referred to the former slave as "Mr. Williams," something the abolitionists just could not bring themselves to do. They called him "James," the way white men usually referred to black men. But Larimer correctly exposed Williams's birth name, Shadrach Wilkins, and the name and location of his Alabama owner, Mr. Tate, whose post office "was a little place called Selma" (though he still erred in saying the county was Greene rather than Dallas). The bulk of his generally accurate letter revealed the gaps that Williams had created when he omitted any references to the Janeys and Tate as well as the fact that Williams had been accused—though not prosecuted—in a poisoning plot. In the same article with Larimer's letter, Rittenhouse published a letter from Henry S. Brooke of Richmond, denying an incident involving Brooke and Williams's unnamed brother, and another letter from a Powhatan resident, with more of the usual rebuttals from that county.

But just when Rittenhouse had finally uncovered the name of Williams's real master in Alabama and the location near Selma where he had actually been enslaved, the editor suddenly got busy. "We have not now time to pursue this matter," he wrote, as he printed the letter. Although he had investigated tenaciously until now, he did not bother to write Mr. Tate, in care of the Selma post office fifty miles away, to inquire if his overseer and neighbors had treated their slaves as horribly as Williams claimed. Carefully stopping while he was ahead, he published Larimer's letter as his crowning achievement and demanded the "full refutation of one of the most abandoned fabrications and attrocious calumnies of the times."

With Williams now safe from recapture in some unknown English colony, one might expect the abolitionists' greatest frustration would be an inability to extract the truth from Tate and his neighbors, who would surely refuse to give any incriminating evidence about themselves. Instead, Birney and Tappan took the opposite tack. Still hoping that the narrative contained the complete truth or nothing, they concluded that this George T. F. Larimer obviously was not the George Larrimore they were looking for, nor had he correctly identified the slave they knew. "There is not, except in the *surname*, a single point of coincidence between the writer, and James's young master . . . The single point on which the identity of the two [slaves] is made to rest is that they both had wives named *Harriet*."

Desperate to get a final jab at the slave owners, they noted "the unlawful conduct" of Mrs. Janey, who had sold her slave out of state after his attempt to poison Dr. Roy, "thus screening from punishment, one who had committed an enormous crime," and selling him to Mr. Tate, "who, for aught that appears, was ignorant of the character of 'Shadrak Wilkins,' and from whose service the said Shadrak did finally and successfully elope." With that odd expression almost of sympathy toward Tate on the loss of his errant servant—who surely was not their honest James—the investigation wound down.

Rittenhouse kept a strategic silence on behalf of the southerners. Birney and Tappan, acting as the investigating committee for the American Anti-Slavery Society, continued writing fruitless letters to ferret out the illusive Larrimore family of Powhatan County while holding in mind their long-term goal: to protect the reputation of the society, not necessarily to defend this particular narrative. Nevertheless, they were not ready to abandon their faith in Williams yet, and in fact their hunch in August 1838 about the core truth of the narrative was absolutely correct: "That James was a slave—that he was brought up or resided in Virginia—that he was transferred to the planting

South—that he was acquainted with the usages and conduct of large plantations there—that he had an opportunity of becoming acquainted with the atrocities (if any such are practiced) by overseers entrusted with the management of large estates—that he suffered himself much in his person from the cruelty of an overseer or master, of which his back gave shocking proof—that he made his escape from the far South (most probably from some part of Middle or South Alabama) we think is sufficiently certain."[40]

At the end of September they still held out hope, hinting they might later publish the names of some people who knew the Larrimore family, not making clear whether they referred to Larrimore of Powhatan or Larimer the Essex letter writer:

> [A] gentleman and lady, from Virginia, who were recently in this city, declared, after reading the Narrative, that they believed it to be substantially true; that they knew the parties mentioned generally; that the lady knew the wife of George Larrimore, Jr. (supposed to be Lorimer) and declared that such was the accuracy of the delineation of her character, that she would have recognized it without her name being mentioned. A gentleman of high respectability in this State, has a letter from a friend in Virginia, to whom he wrote inquiring as to the truth of the Narrative, stating that he has no doubt of its truth, and is acquainted, either personally or by reputation, with all the persons mentioned in it, as living in that quarter, except Larrimore. A lady of Virginia, now in this city, who is extensively acquainted in her own State, has declared that she knew all the persons named in the Narrative as living in Virginia, except Larrimore, and she knew him by reputation; that she knew, the estate on which James lived, and had no doubt of the truth, generally, of the Narrative.[41]

But as more responses arrived, things looked bleaker. Seven men wrote back, all denying any existence of the Larrimores and related families of Powhatan County or other details surrounding the Virginia portion of the narrative. The anonymous supporters either backed down or perhaps clarified they were talking about Larimer the letter writer, whom the abolitionists had insisted was the wrong man.

The American Anti-Slavery Society realized their investigation was failing. It would be better to admit defeat than to drag out the embarrassment. Concluding there was no doubt that "one of the parties has intentionally misrepresented," Birney and Tappan reassured the readers of the society's newspaper, the *Emancipator,* that they had not succumbed to the "prevailing prejudice, which would lead them to decide *of course,* or hastily, against a *black,* where his testimony was contradicted by a *white.*" But in the end they needed to do so, and without waiting for replies from Alabama, they concluded that "they cannot with propriety ask for the confidence of the community in any of the statements contained in the narrative." The Executive Committee approved the final announcement to end the debacle, which appeared in the October 25, 1838, *Emancipator:* "Resolved . . . that the publishing agent be directed to discontinue the sale of the work."[42]

Even after giving in only seven months following Rittenhouse's first objection, the society had to live with the fiasco. The following year a critic highlighted the damage:

> Some of the most influential literary emissions of the American Anti-Slavery Society are purely fictitious, and generally so exaggerated and highly coloured, or so unfaithful in not giving the whole truth, as to misrepresent the truth. "The narrative of James Williams," which has probably had more influence, and excited more feeling, than any other single document, and which was thought of sufficient importance to be made conspicuous in the last Annual Report of the Society, by devoting one third of a page to *attest its veracity,* notwithstanding the Abolitionists had been sufficiently advised, *that it was false.* They have at last been forced to make public confession, *that it is a fiction!* It is impossible to say, what proportion of the issues of this Society are of this character . . . but the exceeding avidity of the Abolitionists to take up and accredit such stories as "the Narrative of James Williams," directly in the face of rebutting and conclusive evidence, and the strong temptations in such circumstances to fiction, may fairly establish the presumption, that many of their issues are purely fictitious.[43]

THE REAL JAMES WILLIAMS

So who was this man, James Williams, and what was his actual story? The narrative offers clues that help fill in part of the outline of his life during the years of the narrative, but research from sources other than his own words gives a much fuller picture. Most of the period until the summer of 1835 is covered only briefly here, as it is discussed and sourced thoroughly in the notes to the narrative. The poisoning incident in 1834 and Williams's adventures after he escaped from Alabama, which he omitted from the narrative, are recounted in more detail here because they do not fit as well within the scope of the narrative's annotation.

Williams was born Shadrach Wilkins, along with his twin brother Meshech, to an enslaved woman, probably on a plantation in Essex County, Virginia, between 1805 and 1810. He grew into a young man "every way well proportioned" and evidently made the most of his natural advantages. His "neatness & activity," as one observer noted,[44] must have gained him favor as a servant among the politically influential families of Essex. Additionally, he apparently worked to ingratiate himself with his owners by displaying the personality they wished to see while hiding his own thoughts. Alluding to this talent under worse circumstances, he told how he had humored Huckstep the overseer: "Oh! how often have I laughed, at such times, when my heart ached within me."[45] As an accomplished household servant, he had probably felt in reality what he said in the narrative: "The early years of my life went by pleasantly. The bitterness of my lot I had not yet realized."[46]

He most likely lived near Tappahannock or Loretto, or possibly at times in Richmond, serving one or more families. Sometime before 1832, French-born Joseph Janey purchased him and brought him to Monte Verde plantation, overlooking the Rappahannock River near Bowler's Wharf, still in Essex County. Shadrach and his wife, an enslaved woman named Harriet, lived together there, while his sister was owned a few miles away at Rose Hill. Other relatives whom he mentioned in the narrative may have lived in the surrounding area.

When Joseph Janey died in 1832, Shadrach and Harriet's ownership passed to Janey's widow, Adelaide, a Frenchwoman from New Orleans who continued to manage the plantation. Her widowed daughter from her first marriage, Virginia Collins, also lived at Monte Verde. In the spring of 1833 Mrs. Collins's new husband, George Larimer, moved in too, becoming the only man in the Janey-Larimer family. Just as Shadrach later claimed to have played a role to please his overseer, he apparently had been successfully hiding some side of himself from Mrs. Janey as well. She must have trusted him because she had chosen him as her carriage driver, but that ended abruptly after she discovered what he did on August 7, 1834.[47]

POISONING PLOT

Warner, the slave of neighbor Dr. Augustus Gustavus Dunbar Roy, had attempted to run away, but he was caught and returned the same day. Angry and afraid of Dr. Roy's whipping, he decided to poison his master and mistress. The Roys had married earlier that year in March, and she was three or four months pregnant with their first child.[48]

Warner obtained some powders, probably from Dr. Roy's stock of medicines, including cobalt. It may have been an impure form containing arsenic and therefore harmful enough, but he also consulted with Shadrach next door, who obliged him by digging a better poison, which the slaves called "hug root," from a swampy area near one of the Monte Verde slave cabins—surely not the sort of activity Mrs. Janey would have expected from a trusted carriage driver.

Warner started the process of extracting the poison by steeping the root in a vial while plotting how to administer it. He discussed his plans in his master's kitchen with two other slaves owned by Dr. Roy, Tabby and Harriet, who had access to the Roys' food. This Harriet was a different woman than Shadrach's wife. Tabby helpfully suggested ways to administer the hug root, combining truly deadly suggestions, such as adding it to the Roys' milk, with the magical but actually harmless idea of laying it under a doorway that the Roys would cross, a common superstition.[49]

Harriet gave the first unsupportive response, announcing she would tell their owners. Despite Warner's threat that he would kill her too, she informed Mrs. Roy. On August 11 Dr. Roy confronted Warner, who confessed the entire plan, including the fact that Shadrach had helped. Soon afterward, the doctor must have informed his neighbors of the peril lurking in both their households. Being poisoned by one's own servants was a long-standing fear among slave owners.

More than just nearby residents, the Larimers and Janeys had known the Roys for years. In 1819 Dr. Roy's father had appointed Larimer's father as one of the men to divide up his estate, and Dr. Roy had witnessed the will of Mrs. Larimer's first husband in 1826.[50] Perhaps skeptical at first that his mother-in-law's servant would do such a thing, Larimer went down to the swampy area and found verification: the discarded tops of some dug-up roots. He took the stalks back to the doctor, who confirmed that the mysterious hug root was deadly poisonous hemlock. Dr. Roy reported the situation to the sheriff, who arrested all the slaves involved, including Shadrach.

Justice came swiftly. A week later the Essex County Court of Oyer and Terminer in Tappahannock found Warner and Tabby guilty and sentenced them to be hanged, but the ruling was subsequently reduced to transportation out of the country. The state sold them in October and reimbursed Dr. Roy for their value. The court offered no peace of mind for the Larimer-Janey household. Shadrach and another of Janey's slaves were also brought to the bar the same day, but the attorney for the commonwealth declined to prosecute. Austin Brockenbrough signed off on the court's decision to set them free—from being prisoners, not from being slaves. Larimer wrote, "Had Shadrach been tried, there is scarcely a doubt, but that he would have been hanged."[51] Mrs. Janey determined to do the next best thing to secure the family's safety: sell Shadrach herself, far south, where there was a ready market for slaves on the brutal cotton plantations.

Shadrach surely did not want to go. As he wrote in the narrative: "It is an awful thing to a Virginia slave to be sold for the Alabama and Mississippi country. I have known some of them to die of grief, and others to commit suicide, on account of it."[52] He may have hoped that he could talk his way out of it, as he had perhaps talked his way out of being prosecuted, but to no avail. Mrs. Janey sold his wife, Harriet, and infant son, Ben, along with him "rather than separate her from her husband," as Larimer explained, even though Harriet had not been implicated.[53] Keeping a family together was considered a duty of conscientious owners, but Mrs. Janey and Larimer also probably did not want a resentful spouse left behind, who might be as acquainted with the uses of hug root as her husband.

Shadrach, Harriet, and Ben's new master, Caleb Tate of Dallas County, Alabama, owned about a thousand acres in the midst of the profitable cotton-growing region. The story that Shadrach would tell later, inspired by his time on Tate's plantation, formed the heart of his narrative. There is no evidence to indicate whether Shadrach worked there specifically as a driver supervising other slaves, as he claimed in the narrative, though his qualifications made it possible, especially if no one had disclosed the poisoning incident. He had the ability to get whites to trust him, an air of enthusiasm that made him valuable as more than a field hand, and skill with a whip from his work as a carriage driver.

In the narrative Williams claimed to have been enslaved in Alabama from the fall of 1833 to the summer of 1837, almost four years, hence the subtitle "for Several Years a Driver on a Cotton Plantation," but he actually stayed on Tate's plantation only about a year, probably arriving in the fall of 1834. He, his wife, and toddler son attempted twice to escape as a family. The first time they used the aliases Ben and Eliza Jonson but were recaptured. Their second attempt, begun on the night of August 23, 1835, may have given them a taste of freedom for more than a month. Tate kept advertising for them into October and finally recovered them.[54]

ESCAPE FROM ALABAMA

On Shadrach's third attempt at escape, the night of October 16, 1835, he left behind the family that Mrs. Janey had tried to keep with him and fled with another enslaved man named William. Rumors abounded that abolitionists and criminals lurked in Dallas County and south-central Alabama in general, enticing away slaves. Shadrach wound up in the company of one, a white abolitionist con man named James B. White, who went by the alias "John Smith."[55]

White had approached abolitionists in New York, claiming to be an experienced conductor who escorted runaway slaves to Buffalo and Canada and requesting donations to fund another trip south to free more. The New York abolitionists did not trust him enough to open their pocketbooks, but he enjoyed sufficient success in Philadelphia, and true to his word, when he had enough subscription money in hand, he headed south. There he found Shadrach, whose talent for acting and deception complemented his own. Shadrach needed an alias himself, so he chose "James Williams."

Slowly, they worked their way northward, paying their way with a ruse made famous by the recently broken-up Murrell gang.[56] White posed as John Smith, who claimed to be the lifelong owner and companion of Shadrach, who portrayed James Williams, his loyal slave. "Smith" would offer to sell "James" to a farmer, pocket the money, then help him escape, and they would travel on again, repeating the scam elsewhere, perhaps under several names. Because they claimed to have been raised together, Williams may already have been practicing a version of the story that he would tell to the abolitionists in New York, about being raised from childhood with his master George Larrimore.

The scheme worked well until they reached Baltimore. There, on April 12, 1836, almost six months after Williams had run away, White offered to sell Williams to a man named James Franklin Purvis. As always, the deal was an attractive one. The handsome slave came with a signed certificate from his lifelong owner, vouching for his character, and the asking price of seven hundred dollars was reasonable, considering his quality. Purvis agreed to the deal, accepted custody of Williams, and locked him in his private jail. Whether the con man White knew it, Purvis was not a trusting farmer but a major trader, buying slaves for the New Orleans market, so there was little chance that Williams could escape before being sent to the Deep South again.

Williams panicked. Convinced that the fake abolitionist had deliberately sold him where there was no opportunity to escape, during their final scam just before they would have reached the free state of Pennsylvania, Williams told all to his new master. He probably spun the story to emphasize his own helplessness as the pawn of an evil slave stealer, both to retaliate against White and to vie for a trip back to his family on Tate's plantation rather than be sold at auction. Faced with this surprising revelation, Purvis contacted the city police. The next day Officer Simeon Hays arrested the suspicious seller before he could leave town, searched him, and found incriminating papers, including a list of the original subscriptions from abolitionists to pay for the trip.

Caught red-handed, White confessed, portraying himself as an idealistic abolitionist rather than a slave stealer. Perhaps he *had* made an honest mistake and was indeed still working for Williams's benefit, given his claim that "he was on his way to Alabama for the purpose of liberating said James alias Shadrick's wife and children to take them likewise to Buffalow." But the game was over. Shadrach's wife, Harriet, toddler Ben, and another child named Chastine would remain enslaved on the plantation until Tate's death in 1841, when their ownership would pass to Tate's children. Williams would never see them again. Officials placed Williams in the Baltimore jail while the courts sorted out the mess and contacted the rightful owner.

A few weeks later, on June 2, 1836, Williams recognized a familiar face. Robert Tate, his owner's twenty-eight-year-old son, had come from Alabama as a representative of his father to reclaim him.[57] But Williams was not going home. The Tates apparently had become tired of dealing with a chronic runaway. After being swindled once, Purvis also did not want to buy the slave, even from his legitimate owner, so Tate contacted another Baltimore trader, Hope Hull Slatter.

Originally from Georgia, Slatter had built a new private jail on Baltimore's Pratt Street to hold slaves waiting sale. He advertised that summer: "Cash and the highest prices will at all times be given for likely slaves of both sexes, with good and sufficient titles. Persons having such property to dispose of would do well to see me before they sell, as I am always purchasing for the New Orleans market." A history of running away would not deter him; he claimed, "Such security and confidence I have in my building that I hold myself bound to make good all jail-breaking or escapes from my establishment."[58]

Although Slatter presented himself as courteous and impeccably moral, he would always be snubbed by Baltimore's finer society due to his profession as a slave trader. One of the few sympathetic descriptions of him comes from a surprising source, Joseph Sturge, who received James Williams in Liverpool after he fled New York, and John Greenleaf Whittier. The two abolitionists visited Slatter out of curiosity in 1841, never realizing he had once owned the enslaved man they both knew, nor that his brother S. F. Slatter still legally had title to him, though Williams was long out of the country.

Slatter made a more favorable impression than they expected, convincing them a trader was no worse than an owner. He explained "that the negroes were better off when he sold them than they were in the hands of those of whom he purchased them" and that "he had never sworn an oath, nor committed an immoral act in his life," though Whittier noticed he would not look them in the face as he spoke.[59]

Five years earlier, in the summer of 1836, Williams had waited in the Baltimore jail as Tate and Slatter haggled over his price, while another man named Henry F. Peterson looked on. Peterson traveled extensively in connection with the slave trade and may have been either Slatter's friend or agent.[60] Finally, Slatter agreed to the sale, and the jailer released Shadrach Wilkins—no longer able to call himself James Williams—into his new owner's custody.

Slatter was probably unaware of the poisoning incident back in Virginia, but Tate or the court officials surely informed him of this slave's recent history as a repeated runaway. Nevertheless, Shadrach appeared a day or two later "at the house" of Mr. Slatter when Peterson came to visit.[61] Peterson could have meant the phrase in the sense of "house of business" to refer to Slatter's private slave jail, but Shadrach also may have used his talents to improve slightly his poor situation. Enticing his new owner with tales of his expertise as the servant of upper-class Virginians and performing a convincing show of devotion and loyalty, he may have persuaded the slave trader to unlock him at least part of the time and employ him as a servant in his own home.

For a while Shadrach either resigned himself to his circumstances or had no opportunity for escape because he remained four months in Baltimore, less than a hundred miles from the heart of the Quaker communities and freedom in Pennsylvania. In early fall, two years after he had first been sent to Alabama, he heard the heartrending news again: he would be sold down south once more, this time to Slatter's brother in New Orleans, coincidentally named Shadrach F. Slatter. The brother, also a trader, would most likely sell him to some unknown final buyer in Louisiana.[62] In early October of 1836, at the start of the annual shipping season for sending slaves south, Slatter, again accompanied by Henry Peterson, took Shadrach and several other enslaved people to Alexandria, where they were put aboard a brig to New Orleans, destined for another slave pen and resale.

In Louisiana the southern Slatter brother apparently recognized the handsome slave's potential and perhaps marketed him as an experienced man-servant, waiter, or dining room servant, a background that in the narrative Shadrach claimed he had had in Virginia.[63] Within a few weeks a buyer showed up.

Irish-born Charles Armstrong, about forty years old, was in the midst of a long career as the keeper of New Orleans coffee shops (which were more like bars), restaurants, and hotels.[64] Armstrong's previous enterprise had ended dramatically, when the Planter's Hotel collapsed in the middle of the night a year and a half earlier, making news nationwide. As far away as New York, a struggling young lithographer, Nathaniel Currier, published a print showing the "Ruins of the Planter's Hotel, New Orleans, which fell at two o'clock on the morning of the 15th of May 1835, burying 50 persons, 40 of whom escaped with their lives." The surprising public appetite for such a newsworthy scene inspired Currier to begin selling similar lithographs, later forming the partnership Currier & Ives.[65]

Undismayed by the spectacular failure of the Planter's Hotel, Armstrong would continue in the restaurant and hotel business into the 1850s, and he needed good servants. He purchased Shadrach for $1,600, a price that surely netted the Slatter brothers a profit, though it may not have been accompanied by a full disclosure of Shadrach's history. For a skilled servant, the cost would be reasonable, but "$1600 for a runaway negro[,] the inmate of Baltimore prison for crime or otherwise[,] would seem to be an exhorbitant estimate," as a lawyer commented afterward.[66]

Finally away from the Slatter brothers' slave-trading pens and in the hands of a more lax master, Shadrach seized his chance. On January 10, 1837, he sneaked away from Armstrong, slipped down to the levee, and hid on board the steamboat *Henry Clay.*

ESCAPE FROM NEW ORLEANS

Captain John Alexander Holton of Kentucky was actually a friend of politician Henry Clay, hence the choice of his boat's name. The steamer would be leaving New Orleans the next day for Louisville on one of its regular runs carrying passengers and cargo between the two cities.[67] Fifty years old, Captain Holton had commanded boats on the Mississippi even before steam, drifting freight from Frankfort, Kentucky, to New Orleans on a flatboat as a teenager and then walking and riding home. After fighting in the War of 1812, he returned and began his long career as a steamboat captain, still maintaining his family home at the Forks of Elkhorn in Franklin County, Kentucky.[68]

Shadrach may have known the boat's destination because the big 424-ton *Henry Clay* "had the highest reputation of any boat on the river, having made ninety-six trips without accident; a rare feat on this dangerous river," according to a passenger in 1835, or he may have chosen it by luck.[69] But he surely knew that captains guarded against runaway slaves using northbound boats for escape, so he needed to conceal himself carefully. In fact, he hid himself so well that the question of whether someone could possibly do it so completely became a central point in a Louisiana Supreme Court case and set a minor precedent about negative evidence.[70]

William Holton, the *Henry Clay*'s first mate and brother of the captain, "took much pains to ascertain who was on board and particularly if there were any run away negroes," but he did not find Shadrach. Thomas D. Cox, the second mate, also saw no sign of him. Nicolas C. Snethen, the boat's second clerk, recalled that "it was his particular duty to know who was on board the boat at the time of her departure and during her trip[;] that he caused the deck passengers to be mustered several times during the trip[;] it was his duty which he faithfully performed to examine the boat that there might be no run away slaves on board—that he has no recollection of the boy Shadrack being on board, [and] he feels confident he was not."[71]

Hiding was not the only challenge for a person seeking freedom. The boat would not pass the first free state, Illinois, for more than a week, so at some point Shadrach needed to come out for food and water. The only other African American passengers on board this trip were the servant of Captain Slade of Mobile, who had bought a cabin ticket in New Orleans, and Sanders, the steward of the steamboat *St. Lawrence*, who boarded at the mouth of the White River, about halfway between New Orleans and the mouth of the Ohio River.[72]

The men in charge of keeping runaways off the *Henry Clay* noticed those two legitimate passengers and confirmed that no other men of color lurked on board, except of course those connected to the boat.

The hardworking black crew, tending to the needs of the boat and its passengers, were all but invisible to the white employees as long as they did their jobs, so no one noticed that the *Henry Clay* seemed to have gained an extra one. From a distance the new waiter, "Jim Thornton," resembled the free cook Bob, a tall, "handsome well formed" mulatto in his late twenties, so at a glance or after dark some may have even mistaken him for Bob.[73] Under his new name the runaway Shadrach Wilkins, alias Jim Thornton, pitched into his volunteer work with enthusiasm, serving meals to passengers while he sneaked his own bites to eat throughout the long, hectic workdays. The *Henry Clay* had an "almost interminable table in the cabin. This table, long as it was, would not hold all the company. Many had to wait till seats were vacated." Service began with breakfast at seven in the morning and did not end until after supper, which started twelve hours later.[74]

After about a week of steaming upriver, the crew and passengers caught their first glimpse of Illinois. Shadrach, who had never seen a free state before, may have felt like Harriet Martineau, who rode the *Henry Clay* from New Orleans in 1835: "How some of us fixed our eyes on the shores of free Illinois! After nearly five months of sojourn in slave-land, we were now in sight of a free State once more. I saw a settler in a wild spot, looking very lonely among the tall trees; but I felt that I would rather be that man than the wealthiest citizen of the opposite State, who was satisfied to dwell there among his slaves."[75] Shadrach apparently wanted to get as far north as possible or perhaps had no chance to leave without rousing suspicion, so he stayed on board.

Almost 1,200 miles from New Orleans and now on the Ohio River, the *Henry Clay* reached the mouth of the Cumberland River, which flowed through Tennessee and Kentucky. At its outlet it formed the well-known Cumberland bar in the Ohio River, narrowing the passage. On this trip low water forced the big *Henry Clay*, along with other boats, to stop and wait before they could make the final 330 miles up the Ohio to Louisville. The man known as Jim Thornton dutifully served dinner to the passengers, but he and they were restless to continue.

Meanwhile, the little seventy-five-ton steamboat *Wave* had been paddling down the Cumberland from Nashville.[76] It reached the Ohio River and pulled alongside the *Henry Clay* for the night. Despite being shorthanded, with only one of the usual two pilots and a steward who was sick, the *Wave*'s captain informed the *Henry Clay*'s captain that he planned to leave for Louisville the next morning, despite the low water. Did any of the *Henry Clay*'s passengers want to transfer to the *Wave* and continue? Several did. The *Henry Clay*'s Captain Holton also remarked that some of his crew would like to continue too. Captain Spalding of the *Wave* remembered that Holton "requested me to let such as I should need[,] work their passage[,] the rest pay," though Holton was vague about exactly which crew members he was referring to.[77]

Probably determined to get the most for his generosity, Spalding sized up the four African American men who wanted on board and may have picked the two most energetic to work for their passage. At least the choice of one was easy. Both Spalding and the pilot noticed Jim Thornton's diligence. The pilot described him: "rather tall . . . about 5 feet 9 or 10[,] of a copper color[,] wore his hair well combed back from his face & was remarked on board the Wave for his neatness & activity in acting as a Waiter."[78] Someone reliable who could wait on tables unsupervised would be especially useful, given the illness of the *Wave*'s steward. The captain offered free passage to Jim Thornton and another man if they would work, asking payment from the other two. The next morning Jim Thornton eagerly carried bags for the white passengers who wanted to transfer from the *Henry Clay* and then resumed his duties as a waiter, while the *Wave* steamed toward Louisville.

Meanwhile, another steamboat, the *Mississippi*, had left New Orleans about the same time as the *Henry Clay*. At Vicksburg a passenger boarded for a trip up the Mississippi and Ohio Rivers to Wheeling, Virginia: Henry F. Peterson, the same man who had stood by as Hope H. Slatter purchased Shadrach from Robert Tate in Baltimore seven months earlier and who had watched him being shipped south to Slatter's brother. Peterson transferred from the *Mississippi* to the *Tuscarora* near Paducah, but after less than a day the *Tuscarora* ran aground below Shawneetown, Illinois. The *Wave* came steaming past, and just as Captain Spalding had offered to help the passengers of the halted *Henry Clay*, he offered to take on the *Tuscarora*'s stranded passengers too. Fate had brought Peterson and Shadrach, alias Jim Thornton, face to face again.

As soon as Peterson stepped on board the *Wave*, he saw Shadrach, spoke to him, and recognized him. He hurried to Captain Spalding and "told him that the boy belonged to Mr. S. F. Slatter of New Orleans; that [he] was of opinion he had run away, and that Capt Spalding ought to have him arrested."[79] Aiding a runaway was a crime, not to mention a financial liability to be responsible for the loss of such an expensive slave, but the captain also must have dreaded giving up a good waiter when he was already shorthanded. Happily, he could shift responsibility. He replied "that the boy was put on board his boat by Captain Holton of the Steam boat Henry Clay; and that he did not believe that Captain Holton would have put him on board his boat, if he had not authority to do so; and that as Captain Holton was responsible for the boy in case he should be a slave, he thought he would not arrest him."[80]

The transfer, of course, was not as clear as that. Captain Holton had vaguely indicated some of the servants from the *Henry Clay* wanted passage, and Jim Thornton appeared to be a servant, waiting at the table and carrying baggage, but Captain Spalding even admitted later, "I had no conversation with Capt Holton respecting [Thornton] no more than the balance of the boys that came on board of the Wave."[81] Satisfied he had shifted responsibility well enough, Spalding dismissed his fuming passenger and let his excellent waiter continue to work, until the *Wave* itself became stopped by ice in the evening, just beyond Flint Island, almost a hundred miles below Louisville. There each passenger "had to get on as he could."[82] Jim Thornton slipped off the boat with the other three black men from the *Henry Clay*, ahead of Peterson, who disembarked the next day. It would be the last any of the people from the steamboats saw Shadrach, except possibly for one.

Walter Cox, another white passenger who transferred onto the *Wave* with Peterson, was a friendly bachelor on his way home to Louisville. He lived and worked with Horace B. Hill, of the large commission merchant company H. B. Hill on Main Street, and took his meals at the fashionable Washington Hotel a block away. Not unconcerned with the problems of the colored race, he had donated five dollars to the Colonization Society within the past year.[83] Later he testified that he was "under the impression he has since seen [Jim Thornton] in Louisville Kentucky." But he did nothing to apprehend him, and as far as anyone on the steamboats knew, Shadrach, alias Jim Thornton, had disappeared.

IN CINCINNATI

The next information on Shadrach's whereabouts comes from the letter he sent his enslaved sister back in Essex County, Virginia, almost a year later. In it Shadrach reportedly wrote "that he went to the Mississippi river in a steamboat, and succeeded in getting to Cincinnati, where he remained a short time, and from thence he went on to New York."[84] Apparently, during 1837 he managed to get to Louisville and then traveled the remaining 140 miles upriver to Cincinnati, where he stayed until fall.

Despite being in the free state of Ohio, Cincinnati was hardly a haven for runaways. Slave catchers and kidnappers prowled the wharfs and streets. The black population had dropped to about half of what it had been a decade earlier, thanks to a race riot in 1829 and stricter enforcement of the law requiring each black inhabitant to post a five hundred–dollar bond. Over a thousand residents had left for greener pastures, including a new settlement in Upper Canada.[85] Abolitionists were nevertheless gaining a foothold. The previous year an attempt to publish an antislavery newspaper, the *Philanthropist*, sparked another rampage, during which a mob tore up the press, but the abolitionists persisted, and the *Philanthropist* was a going concern in 1837. The city's busy antislavery society sponsored lectures and sold books from its depository on the corner of Sixth and Main.

Although a budding Underground Railroad network was spreading northward from the banks of the Ohio River, Shadrach chose to stay in the city, evidently earning a living while avoiding slave catchers, kidnappers, and officials who would demand he post bond. Unbeknownst to him, he also narrowly avoided another danger that would have damaged any chance of the American Anti-Slavery Society publishing his narrative the following year.

James G. Birney, one of the abolitionists whom he would encounter in New York City, also lived in Cincinnati in 1837. He was editor of the *Philanthropist* and actively promoted the local and state antislavery societies.[86] If they had met, things might have turned out differently. When Shadrach, alias James Williams, would arrive in New York claiming to be a refugee fresh off an Alabama plantation, Birney could have recognized him as a resident of Cincinnati, immediately throwing doubt on his entire story, in a coincidence as bizarre as when Shadrach had encountered Henry Peterson again.

But apparently, Birney paid little attention to the actual runaways in the city, letting African Americans take care of that, so the two never encountered each other. Another refugee from slavery, a young woman, had also escaped from New Orleans on a steamboat in the middle of January, about the same time as Shadrach, and reached Cincinnati. Birney reported that she "was successfully concealed here by her colored friends." In the same letter he wrote, "The Captain of a Steamboat said at the Exchange a few days ago, that he would give $500 to any one who would prove that I had any hand in persuading a hired slave on his boat to run off—that he would forthwith go and take my life." Birney noted the incident apparently without concern that he could be implicated because, he explained, "such matters are almost uniformly managed by the colored people. I know nothing of them generally till they are passed."[87]

Even if he was not aware of Shadrach or the other runaways in the city, Shadrach may have heard of him. In March a slave catcher discovered that the Birneys' housekeeper was actually an escaped slave. Birney claimed he did not know it, and he actually might not have because she passed as white. He became embroiled in extended legal action that resulted in her being taken back into slavery, while he was found guilty and fined, a decision later overturned on appeal, but the excitement meant Birney's name was in the Cincinnati news all spring.[88] Incessantly busy even beyond his publishing duties and lawsuit appearances, he traveled in the Northeast and then left Cincinnati permanently for New York late in the summer of 1837.

A few months later Shadrach also left for New York, once again using the name James Williams. Both men would both arrive among the members of the American Anti-Slavery Society, Birney in the fall, Williams in the winter. Birney had been invited there to become the new corresponding secretary,[89] but Williams's motives for the move are unknown. His owner Slatter might have sent someone from New Orleans who finally found his track, but for whatever reason he abandoned life in Ohio and headed east. Certainly, slave catchers were close behind when he arrived in New York because the two white men and a colored man who could identify him were on his trail.[90]

Perhaps Williams planned from the beginning to sell his story for a ticket out of the country, or perhaps he only stumbled into the opportunity. Slave autobiographies would become more common later, but in Cincinnati he could have seen at least two recent examples: *The Slave; or, Memoirs of Archy Moore* and *Slavery in the United States: A Narrative of the Life and Adventures of Charles Ball, a Black Man.*[91] Archy Moore was later revealed to be a fictional creation from white author Richard Hildreth, though at the time he was often considered genuine. Regardless, either through luck or design, by the time he reached Carlisle, Pennsylvania, Williams had his story and alias firmly in mind. He recycled not only the name but some of the background he had used when he was traveling with James B. White, describing himself as the longtime property of a master with whom he had been raised, except this time he was alone, and his supposed master, George Larrimore, was in Virginia.

In Carlisle he found the Quaker-run Underground Railroad that led him to the American Anti-Slavery Society, John Greenleaf Whittier, and a chance to trade his story for freedom.

LOUISIANA SUPREME COURT APPEAL

Back in New Orleans, Charles Armstrong, the hotel and restaurant keeper, had no idea what was transpiring on the boats upriver. He only knew that he had just paid sixteen hundred dollars for a supposedly obedient servant, who had immediately absconded. Apparently, he contacted Slatter about getting his money back because Slatter obviously had misrepresented his wares. Around the same time, Slatter must have heard from Henry Peterson, who told the disturbing news about what had happened on the *Wave*.

In an attempt to recoup their loss, Armstrong and Slatter started out aiming a suit at the deep pockets of Captain Holton because the captain was responsible for letting their slave sneak on board in New Orleans. New steamboats of moderate size might be worth forty or fifty thousand dollars, but they wore out quickly and were considered old within five years. The *Henry Clay* was larger than most but was already over four years old, and its value for insurance purposes had dropped to twenty-two thousand dollars.[92] Nevertheless, it was worth more than enough to cover the twenty-five hundred dollars that the court required Holton to put up in case he lost the suit. On March 3, 1837, the sheriff seized the well-known boat, briefly stopping its upriver trips. Holton scrambled to find someone to help him post bond and retook control. On March 10 he filed an answer to the suit, denying the charges and indignantly, but unsuccessfully, demanding a thousand dollars for the trouble of having his boat seized and getting it released.

Williams's life in freedom and the lawsuit continued concurrently, each independent from the other. For most of 1837, while Williams was living in Cincinnati, the New Orleans Parish Court collected depositions from witnesses, now scattered across several states. As the process dragged on, Armstrong became restless over his lost investment. Slatter's Baltimore brother had a policy "never to misrepresent Negroes and to exchange them at any time rather than go to a lawsuit," and the New Orleans brother eventually chose the same course.[93] Rather than making his unhappy customer wait for compensation or, worse yet, risk a suit for misrepresenting the slave, he returned Armstrong's money. Satisfied with his refund, Armstrong dropped out from the plaintiff's side, leaving the suit in Slatter's hand.

In December 1837, when Williams was arriving among the Pennsylvania Quakers, the sheriff seized the *Henry Clay* a second time, and Captain Holton scrambled once again to get it back. On January 3, 1838, while the American Anti-Slavery Society was asking for Williams's story, Captain Holton filed another response, again denying any liability and increasing his counterdemand to two thousand dollars for the trouble of twice having his boat taken. In March 1838, never realizing the connection between the slave they were arguing over and the newly published author James Williams, the lawyers began gathering more witnesses.

About the time Williams arrived in England, Slatter released the captain of the *Wave* from any threat of a suit, and both sides focused on the question of Captain Holton's liability. Almost two and a half years after Williams had sneaked onto the *Henry Clay*, Judge Charles Maurian of the New Orleans Parish Court finally passed judgment. On May 10, 1839, he signed his decision that required Captain Holton to pay Shadrach's value of sixteen hundred dollars plus court costs and ordered his boat be seized once again. Holton requested an appeal, put up the necessary three thousand–dollar bond, and the Louisiana Supreme Court agreed to hear the case, all in the next two weeks. Progress slowed to a crawl once again. Finally, two more years later, in June 1841, the case appeared on the docket.

The supreme court upheld the parish court's decision in a case that would be cited as *Slatter v. Holton* 19 LA 39. Captain Holton needed to pay Slatter sixteen hundred dollars for the loss of Shadrach Wilkins, plus the increasingly heavy court costs. In his decision Judge Alonzo Morphy declared, "However strong may appear the negative proof resulting from the declaration of several witnesses that they did not see the plaintiff's boy on board of the Henry Clay during her voyage from New Orleans to Louisville, it cannot destroy the positive testimony in the record showing that during the trip the boy was acting on board as one of the servants of the boat under the name of Jim Thornton."

Holton's lawyer, Richard H. Chinn, was shocked. Even after the decision he could not believe he had lost. He wrote the judge an impassioned letter in July, declaring, "After more than thirty years of attendance upon the courts, my recollection does not furnish me with a case in which I have been twice so much surprised."[94] There was no proof that Shadrach had belonged to Slatter, though the refunded money indicated as much, but more important, there was no evidence he had left Louisiana on the *Henry Clay* and in fact strong evidence that he had not because no one had found him on board until after the boat was out of the Louisiana court's jurisdiction, despite searching diligently.

Chinn was a friend as well as a lawyer of his client. They had both served in the War of 1812 and survived capture at the devastating Battle of Raisin River.[95] All the testimony indicated Holton was an honest man. He begged the judge: "If such men as Holton are to be thus driven from our western waters what will be the inevitable effect, neither the lives or property of the community will have that protection slight as it is which has heretofore existed. The whole business of stream navigation will be thrown upon the reckless profligate and abandoned mercenaries who may take the chances of conviction or acquittal upon doubtful testimony & make their calculations and charges according."

The ten-page request wound up filed with the rest of the case, marked simply "Rehearing refused." James Williams's impact in the United States had come to a close, and steamboat transportation managed to survive. Yet the problem of negative evidence was a suitable legacy, haunting Williams's life for the next 170 years.

FICTION AND REAL LIFE

Because investigators found little evidence connecting his narrative to real people or events, Williams's very existence as an enslaved man came under doubt, affecting not only the reaction to his story but also the lives of future enslaved people who escaped. In many states blacks were not allowed to testify against whites, but abolitionists apparently felt they could overcome any comparison to a court of law by endorsing Williams's testimony themselves. Yet as later events showed, just the opposite was true: the public wanted to judge the character of former slaves firsthand. They might be willing to trust an honest-sounding black person, but the endorsement of biased whites fueled their skepticism.

Realizing the mistake too late, James Birney and Lewis Tappan suggested, "If we could have satisfactory assurance that [Williams] would be safe as a freeman in New York from the claims of the slave-holder, the Executive committee ought to proceed to make inquiry for the place of his residence, that he might be brought back and subjected to the most rigid cross-examination that those who dispute his story could impose."[96] But they barely had been able to keep Williams secure from slave catchers long enough for him to tell his story. Confident neither in his safety nor perhaps in his success under cross-examination, the abolitionists left him to his anonymity in some English colony.

They learned their lesson, however. The next escapees who wanted to tell their stories were expected to do so on stage, and the public responded enthusiastically. Historian William L. Andrews has noted: “That the major slave narratives of the 1840s were produced by seasoned veterans of the abolitionist lecture circuit, not by lonely fugitives like James Williams newly arrived from the South, had much to do with their appeal to white audiences.”[97] Andrews mentioned Frederick Douglass, William Wells Brown, and Henry Bibb, who lectured four years or more before publishing their life stories. Not only did this give whites a chance to convince themselves of the former slaves’ honesty; it also gave later black authors more time to practice before dictating or writing for publication. Williams, however, had not entirely omitted this aspect of his performance. He had tried out his new alias and some of his childhood story when traveling across the South with James B. White, before needing to present it consistently, beginning on the Underground Railroad in Pennsylvania.

“From the troubled history of James Williams, both fugitives and abolitionists learned the importance of allowing audiences to watch and question fugitive narrators,” historian Ann Fabian has observed. Yet this also meant that escapees needed to alter their goals if they were to be content, trapped in limbo on the lecture circuit, “no longer enslaved, to be sure, but suspended somewhere between slavery and freedom.”[98] Later freedom seekers such as Frederick Douglass allied themselves with the abolitionist movement, willingly putting themselves on display to further the rights of their race.

Yet Williams never had to trust whites to that extent, nor did he bare his whole existence for them. He obviously simplified, romanticized, adapted, and edited his real life to create a narrative hovering between fiction and autobiography. He probably saw the days of dictation not as an outpouring of pent-up memories but as a means to an end, yet another facade to please another set of white men in order to get what he wanted: freedom. But we now know that he really had been enslaved in Virginia, sent to Alabama, and escaped from there.

Parts of the narrative may reflect incidents Williams had heard about but did not participate in directly, such as the story of the enslaved boy who walked to school each day with the young master born at Mount Pleasant.[99] Other parts touched on things he had experienced but did not admit—being recaptured, confined in a trader’s jail, or sold south to a new owner.[100] Other elements can be documented to his real life. Goldsby and Sturdivant, for example, the nearby planters in Alabama whom Williams named, were in fact neighbors and friends of his owner there. George Larimer married a widow in Virginia with the Anglican name of Virginia Garland Collins, but she was nonetheless "a French lady of one of the first families" of New Orleans, exactly as Williams stated.[101]

The narrative can therefore be read now in several ways: as a necessary part of Williams's performance that he had been presenting to abolitionists since at least Carlisle, Pennsylvania, culminating in a ticket to freedom in Liverpool; as a collection of his insights as an enslaved man, intermingled with fiction; and as a repository of things he witnessed, heard about, heard rumors of, or imagined, which he thought believable and worthwhile to tell.

This annotation provides extensive historical information, both specific to Williams and supplementary to what he told. Categorizing every incident is still impossible, but the narrative as a whole can now be weighed against the author's real life and read as a testament to the memory, observation, imagination, and talent of an early black author who was also an American slave.

Note: Several editions, including excerpts, were published in 1838, varying mainly in their pagination. This annotation is based on the edition marked:

NEW YORK:
PUBLISHED BY THE AMERICAN ANTI-SLAVERY SOCIETY,
NO. 143 NASSAU STREET.
BOSTON:
ISAAC KNAPP, 25 CORNHILL
1838.

Stereotyped at Geo. A. & J. Curtis's
Type & Stereotype Foundry.—Boston.

NOTES

1. James G. Birney and Lewis Tappan, "Alabama Beacon versus James Williams," *Emancipator*, August 30, 1838, reprinted in the *Friend of Man*, September 19, 1838.

2. See appendix C. Noah Webster's 1831 *Dictionary of the English Language* defined *likely* to mean "having good qualities."

3. R. C. Smedley, *History of the Underground Railroad in Chester and the Neighboring Counties of Pennsylvania* (Lancaster, Pa.: Office of the Journal, 1883), 194; Joan M. Jensen, *Loosening the Bonds: Mid-Atlantic Farm Women, 1750–1850* (New Haven: Yale University Press, 1988), 176–78.

4. *Proceedings of the Pennsylvania Convention, Assembled to Organize a State Anti-Slavery Society, at Harrisburg, on the 31st of January and 1st, 2d and 3d of February 1837* (Philadelphia: Merrihew & Gunn, 1837), 4, 32–33.

5. John W. Blassingame, "Using the Testimony of Ex-Slaves: Approaches and Problems," reprinted in Charles T. Davis and Henry Louis Gates Jr., *The Slave's Narrative* (New York: Oxford University Press, 1985), 81.

6. K. K. Ruthven, *Faking Literature* (Cambridge: Cambridge University Press, 2001), 101.

7. Laura Browder, *Slippery Characters: Ethnic Impersonators and American Identities* (Chapel Hill: University of North Carolina Press, 2000), 27–31.

8. Lydia Maria Child to Angelina Grimké, December 1838, qtd. in Ann Fabian, *The Unvarnished Truth: Personal Narratives in Nineteenth-Century America* (Berkeley: University of California Press, 2000), 93.

9. Lara Langer Cohen, *The Fabrication of American Literature: Fraudulence and Antebellum Print Culture* (Philadelphia: University of Pennsylvania Press, 2012), 118–21.

10. Henry S. Brooke, qtd. in Birney and Tappan, "Alabama Beacon versus James Williams."

11. JB [James Birney], "Narrative of James Williams," *Liberator*, September 28, 1838.

12. William Still, *Still's Underground Rail Road Records* (Philadelphia: William Still, Publisher, 1886), 647; R. C. Smedley, *History of the Underground Railroad*, 57.

13. Ibid.

14. H. R. Howard, comp., *The History of Virgil A. Stewart* (New York: Harper & Bros., 1836), 65–66, 251; untitled article about Jeshua Woolley, "who was engaged in endeavoring to decoy several negroes from a plantation by promising to take them to a free state," [Tuscaloosa] *Alabama Intelligencer and State Rights Expositor*, September 12, 1835.

15. Birney and Tappan, "Alabama Beacon versus James Williams"; Still, *Still's Underground Rail Road Records*, 644–49; Smedley, *History of the Underground Railroad*, 53–58.

16. Birney and Tappan, "Alabama Beacon versus James Williams"; Smedley, *History of the Underground Railroad*, 88; *Narrative of James Williams*, 13.

17. Birney and Tappan, "Alabama Beacon versus James Williams"; Smedley, *History of the Underground Railroad*, 143; Still, *Still's Underground Rail Road Records*, 749.

18. Birney and Tappan, "Alabama Beacon versus James Williams."

19. *Narrative of James Williams*, 61; see p. 128 for speculation that the conductor might have been James Mott; Robert J. Vandewater, *The Tourist, or Pocket Manual for Travellers on the Hudson River* (New York: Harper & Bros., 1839), 7.

20. See *Narrative of James Williams*, 132–33.

21. John Albree, ed., *Whittier Correspondence from the Oak Knoll Collections, 1830–1892* (Salem, Mass.: Essex Book and Print Club, 191), 50.

22. Birney and Tappan, "Alabama Beacon versus James Williams."

23. *Narrative of James Williams*, 131.

24. Birney and Tappan, "Alabama Beacon versus James Williams."

25. *Narrative of James Williams*, 131; Whittier to T. Y. Holbrown, June 31, 1886, qtd. in A.S.W. Rosenbach, *A Catalogue of the Books and Manuscripts of Harry Elkins Widener* (Philadelphia, Printed for the author, 1910), 2:273.

26. Birney and Tappan, "Alabama Beacon versus James Williams."

27. *Narrative of James Williams*, 30; George Larimer, qtd. in Birney and Tappan, "Alabama Beacon versus James Williams." See appendix A.

28. *Narrative of James Williams*, 29.

29. Theodore D. Weld to James G. Birney, January 12 and February 5, 1838, qtd. in *Letters of James Gillepsie Birney, 1831–1857*, ed. Dwight L. Dumond, 1: 446, 451 (New York: Appleton-Century, 1938).

30. Birney and Tappan, "Alabama Beacon versus James Williams."

31. Ibid.

32. Ibid.

33. Rittenhouse's mother, Harriet Beverly, was born in Essex County, Virginia, where Williams lived before being sold to Alabama, but Rittenhouse himself never lived there, and his parents died when he was a boy, so he does not seem to have had any personal acquaintance with other Essex County residents.

William Edward Wadsworth Yerby, *History of Greensboro, Alabama from Its Earliest Settlement* (Montgomery, Ala.: Paragon Press, 1908), 39; 1860 U.S. Federal Census, Charlestown, Middlesex County, Mass.; 1870 U.S. Federal Census, Philadelphia Ward 26, District 87, Pa.; "Appointments by the President," *New-Yorker*, August 1, 1840, 315; "Senate Bill, No. 251, for the relief of John B. Rittenhouse," Reports from the Committee on Naval Affairs, *Index to the Reports of the Committees of the Senate of the United States for the First Session of the Thirty-Sixth Congress* (Washington, D.C.: George W. Bowman, 1860); James H. Bull, *Record of the Descendants of John and Elizabeth Bull* (San Francisco: Shannon-Conmy, 1919), 2:59.

34. John B. Rittenhouse, qtd. in Birney and Tappan, "Alabama Beacon versus James Williams."

35. Birney and Tappan, "Alabama Beacon versus James Williams."

36. The Janey family is discussed in more detail in the notes for relevant pages throughout the narrative.

37. John B. Rittenhouse, qtd. in Birney and Tappan, "Alabama Beacon versus James Williams."

38. More information on the neighboring Alabamans is provided in the notes to the pages on which they were first mentioned in the narrative: Flincher, 35; Goldsby, 37; Huckstep, 35; Crop, 40; Sturtivant, 40; Ludlow, 52.

39. For simplicity's sake the annotation uses *Larimer* to refer to the real man, because that alternate spelling is the one that both Rittenhouse and the abolitionists used, and *Larrimore* to refer to the fictionalized man as described in the narrative.

40. The argument between Rittenhouse and the abolitionists, including this quote, is from their exchanges reprinted in Birney and Tappan, "Alabama Beacon versus James Williams."

41. JB [James Birney], "Narrative of James Williams," *Liberator*, September 28, 1838.

42. James G. Birney and Lewis Tappan, "Statement Authorized by the Executive Committee," *Emancipator*, reprinted in *The African Repository and Colonial Journal* (June 1839): 163; P. K. Foley, "Whittier and the 'Narrative of James Williams,'" *Nation*, April 29, 1897, 321.

43. Calvin Colton, *Abolition a Sedition. By a Northern Man* (Philadelphia: Geo. W. Donohue, 1839), 106.

44. The quoted descriptions are from statements by Walter Cox and William M'Bride, transcribed in appendix E.

45. *Narrative of James Williams*, 37.

46. Ibid., 30.

47. A transcript of the resulting trial appears in appendix B.

48. "Dr. Augustus Gustavus Dunbar Roy married Lucy Carter Garnett, March 6, 1834, Stock Hill, Essex County, Va., by Rev. Richard Claybrook; issue, John Beverly Roy, born January, 1835, at Bowlers, Essex County, Va." Alfred Bagby, *King and Queen County, Virginia* (New York: Neale Publishing Co., 1908), 355.

49. According to trial testimony: "Tabby further said if the poison was put in the milk, it would certainly kill . . . Tabby further remarked to Warner, that he knew where his master and Mistress visited that if he would go and lay the poison at the door it would take away the use of their Master and Mistresses limbs." The second method was an example of a "trick" in the Obeah tradition. The two suggestions echoed Samuel A. Cartwright's observation that Louisiana slaves believed that in certain instances "some enemy on the plantation or in the neighborhood [had] tricked them, that is, laid poison for them to walk over, or given it to them in their food or drinks." Cartwright, "Report on the Diseases and Physical Peculiarities of the Negro Race," *New Orleans Medical and Surgical Journal* (May 1851): 705.

50. Will of Beverly Roy, "King and Queen County: Records Concerning 18th Century Persons," *Virginia Colonial Abstracts* (Baltimore: Genealogical Publishing Co., 1988), 2:171; Will of Thomas Collins Jr., Lost Records Localities Collection, King and Queen County, Digital Collections, Library of Virginia, www.lva.virginia.gov (accessed November 19, 2011).

51. The only unclear statement in Larimer's letter was the timeline. Larimer wrote, "Had Shadrach been tried, there is scarcely a doubt, but that he would have been hanged, as it appears from the testimony in the case, after he was sold, that he was the principal one in the business." The trial of Warner and Tabby occurred the same day that Williams was released, and Williams was actually present in court, so he must have been sold south after the trial. Thus, there could be no "testimony in the case, after he was sold," unless Larimer was referring to informal discussion by the witnesses after the case had been settled in court. George Larimer, qtd. in Birney and Tappan, "Alabama Beacon versus James Williams." See appendix A.

52. *Narrative of James Williams*, 32.

53. See appendix A.

54. See Caleb Tate's runaway ads in appendix C.

55. See Larimer's letter in appendix A, Caleb Tate's last runaway ad in appendix C, and legal papers concerning James B. White and Williams's detention in Baltimore in appendix D. He was probably not the same man as the James White of Springfield, N.J., who was active at the American Anti-Slavery Society's meetings in the 1830s. That James White was present at a meeting in New York on May 10, 1836, the same time James B. White was involved in legal trouble in Baltimore. *Third Annual Report of the American Anti-Slavery Society* (New York: William S. Dorr, 1836), 25.

56. See *Narrative of James Williams*, 129.

57. Both Henry Peterson and George Larimer (see appendix E) stated that "Mr. Tate" was in Baltimore to reclaim and sell Shadrach, but Caleb Tate appeared before a judge in Montgomery County, Alabama, at about the same time (see appendix D). Apparently, he sent his son Robert to Baltimore, and that is whom the men were referring to because a note beside Shadrach Wilkins's name in the jail records stated that Shadrach was "charged with being a runaway confessing his master to be Robert Tate in Alabama."

Although Caleb Tate was the owner, based on newspaper advertisements and court records (see appendixes C and D), if he sent his son to Baltimore to act as his agent, the clerk recording the disposition of the case might not have realized that another Tate with a different first name was the actual owner. Baltimore City and County Jail Runaway Docket, 1832–36, April 13, 1836, docket no. 928, Maryland State Archives, Annapolis.

58. "Historical Value of Iowa Newspapers," *Annals of Iowa* (October 1896): 561.

59. Henry Richard, *Memoirs of Joseph Sturge* (London: S. W. Partridge, 1864), 233; Joseph Sturge, *A Visit to the United States in 1841* (London: Hamilton, Adams, & Co., 1842), 30–34.

60. H. F. Peterson was listed as a "negro dealer" in Cohen's *New Orleans & Lafayette Directory* for 1851. A man with the same name had also purchased and sold a slave from the Baltimore jail in June 1837.

61. Statement of Henry F. Peterson transcribed in appendix E.

62. See appendix E for testimony concerning events in Louisiana and on the Mississippi River.

63. *Narrative of James Williams,* 31.

64. Charles Armstrong, coffeehouse, 43 Chartres, *1832 New Orleans City Directory,* files.usgwarchives.net/la/orleans/history/directory/1832nocd.txt (accessed November 19, 2011); Charles Armstrong, Exchange Saloon & Restaurant, 18 Royal, *Cohen's New Orleans & Lafayette Directory for 1851,* files.usgwarchives.net/la/orleans/history/directory/1851cdab.txt (accessed November 19, 2011); Charles Armstrong, 53, hotel keeper, 1850 United States Federal Census, Municipality 1 Ward 1, New Orleans.

65. "New-Orleans, May 15th—Awful Catastrophe," *American Railroad Journal, and Advocate of Internal Improvements,* May 30–June 5, 1835, 349; "Currier & Ives—The History of the Firm," Currier and Ives Foundation, www.currierandives.com/history.html (accessed November 25, 2011).

66. Statement of Richard H. Chinn, transcribed in appendix E.

67. "Arrived To Day . . . Steamer Henry Clay, Holton, from Louisville: cargo—pork lard, beef, bacon, apples, &c.," *New Orleans Courier,* February 27, 1837, 3; "Reminiscences of C. C. Cox," *Quarterly of the Texas State Historical Association* (October 1902): 115. This *Henry Clay* was a different boat than the steamer *Henry Clay* that plied the route between Buffalo and Detroit under Captain Walter Norton at about the same time.

68. "Captain John A. Holton, The Forks of Elkhorn" and "Death of Captain John A. Holton," qtd. in "Famous Steamboats and Their Captains on Western and Southern Waters," in Ella Hutchison Ellwanger, *Register of the Kentucky State Historical Society* (May 1920): 37–40.

69. Harriet Martineau, *Retrospect of Western Travel* (London: Saunders & Otley, 1838), 2:161. Some editions with the same publication information begin volume 2 with the chapter "Mississippi Voyage," so the quote appears on p. 5 rather than p. 161.

70. "Positive testimony cannot be destroyed by the negative proof of witnesses who testified that they did not see a certain slave on board the defendant's steamboat.—Slatter v. Holton, 19 La. 39." *United States Circuit Courts of Appeals Reports* (St. Paul, Minn.: West Publishing Co., 1915), 136:10.

71. The witnesses' statements are transcribed in appendix E.

72. All distances on the river are based on Samuel Cummings, *Charts of the Ohio River and of the Mississippi* (Cincinnati: George Conclin, 1848).

73. Statement of William Holton, transcribed in appendix E.

74. Harriet Martineau, *Retrospect of Western Travel,* 2:165, 166, 170.

75. Ibid., 2:197.

76. Tonnages of steamboats are from W. G. Lyford, *The Western Address Directory* (Baltimore: Jos. Robinson, 1837), 464, 468.

77. Statement of Ulysses Spalding, transcribed in appendix E.

78. Statement of William M'Bridge, transcribed in appendix E.

79. Statement of Henry F. Peterson, transcribed in appendix E.

80. Ibid.

81. Statement of Ulysses Spalding, transcribed in appendix E.

82. Statement of Walter Cox, transcribed in appendix E.

83. *Diary of William Fairfax Gray, from Virginia to Texas, 1835–1837,* William P. Clements Center for Southwest Studies, Southern Methodist University, Dallas, smu.edu/swcenter/FairfaxGray/wg_011.htm (accessed November 25, 2011); "Contributions," *African Repository Colonial Journal* (October 1836): 327; W. G. Lyford, *The Western Address Directory* (Baltimore: Jos. Robinson, 1837), 372; *The Louisville Directory for the Year 1832* (Louisville: Richard W. Otis, 1832), 42, 81, 85; "The Original Galt House," *History of the Ohio Falls Cities and Their Counties* (Cleveland: L. A. Williams & Co., 1882), 1:278.

84. See appendix A.

85. Nikki M. Taylor, *Cincinnati's Black Community, 1802–1868* (Athens: Ohio University Press, 2005), 50–79.

86. William Birney, *James G. Birney and His Times* (New York: D. Appleton & Co., 1890), 256–68. Birney discussed progress in Cincinnati during 1837 in his letters, qtd. in Dumond, *Letters of James Gillespie Birney,* vol. 1.

87. James Birney to Lewis Tappan, February 27, 1837, in Dumond, *Letters of James Gillespie Birney,* 1:376.

88. Even in 1890, when Underground Railroad conductors might be hailed as heroes, his son still maintained the family had thought she was white. Birney, *James G. Birney and His Times,* 262; Jules Lobel, *Success without Victory* (New York: New York University Press, 2003), 52–57; *Speech of Salmon P. Chase in the Case of the Colored Woman, Matilda* (Cincinnati: Pugh & Dodd, 1837). The case was reported in numerous newspaper articles, such as "The Birney Case Again," *Cincinnati Daily Gazette,* April 7, 1837; "The Birney Case Once More," *Cincinnati Daily Gazette,* April 10, 1837.

89. Birney, *James G. Birney and His Times,* 275–76. Letters to and from Birney, T. D. Weld, and Lewis Tappan in the summer of 1837, qtd. in Dumond, *Letters of James Gillespie Birney,* vol. 1 (New York: Appleton-Century, 1938).

90. *Narrative of James Williams,* 131; Birney and Tappan, "Alabama Beacon versus James Williams."

91. Both were advertised for sale in the *Philanthropist*, at least as early as June 9, 1837, through the end of the year.

92. "Dots and Lines—No. IV," *Ladies' Companion* (September 1839): 243; Lyford, *Western Address Directory*, 464.

93. Slatter's salesman, qtd. in Walter Johnson, *Soul by Soul: Life Inside the Antebellum Slave Market* (Cambridge: Harvard University Press, 1999), 132.

94. Chinn's letter appears as the final communication in *Slatter v. Holton*, docket no. 2894, Eastern District, June 1841, Supreme Court of Louisiana 19 LA 39, Earl K. Long Library, University of New Orleans, http://libweb.uno.edu/jspui/handle/123456789/12613 (accessed October 23, 2011).

95. Chinn wrote, "Having known the defendant and his principal witness since the war of 1812 in most of the relations of life." *Slatter v. Holton*, p. 00997, Earl K. Long Library, University of New Orleans, http://libweb.uno.edu/jspui/handle/123456789/12613 (accessed October 23, 2011); Garrett Glenn Clift, *Remember the Raisin!* (1961; repr., Baltimore: Genealogical Publishing Co., 2002), 192, 220.

96. Birney and Tappan, "Alabama Beacon versus James Williams."

97. William L. Andrews, *To Tell a Free Story: The First Century of Afro-American Autobiography, 1760–1865* (Champaign: University of Illinois Press, 1986), 100.

98. Fabian, *Unvarnished Truth*, 85.

99. See *Narrative of James Williams*, 75.

100. See ibid., 59 and 118.

101. See ibid., 33.

NARRATIVE

OF

JAMES WILLIAMS,

AN

AMERICAN SLAVE,

WHO WAS FOR SEVERAL YEARS A DRIVER ON A COTTON PLANTATION IN ALABAMA

Oh the slave, who toils from the rising sun to sundown—who labors in the cultivation of a crop whose fruits he may never reap—who comes home at nightfall weary, faint, and sick of heart, to find in his hut creatures that are to run in the same career with himself,—will you not tell him of a period when his toil shall be at an end? Will you not give him a hope for his children?

—*Speech of O'Connell. London*, 1833.[1]

PREFACE

[JOHN GREENLEAF WHITTIER]

"American slavery," said the celebrated John Wesley, "is the *vilest* beneath the sun!"[2] Of the truth of this emphatic remark no other proof is required than an examination of the statute books of the American slave states. Tested by its own laws, in all that facilitates and protects the hateful process of converting a man into a "*chattel personal*";[3] in all that stamps the law-maker and law-upholder with meanness and hypocrisy, it certainly has no present rival of its "bad eminence";[4] and we may search in vain the history of a world's despotism for a parallel. The civil code of Justinian never acknowledged, with that of our democratic despotisms, the essential equality of man. The dreamer in the gardens of Epicurus recognized neither in himself, nor in the slave who ministered to his luxury, the immortality of the spiritual nature. Neither Solon nor Lycurgus taught the inalienability of human rights.[5]

The Barons of the Feudal System, whose maxim was emphatically that of Wordsworth's robber,[6]

> "That he should take who had the power,
> And he should keep who can,"

while trampling on the necks of their vassals, and counting the life of a man as of less value than that of a wild beast, never appealed to God for the sincerity of their belief that all men were created equal. It was reserved for American slave-holders to present to the world the hideous anomaly of a code of laws, beginning with the emphatic declaration of the inalienable rights of all men to life, liberty, and the pursuit of happiness, and closing with a deliberate and systematic denial of those rights, in respect to a large portion of their countrymen; engrossing on the same parchment the antagonist laws of liberty and tyranny. The very nature of this unnatural combination has rendered it necessary that American slavery, in law and in practice, should exceed every other in severity and cool atrocity. The masters of Greece and Rome permitted their slaves to read and write, and worship the gods of paganism in peace and security, for there was nothing in the laws, literature, or religion of the age to awaken in the soul of the bondman a just sense of his rights as a man. But the American slave-holder cannot be thus lenient. In the excess of his benevolence, as a political propagandist, he has kindled a fire for the oppressed of the old world to gaze at with hope, and for crowned heads and dynasties to tremble at; but a due regard to the safety of his "peculiar institution" compels him to put out the eyes of his own people,[7] lest they too should see it. Calling on all the world to shake off the fetters of oppression, and wade through the blood of tyrants to freedom, he has been compelled to smother in darkness and silence the minds of his own bondmen, lest they too should hear and obey the summons, by putting the knife to his own throat. Proclaiming the truths of Divine Revelation, and sending the Scriptures to the four quarters of the earth, he has found it necessary to maintain heathenism at home by special enactments, and to make the second offence of teaching his slaves the message of salvation punishable with *death!*[8]

What marvel then that American slavery, even on the *statute book,* assumes the right to transform moral beings into brutes;*—that it legalizes man's usurpation of Divine authority: the substitution of the will of the master for the moral government of God;—that it annihilates the rights of conscience; debars from the enjoyment of religious rights and privileges by specific enactments; and enjoins disobedience to the Divine Lawgiver;—that it discourages purity and chastity, encourages crime, legalizes concubinage; and, while it places the slave entirely in the hands of his master, provides no real protection for his life or his person.

[*Footnote in original preface:* *The *cardinal principle* of slavery, that a slave is not to be ranked among sentient beings, but among things, as an article of Property, a chattel personal, obtains as undoubted law, in all the slave states. (Judge Stroud's sketch of Slave Laws, p. 22.)][9]

But it may be said, that these laws afford no certain evidence of the actual condition of the slaves: that, in judging the system by its code, no allowance is made for the humanity of individual masters. It was a just remark of the celebrated Priestley, that "no people ever were found to be better than their laws, though many have been known to be worse."[10] All history and common experience confirm this. Besides, admitting that the legal severity of a system may be softened in the practice of the humane, may it not also be aggravated by that of the avaricious and cruel?

But what are the testimony and admissions of slave-holders themselves on this point? In an Essay published in Charleston, S. C., in 1822, and entitled "A Refutation of the Calumnies circulated against the Southern and Western States," by the late Edwin C. Holland, Esq., it is stated, that "all slave-holders have laid down non-resistance, and perfect and uniform *obedience* to their orders, as fundamental principles in the government of their slaves"; that this is "a *necessary* result of the relation," and "*unavoidable.*"[11] Robert J. Turnbull, Esq., of South Carolina, in remarking upon the management of slaves, says, "The only principle upon which any authority over them (the slaves) can be maintained is *fear,* and he who denies this has little knowledge of them."[12] To this may be added the testimony of Judge Ruffin, of North Carolina, as quoted in Wheeler's Law of Slavery, p. 247. "The slave, to remain a slave, must feel that there is *no appeal from his master.* No man can anticipate the provocations which the slave would give, nor the consequent wrath of the master, prompting him to BLOODY VENGEANCE on the turbulent traitor, a vengeance *generally* practiced with impunity by reason of its *privacy.*"[13]

In an Essay on the "improvement of negroes on plantations," by Rev. Thomas S. Clay, a slave-holder of Bryan County, Georgia, and printed at the request of the Georgia Presbytery, in 1833, we are told, "that the present economy of the slave system is *to get all you can* from the slave, and give him in return *as little as will barely support hint in a working condition!*" Here, in a few words, the whole enormity of slavery is exposed to view: "to *get all you can* from the slave"—by means of whips, and stocks and irons—by every device for torturing the body, without destroying its capability of labor; and in return give him as little of his coarse fare as will keep him, like a mere beast of burden, in a "*working condition.*" This is slavery, as explained by the slave-holder himself.

Mr. Clay further says: "*Offences against the master* are more severely punished than violations of the law of God, a fault which affects the slave's personal character a good deal. As examples we may notice, that *running away* is more severely punished than adultery." "He (the slave) only knows his master as lawgiver and executioner, and the *sole object of punishment* held up to his view, is to make him *a more obedient and profitable slave.*"[14]

Hon. W. B. Seabrook, in an address before the Agricultural Society of St. Johns, Colleton, published by order of the Society, at Charleston, in 1834, after stating that, "as Slavery exists in South Carolina, the action of the citizens should rigidly conform to that state of things," and that "no *abstract opinions of the rights of man* should be allowed in any instance to modify the *police system of a plantation*," proceeds as follows: "*He (the slave) should be practically treated as a slave*, and thoroughly taught the true cardinal principle on which our peculiar institutions are founded, viz., that to his owner he is bound by the law of God and man; and that no human authority can sever the link which unites them. The great aim of the slave-holder, then, should be to keep his people in strict *subordination*. In this, it may in truth be said, lies his *entire duty*." Again, in speaking of the punishments of slaves, he remarks: "If to our army the disuse of THE LASH has been prejudicial, to the slave-holder it would operate to deprive him of the MAIN SUPPORT of his authority. For the first class of offences, I consider imprisonment in THE STOCKS* at night, with or without hard labor lay day, as a powerful auxiliary in the cause of *good* government." "*Experience* has convinced me that there is no punishment to which the slave looks with more horror, than that upon which I am now commenting (the stocks,) and none which has been attended with happier results."[15]

[*Footnote in original preface:* *Of the nature of this punishment in the stocks, something may be learned by the following extract of a letter from a gentleman in Tallahasse, Florida, to the editor of the Ohio Atlas, dated June 9, 1835: "A planter, a professor of religion, in conversing upon the universality of whipping, remarked, that a planter in G——, who had whipped a great deal at length got tired of it, and invented the following *excellent* method of punishment, which I saw practised while I was paying him a visit. The negro was placed in a sitting position, with his hands made fast above his head, and his feet in the stocks, so that he could not move any part of the body. The master retired, intending to leave him till morning, but we were awakened in the night by the groans of the negro, which were so doleful that we feared he was dying. We went to him, and found him covered in a cold sweat, and almost gone. He could not have lived an hour longer. Mr. —— found the 'stocks' such an effective punishment, that it almost superseded the whip."][16]

There is yet another class of testimony quite as pertinent as the foregoing, which may at any time be gleaned from the newspapers of the slave states—the advertisements of masters for their runaway slaves, and casual paragraphs, coldly relating cruelties, which would disgrace a land of Heathenism. Let the following suffice for specimen:

To the Editors of the Constitutionalist;

AIKEN, S.C., Dec. 20, 1836.

I have just returned from an inquest I held over the dead body of a negro man, a runaway, that was shot near the South Edisto, in this District (Barnwell,) on Saturday morning last. He came to his death by his own recklessness. He refused to be taken alive; and said that other attempts to take him had been made, and he was determined that he would not be taken. When taken, he was nearly naked—had a large dirk or knife, and a heavy club. He was, at first (when those who were in pursuit of him found it absolutely necessary,) shot at with small-shot, with the intention of merely crippling him. He was shot at several times, and at last he was so disabled as to be compelled to surrender. He kept in the run of a creek in a very dense swamp all the time that the neighbors were in pursuit of him. As soon as the negro was taken, the best medical aid was procured, but he died on the same evening. One of the witnesses at the inquisition stated that the negro boy said that he was from Mississippi, and belonged to so many persons he did not know who his master was: but again he said his master's name was *Brown*. He said his own name was Sam; and when asked by another witness who his master was, he muttered something like Augusta or Augustine. The boy was apparently above 35 or 40 years of age—about six feet high—slightly yellow in the face—very long beard of whiskers—and very stout built, and a stern countenance; and appeared to have been run away a long time.

WILLIAM H. PRITCHARD
Coroner (Ex officio,) Barnwell Dist., S.C.

The Mississippi and other papers will please copy the above.—*Georgia Constitutionalist.*[17]

$100 REWARD.—Ran away the subscriber, living on Herring Bay, Anne Arundel Co., Md., on Saturday, 28th January, Negro man Elijah, who calls himself Elijah Cook; is about 21 years of age, well made, of a very dark complexion, has an impediment in his speech, and *a scar on his left cheek bone, apparently occasioned by a shot.*

J. SCRIVENER.

Annapolis (Md.) Rep., Feb. 1837.[18]

$40 REWARD.—Ran away from my residence, near Mobile, two negro men, Isaac and Tim. Isaac is from 25 to 30 years old, dark complexion, scar on the right side of the head, and also one on the right side of the body, occasioned by BUCK SHOT. Tim is 22 years old, dark complexion, scar on the right cheek, as also another on the back of the neck. Captains and owners of steamboats, vessels, and water crafts of every description, are cautioned against taking them on board, under the penalty of the law, and all other persons against harboring or in any manner favoring the escape of said negroes, under like penalty.

SARAH WALSH.

Mobile, Sept. 1.

Montgomery (Ala.) Advertiser, Sept. 29, 1837.[19]

$200 REWARD.—Ran away from the subscriber, about three years ago, a certain Negro man named Ben (commonly known by the name of Ben Fox.) He is about 5 feet 5 or 6 inches high, chunky made, yellow complexion, and has but one eye. Also, one other negro by the name of Rigdon, who ran away on the 8th of this month. He is stout made, tall, and very black, with large lips.

I will give the reward of one hundred dollars for each of the above negroes, to be delivered to me or confined in the jail of Lenoir or Jones County, or *for the killing of them so that I can see them.* Masters of vessels, and all others, are cautioned against harboring, employing, or carrying them away, under the penalty of the law.

W. D. COBB.

Lenoir Co., N. C., November 12, 1836.[20]

BROUGHT TO JAIL.—In Irwinton, Wilkinson County (Ga.) 16th Nov. 1837, a negro man by the name of JACOB, who says he belongs to Heritan Middleton, in Henry County, Alabama. He says he was hired to John Webb, near West Point, in this State. He is about 6 feet high, dark complexion, and slow in speaking.

There are no marks discoverable, *only* he is VERY BADLY SHOT *in the right side and right hand.* The owner or owners are requested to come forward, prove property, pay charges, and take him away.

S. B. MURPHEY, Jailer.
Milledgville [*sic*], Jan. 2, 1838. *Georgia Journal*[21]

[From the *Clinton (Miss.) Gazette,* July 23, 1836.]

WAS COMMITTED to the jail of Covington County, on the 26th day of June, 1836, by G. D. Gere, Esq., a negro man, who says his name is JOSIAH, and says he belongs to John Martin, an Irishman, living in the State of Louisiana, on the west side of the Mississippi river, twenty miles below Natchez. Josiah is 5 feet 8 inches high, heavy built, copper color, his back *very much scarred* with the *whip,* and BRANDED on the thigh and hips in *three* or *four* places; thus (I. M.) or (J. M.;) the M. is very plain, but the I. or J. is not plain: the rim of his right ear has been bit or cut off. He is about 31 years of age, had on, when committed, pantaloons made of bed ticking, cotton coat, and an old fur hat very much worn. The owner of the above described negro is requested to comply with the requisitions of the law in such cases made and provided.

J. L. JOLLEY, Sheriff, C. C.
Williamsburgh, June 28, 1836.[22]

WAS COMMITTED to jail, a negro man, who says that his name is HARRY. Said boy is about 30 years old, light complexion and bald head; has a scar on his left knee; also, one on his forehead, and one on his right hand; *he is very much marked with the whip.* The owner, &c.

B. W. HATCH, Jailer.
Port Gibson (Mi.,) Correspondent, Sept. 16, 1837.

$50 REWARD.—Ran away from the subscriber, a negro fellow named Dick, about 21 or 22 years of age, dark mulatto, has many scars on his back from being *whipped.* The boy was purchased by me from Thomas L. Arnold, and absconded about the time the purchase was made.

JAMES NOE.
Sentinel and Expositor, Vicksburg (Mi.,) Oct. 10, 1837.[23]

[From the *New Orleans Bee,* Oct. 28, 1837.]

$10 REWARD.—Ran away, on the 9th of October, CAROLINE, aged about 38 years; had a collar on with one prong turned down.

T. CUGGY,
Gallatin st., between Hospital and Barracks.[24]

$25 REWARD.—For the black woman, Betsey, who left my house in the Faubourg, McDonnough, about the, 12th inst., when she had on her neck an iron collar; has a mark on her neck and is about 20 years of age.

CHARLES KERNIN.
New Orleans paper, March, 1837.[25]

$50 REWARD.—Ran away from Murot's Plantation, near Baton Rouge, about two months ago, the negro man Manuel. Description—black, 5 feet 4 inches high, about 30 years old, one scar on the forehead, and *much marked with irons.*

New Orleans Bee, May 27, 1837.[26]

COMMITTED to the jail of Pike County, a man about twenty-three or four years old, who calls his name John. The said Negro has a clog of iron on his right foot which will weigh 4 or 5 pounds. The owner is requested, &c.

B. W. HODGES, Jailer.
Montgomery (Alabama) *Advertiser,* Sept. 29, 1837.[27]

$100 REWARD.—Ran away from the subscriber, six weeks ago, two negro men, one a tall fellow, stoops considerably in walking; when spoken to fiercely, looks as if he would sink into the earth. The other is a short stumpy fellow, of a very black or almost blue color, large cheeks, has a scar over one eye; also, *one on his leapfrog the bite of a dog,* and a burn on his body from a piece of *hot iron,* in the shape of a T!

JOHN A. DILLAHUNTY.
New Orleans Bee, Feb. 8, 1837.[28]

A Negro who had absconded from his master, and for whom a reward was offered of $100, has been apprehended and committed to prison in Savannah, Georgia. The editor who states the fact, adds, with as much coolness as though there were no barbarity in the matter, that he did not surrender until he was considerably *maimed by the dogs** that had been set on him,—desperately fighting them, one of which he cut badly with a sword.

New York Commercial Advertiser, June 8, 1827.[29]

[*Footnote in original preface:* *In regard to the use of bloodhounds, for the recapture of runaway slaves, we insert the following from the New York Evangelist, being an extract of a letter from Natchez (Miss.) under date of January 31, 1835: "An instance was related to me in Clairborne County, in Mississippi. A runaway was heard about the house in the night. The hound was put upon his track, and in the morning was found watching the dead body of the negro. The dogs are trained to this service when young. A negro is directed to go into the woods and secure himself upon a tree. When sufficient time has elapsed for doing this, the hound is put upon his track. The blacks are compelled to worry them until they make them their implacable enemies; and it is common to meet with dogs which will take no notice of whites, though entire strangers, but will suffer no blacks beside the house servants to enter the yard."][30]

From the foregoing evidence on the part of slave-holders themselves, we gather the following facts:

1. That perfect obedience is required of the slave—that he is made to feel that there is no appeal from his master.

2. That the authority of the master is only maintained by fear—a "*reign of terror.*"

3. That "the economy of slavery is to *get all you can* from the slave, and give him in return as little as will barely support him in a working condition."

4. That runaway slaves may be shot down with impunity by any white person.[31]

5. That masters offer rewards for "*killing*" their slaves, "*so that they may see them!*"

6. That slaves are branded with hot irons, and very much scarred with the whip.

7. That *iron collars*, with projecting prongs, rendering it almost impossible for the wearer to lie down, are fastened upon the *necks of women*.

8. That the LASH is the MAIN SUPPORT of the slave-holder's authority; but, that the *stocks* are "a powerful auxiliary" to his government.

9. That runaway slaves are chased with dogs—men hunted like beasts of prey.

Such is American Slavery in practice.

The testimony thus far adduced is only that of the slave-holder and wrong-doer himself: the admission of men who have a direct interest in keeping out of sight the horrors of their system. It is, besides, no voluntary admission. Having "framed iniquity by law,"[32] it is out of their power to hide it. For the recovery of their runaway property, they are compelled to advertise in the public journals, and, that it may be identified, they are under the necessity of describing the marks of the whip on the backs of women, the iron collars about the neck, the gun-shot wounds, and the traces of the branding-iron. Such testimony must, in the nature of things, be partial and incomplete. But for a full revelation of the secrets of the prison-house, we must look to the slave himself. The Inquisitors of Goa and Madrid never disclosed the peculiar atrocities of their "hall of horrors."[33] It was the escaping heretic, with his swollen and disjointed limbs, and bearing about him the scars of rack and fire, who exposed them to the gaze and abhorrence of Christendom.

The following pages contain the simple and unvarnished story of an AMERICAN SLAVE,—of one whose situation, in the first place, as a favorite servant in an aristocratic family in Virginia, and afterwards as the sole and confidential driver on a large plantation in Alabama, afforded him rare and peculiar advantages for accurate observation of the practical workings on the system. His intelligence, evident candor, and grateful remembrance of those kindnesses which in a land of slavery made his cup of suffering less bitter; the perfect accordance of his statements (made at different times and to different individuals*) one with another, as well as those statements themselves, all afford strong confirmation of the truth and accuracy of his story. There seems to have been no effort, on his part, to make his picture of slavery one of entire darkness—he details every thing of a mitigating character which fell under his observation; and even the cruel deception of his master has not rendered him unmindful of his early kindness.

[*Footnote in original preface:* *The reader is referred to JOHN G. WHITTIER, of

Amesbury, Mass., or to the following gentlemen, who have heard the whole or part of his story from his own lips: Emmor Kimber, of Kimberton, Pa., Lindley Coates, of Lancaster Co., do.; James Mott, of Philadelphia, Lewis Tappan, Elizur Wright, Jun., Rev. Dr. Follen, and James G. Birney, of New York.[34] The latter gentleman, who was a few years ago a citizen of Alabama, assures us that the statements made to him by James Williams were such as he had every reason to believe, from his own knowledge of slavery in that State.][35]

The Editor is fully aware that he has not been able to present this affecting narrative in the simplicity and vivid freshness with which it fell from the lips of the narrator. He has, however, as closely as possible, copied his manner, and in many instances his precise language. THE SLAVE HAS SPOKEN FOR HIMSELF. Acting merely as his amanuensis, he has carefully abstained from comments of his own.*

[*Footnote in original preface:* *As the narrator was unable to read or write, it is quite possible that the orthography of some of the names of individuals mentioned in this story may not be entirely correct. The name of his master, for instance, may have been either Larrimer or Larrimore.][36]

The picture here presented to the people of the free states is, in many respects, a novel one. We all know something of Virginia and Kentucky slavery. We have heard of the internal slave trade—the pangs of separation—the slave ship with its "cargo of despair,"[37] bound for the New Orleans market—and the weary journey of the chained Coffle to the cotton country. But here, in a great measure, we have lost sight of the victims of avarice and lust. We have not studied the dreadful economy of the cotton plantation, and know but little of the secrets of its unlimited despotism.

But in this narrative the scenes of the plantation rise before us, with a distinctness which approaches reality. We hear the sound of the horn at daybreak, calling the sick and the weary to toil unrequited.[38] Woman, in her appealing delicacy and suffering, about to become a mother, is fainting under the lash, or sinking exhausted beside her cotton row.[39] We hear the prayer for mercy answered with sneers and curses.[40] We look on the instruments of torture, and the corpses of murdered men.[41] We see the dogs, reeking hot from the chase, with their jaws foul with human blood.[42] We see the meek and aged Christian, scarred with the lash, and bowed down with toil, offering the supplication of a broken heart to his Father in Heaven for the forgiveness of his brutal enemy. We hear, and from our inmost hearts repeat, the affecting interrogatory of the aged slave, "*How long, Oh Lord! How long!*"[43]

The Editor has written out the details of this painful narrative with feelings of sorrow. If there be any who feel a morbid satisfaction in dwelling upon the history of outrage and cruelty, he at least is not one of them. His taste and habits incline him rather to look to the pure and beautiful in our nature—the sunniest side of humanity—its kindly sympathies—its holy affections—its charities and its love. But it is because he has seen that all which is thus beautiful and excellent in mind and heart perishes in the atmosphere of slavery; it is because humanity in the slave sinks down to a level with the brute, and in the master gives place to the attributes of a fiend—that he has not felt at liberty to decline the task. He cannot sympathize with that abstract and delicate philanthropy which hesitates to bring itself in contact with the sufferer, and which shrinks from the effort of searching out the extent of his afflictions. The emblem of Practical Philanthropy is the Samaritan stooping over the wounded Jew. It must be no fastidious hand which administers the oil and the wine, and binds up the unsightly gashes.

Believing, as he does, that this narrative is one of truth; that it presents an unexaggerated picture of slavery as it exists on the cotton plantations of the South and West, he would particularly invite to its perusal those individuals, and especially those professing Christians at the North, who have ventured to claim for such a system the sanction and approval of the religion of Jesus Christ. In view of the facts here presented, let these men seriously inquire of themselves, whether, in advancing such a claim, they are not uttering a higher and more audacious blasphemy than any which ever fell from the pens of Voltaire and Paine. As if to cover them with confusion, and leave them utterly without excuse for thus libelling the character of a just God, these developments are making, and the veil rising, which for long years of sinful apathy has rested upon the abominations of American Slavery. Light is breaking into its dungeons, disclosing the wreck of buried intellect—of hearts broken—of human affections outraged—of souls ruined. The world will see it as God has always seen it; and when He shall at length make inquisition for blood, and His vengeance kindle over the habitations of cruelty, with a destruction more terrible than that of Sodom and Gomorrah, His righteous dealing will be justified of man, and His name glorified among the nations, and there will be a voice of rejoicing in Earth and in Heaven. ALLELUIA! THE PROMISE IS FULFILLED!—FOR THE SIGHING OF THE POOR AND THE OPPRESSION OF THE NEEDY, GOD HATH RISEN!

It is the earnest desire of the Editor that this narrative may be the means, under God, of awakening in the hearts of all who read it a sympathy for the oppressed which shall manifest itself in immediate, active, self-sacrificing exertions for their deliverance; and, while it excites abhorrence of his crimes, call forth pity for the oppressor. May it have the effect to prevent the avowed and associated friends of the slave from giving such an undue importance to their own trials and grievances, as to forget in a great measure the sorrows of the slave.[44] Let its cry of wo[e], coming up from the plantations of the South, suppress every feeling of selfishness in our hearts. Let our regret and indignation at the denial of the right of petition be felt only because we are thereby prevented, from pleading in the halls of Congress for the "suffering and the dumb."[45] And let the fact, that we are shut out from half the territory of our country, be lamented only because it prevents us from bearing personally to the land of slavery the messages of hope for the slave, and of rebuke and warning for the oppressor.

New York, 24th 1st. mo., 1838.[46]

NOTES TO THE 2013 EDITION

1. This quotation is from a speech by Irish reformer Daniel O'Connell, one of several speakers at the Anti-Colonization Meeting in Exeter Hall, London, July 13, 1833. Others in attendance included British philanthropist James Cropper, whose son would assist James Williams in Liverpool, and American abolitionist William Lloyd Garrison, who caused a collection of the speeches to be printed in the United States the same year. Williams himself expressed his opinion about the American Colonization Society's plan to send freed slaves to Liberia (p. 31). *Speeches Delivered at the Anti-Colonization Meeting in Exeter Hall, London, July 13, 1833* (Boston: Garrison & Knapp, 1833), 22.

2. John Greenleaf Whittier, who wrote the narrative from James Williams's dictation, composed the preface. This quotation was adapted from a letter written February 24, 1771, by John Wesley, founder of the Methodist Church. A few days before he died, Wesley wrote William Wilberforce: "Go on, in the name of God, and in the power of his might, till even American slavery (the vilest that ever saw the sun) shall vanish away before it." Wilberforce continued to work for the cause of abolition in England, living just long enough to see the passage of the Slavery Abolition Act of 1833, which ended slavery throughout most of the British Empire. John Emory, *The Works of the Reverend John Wesley, A.M.* (New York: B. Waugh & T. Mason), 7:237.

3. *Chattel personal* was the legal term for personal property, as opposed to real estate.

4. The phrase was applied to people or things who achieved distinction in a negative way. It

appeared in John Milton's *Paradise Lost*, bk. 2, "The Argument," lines 5–6: "Satan exalted sat, by merit rais'd / To that bad eminence."

5. Roman emperor Justinian issued his influential civil code in the sixth century C.E. The others attained their fame in the era of ancient Greece. Philosopher Epicurus kept a school in his garden in Athens. Solon and Lycurgus were legislators in Athens and Sparta.

Whittier began his introduction by pointing out the contradiction between legalized slavery and the principle that all men are created equal, but he soon shifted to specific newspaper notices and eyewitness accounts, selected to reinforce the accuracy of Williams's narrative.

When southerners questioned the truth of the narrative, the abolitionists fell back on their strongest point: the cruel treatment *could* have occurred, whether Williams had lied about other things or not: "To corroborate the representation in this respect, the narrative was accompanied by a prefatory essay, in which numerous well authenticated facts connected with American slavery, were brought together and presented in such a manner as to force the belief, that the picture exhibited in the narrative, if not drawn from life, was certainly true to nature. The book was then sent forth, to pass for what it purported to be, and nothing more." James G. Birney and Lewis Tappan, "Alabama Beacon versus James Williams," *Emancipator*, August 30, 1838, reprinted in the *Friend of Man*, September 19, 1838.

6. The oft-quoted lines were from William Wordsworth's poem "Rob Roy's Grave":

> The Creatures see of flood and field,
> And those that travel on the wind!
> With them no strife can last; they live
> In peace, and peace of mind.
>
> For why?—because the good old Rule
> Sufficeth them, the simple Plan,
> That they should take, who have the power,
> And they should keep who can.

—from "Rob Roy's Grave," in *The Complete Poetical Works of William Wordsworth*, ed. Henry Reed (Philadelphia: James Kay, Jun. & Brother, 1837), 200–201.

7. The phrase *peculiar institution* indicated any institution unique to a particular group, though it came to be applied most famously to slavery. Southerners used it to emphasize the necessity of slavery in the South's distinctive economic and geographical situation, a concept that they felt northerners had difficulty understanding.

8. Whittier was referring to the ongoing hostility against abolitionists who sent literature into the South. In the 1830s both federal and state laws had been proposed, banning antislavery materials from the mail, and some were enacted. Even when there was no specific legal prohibition, southerners stopped the mail with violence and intimidation. Less than three years earlier, in July 1835, a mob had destroyed abolitionist pamphlets at the Charleston, South Carolina, post office and burned effigies of leading abolitionists. Postmaster General Amos Kendall commented sympathetically, admitting he could not legally bar abolitionists from sending what they wanted,

though he wrote to the Charleston postmaster, "We owe an obligation to the laws, but a higher one to the communities in which we live."

In 1831 William Lloyd Garrison and Isaac Knapp had been indicted by a North Carolina jury for violating a newly enacted state law "to prevent the circulation of seditious publications." Their crime was mailing copies of the *Liberator* from Boston to North Carolina, though the trial never proceeded because North Carolina officials were unable to extradite them from Massachusetts. Whittier might have been referring to that specific incident because the law they were accused of violating called for whipping and a prison sentence for a first offense and death without benefit of clergy for a second offense.

A similar case occurred the same month James Williams escaped from Alabama and less than a hundred miles away. In September 1835, the Tuscaloosa County circuit court indicted Robert G. Williams of New York for circulating a copy of the *Liberator* that included the statement: "God commands, and all nature cries out, that man should not be held as property. The system of making men property, has plunged 2,250,000 of our fellow countrymen into the deepest physical and moral degradation, and they are every moment sinking deeper." The punishment for a free person encouraging insurrection was death in Alabama even for the first offense, but the outcome of this indictment was the same: the state failed to extradite the accused.

The hostility was not, as Whittier implied, against religious messages specifically. The messages had to be ones that incited insurrection, but since the bloody 1831 rebellion led by slave preacher Nat Turner, slaves, religion, and insurrection were inexorably linked in southerners' minds. Abolitionists used this association to their advantage, casting their activities in the unobjectionable light of merely spreading the Gospel, while southerners focused on the personal dangers they faced if slaves were informed of their equality or the moral wrong of slavery.

William H. Smith, *A Political History of Slavery* (New York: Putnam, 1903), 42–43; James Parton, *Life of Andrew Jackson* (New York: Mason Brothers, 1860), 3:586–87; Phillip I. Blumberg, *Repressive Jurisprudence in the Early American Republic* (Cambridge: Cambridge University Press, 2010), 362–64; "Legislature of New York. Requisition of the Governor of Alabama," *Niles' Weekly Register,* January 23, 1836, 358–60; Harry Toulmin, *A Digest of the Laws of the State of Alabama* (Cahawba, Ala.: Ginn & Curtis, 1828), 224–25; *The American Anti-Slavery Almanac, for 1837* (Cincinnati: Ohio Anti-Slavery Society, 1836), 18.

9. George McDowell Stroud (1795–1875), a Philadelphia judge, wrote his work on the slave laws from an openly abolitionist viewpoint, using the facts to illustrate the inherent evils. Kimber & Sharpless of Philadelphia published the book, the Kimber being Thomas Kimber, a nephew of Emmor Kimber, who assisted Williams during his escape.

After quoting Louisiana law, Stroud wrote: "With respect to the other slave-holding states, as none of these have adopted *entire written codes,* enunciations of such a *general* nature, as are exhibited in the quotations just made from the law of Louisiana, are not to be expected. Nevertheless, the cardinal principal of slavery,—that the slave is not to be ranked among *sentient beings,* but among *things**—is an article of property—a chattel personal,—obtains as undoubted law in all of these states." The asterisk referenced a Maryland law. The author also offered other laws from Kentucky, South Carolina, and Virginia as examples. George M. Stroud, *Sketch of the Laws Relating to Slavery in the Several States of the United States of America* (Philadelphia: Kimber

& Sharpless, 1827), 22–23; Sidney A. Kimber, *A Genealogical History of the Descendants of Richard Kimber* (Boston: Sidney A. Kimber, 1894), 37, 40.

10. Abolitionists often attributed the quote to Joseph Priestley (1733–1804), but it did not appear verbatim in his writings. Priestley expressed a similar, though less strong, sentiment in *The Evidences of Revelation*, sec. 4: "As it is well known that many persons are much worse, so there are others, no doubt, much better than their principles."

11. Edwin Clifford Holland (c. 1793–1824) was a Charleston editor, essayist, and poet as well as "a sort of local terror," according to one brief biography. Trained as a lawyer, he preferred arguing about social and political issues in print. He claimed to have written this particular pamphlet in response to the hostility and ignorance shown by people in the North and East to those in the South and West on the question of slavery.

The full title reads: *A Refutation of the Calumnies Circulated against the Southern & Western States, Respecting the Institution and Existence of Slavery among Them, to Which Is Added a Minute and Particular Account of the Actual State and Condition of the Negro Population. Together with Historical Notices of All the Insurrections That Have Taken Place since the Settlement of the Country.* The author is identified only as "a South-Carolinian" on the cover, but Holland's name appears on the copyright page.

The quoted passage appears on p. 47, in a rebuttal against charges that masters mistreated their slaves. The paragraph begins:

> It is indeed humiliating to the last degree to listen even to such charges as those we have noticed; but it is due to the fair fame of these sections of the Union to demonstrate, that the condition of the slave, so far from partaking of the misery which has been attributed to it, is in every respect preferable to that of the poor laboring class of people of any Government on earth, and that if it were not for foreign, subsidiary causes, he would remain perfectly satisfied with his lot. It is true, indeed, that all slave-holders have laid down non-resistance and the most perfect and uniform obedience to their orders, as fundamental principles in the government of their slaves. This necessarily results from the relation in which they stand, and we might as well denounce that government a despotism, that punishes any infringement of its laws, as to call that a tyranny which is nothing more or less than an authority *unavoidably* arising from the very character of the connexion between master and slave. This authority unquestionably may be abused, but we deny that these abuses have ever been so frequent as to justify the illiberal and unfeeling calumnies of which we complain.

The author then cited his own examples of signed testimonials describing the benevolent treatment of slaves. George Ripley and Charles A. Dana, eds., *The New American Cyclopaedia* (New York: D. Appleton & Co., 1860), 9:234; Edwin C. Holland, *A Refutation of The Calumnies Circulated against the Southern and Western States* (Charleston: A. E. Miller, 1822), 47–48.

12. Robert James Turnbull (1775–1833) was a lawyer in Charleston. His quote appeared in Holland's pamphlet on p. 55, among the testimonials of humane treatment. He described South Carolina slaves' reasonable tasks, sufficient food and clothing, their "cheerfulness and mirth," and explained:

> With all their mirth and merriment, however, they do not seem more contented than they were thirty or forty years ago, when the discipline was more rigid, their labor more constant and their comforts fewer. This is undoubtedly owing to a *relaxation in disipline* [*sic*] which experience abundantly proves has been almost carried *too far.* The regulations that would be applicable to whites entirely fail when applied to the government of slaves. The only principle upon which any authority over them can be maintained is *fear;* and he who denies this, has but little knowledge of them. Where there is this principle in the bosom of a slave, coupled with a strong sense of his inferiority to his master, he is happy and contented, and this is almost universally the case with the *country Negroes.* In his dreams, no visions visit him to remind him of his servitude. Born a slave, he need only be assured that he will be well fed and clothed for life, and worked in moderation, and he will regard himself as the happiest of mortals.

Elizur Wright, editor of the American Anti-Slavery Society's *Quarterly Anti-Slavery Magazine,* critiqued Turnbull's argument more thoroughly in an article, "Pro-Slavery Testimony Examined," published in the October 1835 issue of the quarterly. Holland, *Refutation of the Calumnies Circulated against the Southern and Western States,* 51–56; "Pro-Slavery Testimony Examined," *Quarterly Anti-Slavery Magazine* (October 1835): 94–98.

13. Judge Thomas Ruffin (1787–1870), a North Carolina Supreme Court justice, issued the statement in response to *The State v. Mann,* an 1829 North Carolina trial in which John Mann was accused of assault and battery upon Lydia, an enslaved woman whom he had hired from her owner for a year. Mann attempted to punish her, but she ran off, and when she did not obey his order to stop, he shot and wounded her. He was found guilty and appealed the verdict.

Ruffin reluctantly pointed out that slaves must labor because of their "natural duty," so "the power of the master must be absolute, to render the submission of the slave perfect. I most freely confess my sense of the harshness of this proposition . . . And as a principle of moral right, every person in his retirement must repudiate it. But in the actual condition of things, it must be so. There is no remedy." Whittier had shortened the quote he used. In full it stated:

> The slave, to remain a slave, must be made sensible that there is no appeal from his master; that his person is, in no instance, usurped; but is conferred by the laws of man, at least, if not by the law of God. The danger would be great indeed, if the tribunals of justice should be called on to graduate the punishment appropriate to every temper, and every dereliction of menial duty. No man can anticipate the many and aggravated provocations of the master which the slave would be constantly stimulated, by his own passions, or the instigation of others, to give; or the consequent wrath of the master, prompting him to bloody vengeance, upon the turbulent traitor; a vengeance generally practised with impunity, by reason of its privacy. The court, therefore, disclaims the power of changing the relation in which these parts of our people stand to each other.

Ruffin reversed the earlier judgment, declaring Mann innocent. The outcome was different from the 1834 North Carolina Supreme Court decision in *The State vs. Negro Will, Slave of James*

S. Battle (see p. 119), in which the guilt of the defendant was upheld and limits were placed on the actions a master could take when a slave attempted to run away. Jacob D. Wheeler, *A Practical Treatise on the Law of Slavery* (New York: Allan Pollock Jr., 1837), 246–47.

14. The essay was *Detail of a Plan for the Moral Improvement of Negroes on Plantations. Read before the Georgia Presbytery*, by Thomas S. Clay (1801–49). Clay, one of the largest slave owners in Bryan County, Georgia, attempted to run his plantation, Richmond-on-Ogeechee, as a benevolent but profitable venture, taking a paternalistic view of slavery while preparing for its ultimate demise by training his slaves for eventual freedom.

The first quoted passage came from p. 20, without the emphasis, as part of a paragraph recommending that owners take more interest in finding out and supplying the comforts that their slaves wanted. The second quote, from pp. 17 and 18, was altered slightly and shortened. The original stated:

> Offenses against the master are more severely punished than violations of the law of God, or faults which affect the slave's personal character or good. As examples, we may notice that running away, is more severely punished than adultery, and idleness, than Sabbath breaking and swearing; and stealing from the master, than defrauding a fellow slave. Under the influence of such a code as this, it cannot be a matter of surprize that the negro forms false estimates of the comparative criminality of actions. And further, the general mode of inflicting punishment, tends to confound these distinctions. The whip is the general instrument of correction, and so long as a negro is whipped without discrimination for neglect of work, for stealing, lying, Sabbath breaking and swearing, he will very naturally class them all together as belonging to the same grade of guilt. In a good code of discipline, the punishment will always be suited to the nature and enormity of the crime; and it is highly important that this measure should be well adjusted, for the common people will judge the criminality of the act by the nature and extent of the punishment.
>
> Another error is obvious in the defective presentation of the design of punishment. The negro is seldom taught to feel, that he is punished for breaking God's law. He only knows his *master* as lawgiver and executioner, and the sole object of punishment held up to his view, is to make him a more obedient and profitable slave.

Thomas S. Clay, *Detail of a Plan for the Moral Improvement of Negroes on Plantations* (N.p.: Printed at the request of the Georgia Presbytery, 1833), 17–18, 20; Janet Duitsman Cornelius, *Slave Missions and the Black Church in the Antebellum South* (Columbia: University of South Carolina Press, 1999), 85–87.

15. Whitemarsh Benjamin Seabrook (1793–1855) read his "Essay on the Management of Slaves, and Especially, on Their Religious Instruction" to the Agricultural Society of St. John's Parish, Colleton County, South Carolina. He was president of the society, had served in the state legislature, and was lieutenant governor of South Carolina. The owner of Gun Bluff Plantation on Edisto Island, he was an opponent of the more egalitarian views of Thomas S. Clay (see note 14), making his writing an easy source for abolitionists to find quotes reflecting poorly

on slave owners. Albert J. Raboteau, *Slave Religion: The "Invisible Institution" in the Antebellum South, updated ed.* (Oxford: Oxford University Press, 2004), 169–70; W. B. Seabrook, *Essay on the Management of Slaves, and Especially, on Their Religious Instruction* (Charleston, S.C.: A. E. Miller, 1834).

16. This passage on the cruelty of stocks was probably meant to attest to the realism of the incident Williams related on p. 41. The letter writer was Philemon Bliss (1813–89), a lawyer who was born in Connecticut but practiced in Elyria, Lorain County, Ohio. In 1834 and 1835 he lived on a plantation near Tallahassee, Florida, and wrote back to his brother, Albert A. Bliss, editor of the *Ohio Atlas*, the Loraine County newspaper, about his experiences there. Theodore Dwight Weld, *American Slavery as It Is* (New York: American Anti-Slavery Society, 1839), 102–5; *History of Lorain County, Ohio* (Philadelphia: Williams Brothers, 1879), 48, 57.

17. Although the weekly *Georgia Constitutionalist* was published across the state line, in Augusta, it was only about twenty miles southwest of Aiken, South Carolina. Aiken's own newspaper, the *Aiken Telegraph and Commercial Advertiser*, had been founded the previous year and may have been out of business by December 1836, but the coroner evidently wanted the news spread in the direction of Mississippi anyway, in hopes of discovering the owner of the enslaved man. "About the Aiken Telegraph and Commercial Advertiser," *Chronicling America*, http://chroniclingamerica.loc.gov/lccn/sn92065410/ (accessed October 13, 2011).

18. The original ad also included details of Elijah Cook's clothing and probable destination. He must have been recaptured because a few months later John Scrivener advertised for him again. The later ad, in the June 21, 1837, Baltimore *American and Commercial Daily Advertiser*, omitted the most important fact to the abolitionists, the scar. It stated:

> $150 REWARD—Ranaway from the subscriber, living on Herring Bay, Anne Arundel County Md. on Sunday, 18th June, 1837, a negro man named LIGE, who calls himself Elijah Cook, is about 21 years of age, well made, very dark complexion and an impediment in his speech, about 5 feet 8 or 10 inches high; his clothing a blue cloth coat, yellow and grey pantaloons, cassinet jacket, and a variety of other clothing, and probably has changed his clothing and name to elude detection, and may be furnished with a pass.
>
> He has relations living in the City of Annapolis or its vicinity. I will give $100 reward if taken in the County or State, or $150 if out of the State, in either case to be secured in jail or delivered to me, so that I get him again. All persons are forwarned against harboring or employing him in any way whatever, as I am determined to enforce the law against all offenders.
>
> JOHN SCRIVENER, Sen.

Scrivener ran the same ad again almost three months later, on September 1, 1837, so Cook may have finally succeeded. "Beneath the Underground: The Flight to Freedom," *Maryland State Archives*, www.mdslavery.net/html/mapped_images/mnpage17376.html (accessed October 13, 2011).

19. Abolitionists reprinted at least two different ads by Sarah Walsh seeking her slave Isaac. Five months later, on February 13, 1838, she was advertising for him alone, offering a twenty-five-

dollar reward. He had been missing since his original escape in September. She described similar marks in the later ad: "a scar on his forehead, caused by a blow, and one on his back, made by a shot from a pistol."

Sarah Barnes had married Dennis R. Walsh (or Welsh) of Mobile in 1836, but they were soon embroiled in an acrimonious divorce. She claimed that he "was guilty of such cruel & barbarous conduct towards her that she found it impossible to live with him." Because she brought her own slaves into the marriage and kept her property separate, she filed suit in 1839 to prevent him from treating them as his own until she could get the divorce finalized. A man named Isaac, about twenty-six years old, showed up in the list of her property then, so perhaps she recaptured him, though Tim did not appear in the list. In the 1840 census she was in her forties, living in Mobile with a young white boy (presumably her son) and twenty-nine enslaved people.

Weld, *American Slavery as It Is*, 172–73; Clinton P. King, *Marriages of Mobile County, Alabama, 1813–1855* (Baltimore: Genealogical Publishing Co., 1985), 8; Document no. 507, Records of the Chancery Court, Divorce Cases, University of South Alabama Archives, Mobile, Petition no. 20183911, *Digital Library on American Slavery*, http://library.uncg.edu/slavery/details.aspx?pid=3040 (accessed October 13, 2011).

20. William Donnell Cobb (1805–65) issued the chilling request to see the dead bodies of Ben Fox and Rigdon, under specific legal circumstances. The men had not fled to freedom in the North but instead had been "lurking about in the Counties of Lenoir and Jones, committing acts of felony." Under North Carolina law, in that situation if an appropriate notice was posted, anyone could legally kill them. Cobb took advantage of the law by making a complaint to two justices of the peace, B. Coleman and Jas. Jones. They published a statement as required, dated the same day as Cobb's advertisement, and at that point it became legal for anyone to "kill or destroy said slaves by such means as he or they think fit, without accusation or impeachment of any crime or offence for so doing." Harriet Beecher Stowe, *Dred: A Tale of the Great Dismal Swamp* (London: Sampson Low, Son & Co., 1856), 2:375–76; Henry Potter, *Laws of the State of North-Carolina* (Raleigh: J. Gales, 1821), 1:165.

21. Irwinton was about 140 miles east of West Point. Williams had fled east across Georgia, over a similar route, two years before the man named Jacob in this ad did. John Claiborne "Bridger" Webb (1790–1840) served as an officer in both the War of 1812 and the Creek War and in 1838 was president of the West Point Land Company and a member of the Georgia legislature. He was born in Elbert County, Georgia, the same county that Williams's owner, Caleb Tate, had lived in before moving to Dallas County, Alabama. Tate married a Middleton, but there is no other information available on "Heritan Middleton." Solomon B. Murphy was also the sheriff and a slave owner himself.

Jack Webb, "John Claiborne 'Bridger' Webb," Webb Family of Georgia, http://wc.rootsweb.ancestry.com/cgi-bin/igm.cgi?op=GET&db=jackwebb48&id=I01801 (accessed October 14, 2011); "Wilkinson County, Ga. News Articles 1820s–1830s," Georgia Genealogy, www.georgia-genealogy.org/wilkinson/news1820s-1830s.html (accessed October 14, 2011); 1840 Georgia Federal Census, District 327, Wilkinson County.

22. Josiah would have traveled over one hundred miles in a generally eastern direction. The J.M. brand apparently signified the initials of his owner, John Martin. Gilbert D. Gere and James L. Jolley (or Jolly) were both locally influential citizens and were among the commissioners

appointed to organize the counties of Smith, Scott, and Neshoba in 1833. T. J. Fox Alden and J. A. Van Hoesen, *Digest of the Laws of Mississippi* (New York: Alexander S. Gould, 1839), 321.

23. In another ad for Dick, placed in the August 22, 1837, *Sentinel* of Vicksburg, Mississippi, James Noe gave his address as Red River Landing, Louisiana. A man with the same name owned property near Vicksburg, 130 miles to the north. Weld, *American Slavery as It Is*, 63.

24. The full advertisement read:

$10 REWARD.

RANAWAY on the 9th of October, the negress CAROLINE, aged about 38 years, stout, 5 feet 5 inches high, awkward feet clumsy ankles and turns out her toes greatly in walking; she is black, had a collar on with one prong turned down, speaks English only; she had a sore on her left chin. She is supposed to be in the third municipality, lurking round the wash houses, also has been seen several times seeking for days work; and had a pair of French bootes with her.

T. CUGGY,
Gallatin st. between Hospital and Barracks.

Abolitionists corroborated the use of pronged iron collars for discouraging runaways with other examples, such as ads like those following this one, or a report published in 1838 from William Armstrong of Marietta, Ohio, who had been to New Orleans as a boat captain: "In New Orleans he saw several with iron collars, with horns attached to them. The first he saw had three prongs projecting from the collar ten or twelve inches, with the letter S on the end of each. He says iron collars are quite frequent there." Weld, *American Slavery as It Is*, 73–75.

25. The ad appeared in the *New Orleans Bee* of June 9, 1837, and similar dates, obviously referring to an escape in an earlier month, not June 12:

REWARD

$25 Reward for the black woman BETSY who left my house, in Faubourg, McDonough, about the 12th of the present month, when she had on her neck an iron collar, has a mark on her left cheek, is about 20 years old, 5 feet 4 inches high, when she ranaway, was well dressed. She was seen two days past at the lower Railroad and had not her collar on her neck.

CHARLES KERNIN
Parish of Jefferson

The subscriber's name may have been Kernion, of the old New Orleans Hutchet de Kernion family, though the abolitionists copied it as it appeared in the newspaper.

26. The ad, which appeared May 29, 1837, and similar dates in the *New Orleans Bee*, stated:

$50 REWARD

RANAWAY from A. Murot's plantation, near Baton Rouge, about two months ago, the negro man, Manuel. Description—black, 5 feet 4 inches high, about 30 years old, one scar on the forehead, and much marked with irons. A few days before he absconded, he was seen about the county with pistols, a gold watch, and a large amount of money in bank notes, which he must have robbed some where. He was engaged some weeks in peddling along the river, among the negroes, and was very nearly taken once or twice. He has been seen two days ago on the river, very genteely dressed and stated that the flat boatmen who had brought him down from Baton Rouge, were to carry him to Cincinnati. He is very plausible, speaks French and English; and is no doubt furnished with every kind of necessary papers. The attention of the captains and clerks of steamboats is called to the present. The reward will be given to lodge him in jail.

Plantation owner A. Murot may have been Achille Murat, nephew of Napoleon, who owned a large sugar plantation near Baton Rouge in the late 1830s. Lois Elmer Bannon, Martha Yancey Carr, and Gwen Anders Edwards, *Magnolia Mound: A Louisiana River Plantation* (Gretna, La.: Pelican Publishing Group, 1984), 45–47; "Parish Court (Orleans): Change of Domicile Records," *New Orleans Public Library,* http://nutrias.org/~nopl/inv/vcp/vcp6.htm (accessed October 15, 2011).

27. Pike County was located southeast of Montgomery, Alabama. Burwell W. Hodges was the sheriff. Martha Thayer, "John F. Shields, Patented Land, Pike, AL," USGenweb Archives, http://files.usgwarchives.net/al/pike/deeds/jfshields2.txt (accessed October 15, 2011).

28. The *T* brand may have stood for *thief,* a method of punishment with a long tradition. Alabama law, for example, stated that any horse thief could be fined up to five hundred dollars, receive thirty-nine lashes, be imprisoned up to twelve months, and "be branded on the face, or in the right hand, as the court shall think fit, with the letter T." John G. Aikin, *A Digest of the Laws of the State of Alabama* (Tuscaloosa, Ala.: D. Woodruff, 1836), 103.

29. Whittier and other abolitionists who reprinted this short article from the *New York Commercial Advertiser* probably assumed it illustrated yet another example of cruelty to a man whose only crime was wanting to be free. But like James Williams's own story, the truth was more extensive and complex. The editor of the *Commercial Advertiser,* William Leete Stone, was an active abolitionist, so either he or a similar-thinking copywriter may have approved of the omission, even if he had read the full story in a southern newspaper.

An example of the original story appeared in the May 29, 1827, *City Gazette* of Charleston: "*A Villain Caught*—The negro fellow Prince, for whom the Justices of the inferior Court of this county lately offered a reward of $100, was taken last evening near Bonaventure by Mr. Wm Richardson, and is safely lodged in jail. He was armed with a pistol and sword, and did not surrender until he was considerably maimed by the dogs that had been set upon him, desperately fighting them, one of which he badly cut with the sword. Prince has been runaway for some time, and is charged with murdering a negro fellow." His victim, named July, belonged to a Mr. Gnann, perhaps one of the many residents by that name in nearby Effingham County, Georgia. Prince belonged to a man called Murell, a name found in both Savannah and Effingham.

The June 20, 1827, *Carolina Gazette,* also of Charleston, reported the result of the trial: "The negro man Prince, convicted of the murder of his companion July, was yesterday sentenced to be hung on Friday, the 29th inst." Before the sentencing a member of the court addressed Prince: "The dread of your violence appears to have been the chief bond of [your fellow slaves'] submission; and the principal cause of your hand not being arrested, whilst inflicting your death blows upon the victim of your resentment. Your heart seems to have been steeled against compassion on the occasion, for you were alike insensible to the prayers of the defenceless being whose life you sought, and the entreaties of your comrades."

The full story would have presented a quandary for abolitionists. Despite all the innocent men who were maimed by dogs simply for seeking freedom, there were a few, such as Prince, whose cruelty seemed to match that of his owners, yet one could also argue that the inhumanity of being enslaved encouraged such brutality and lessened the blame. James Williams, acquainted firsthand with such complexities, must have understood the same problem and realized a simple story would sell better to the abolitionists, so he chose to tell one, omitting his own involvement in attempted poisoning.

30. The letter may have been from Asa A. Stone, who was in Natchez at the time and who wrote other letters to the *New York Evangelist* a few months later. Whittier apparently included the quote to support the accuracy of Williams's description of bloodhounds on pp. 40–41 and 55–56.

31. Legally, this was not always true, but the common practice was illustrated by the many reports of runaways with gunshot wounds on the previous pages.

32. The quote was a reference to Psalm 94, verse 20, translated in the King James Version of the Bible as "Shall the throne of iniquity have fellowship with thee, which frameth mischief by a law?" The slightly altered phrasing, "framed iniquity by law" or "a law," showed up in other contemporary writing.

33. This was perhaps a direct reference to a poem by Thomas Campbell published in the *New Monthly Magazine and Literary Journal* on November 1, 1823, which included the lines: "Go to your bloody rites again;—bring back / The hall of horrors and the assessor's pen." The poem would have been inspiring to abolitionists, with its hopeful conclusion:

> Still in your prostrate land there shall be some
> Proud hearts, the shrines of Freedom's vestal flame.
> Long trains of ill may pass unheeded, dumb,
> But vengeance is behind, and justice is to come.

34. James Birney and Lewis Tappan explained the connection of most of these men in an article that appeared in the *Emancipator* ("Alabama Beacon versus James Williams"), after the truth of the narrative was questioned.

> In the latter part of December last [1837], a letter was received by Lewis Tappan from Emmor Kimber, of Kimberton, near Philadelphia, informing him that James Williams was at his house, and would soon be in New York on his way, escaping still further from the region of slavery, and from the danger of being re-taken. It further stated that James had arrived at Carlisle [Pa.] on the 9th December—that he had there received friendly assistance, and had been enabled to reach the house of Daniel Gibbons on the 15th, where he had to remain several days on account of his feet which had become sore; that on the 20th Joseph Gibbons conveyed him to Lindley Coates' where he staid two nights; that on the 22d he reached John Vicker's, where he again rested till the 25th, when

he came on to Kimberton. Mr. Kimber's letter also contained the heads of Jame's [*sic*] history, which the latter had related to him while at his house. *They* were sent on with a view not only of interesting before hand, the friends of the oppressed here in his safety, but that it might be seen whether any account of his adventures that he might give in New York differed from that which he had already given. On his arrival, James received the hospitality of John W. Hill, at whose house, with the exception of two or three nights passed at the houses of others friendly to him, remained about three weeks (all the time he was in New York) and until he sailed in one of the regular packets for Liverpool.

Whilst James was here, he was visited by many of the friends of the slaves, among them we now remember the Rev. Charles Follen, Theodore D. Weld, John G. Whittier, Elizur Wright, Jr., Rev. E. F. Hatfield, the editor of this paper [Theodore D. Weld], and the undersigned [James G. Birney and Lewis Tappan]. To them he rehersed [*sic*] his adventures—corresponding with remarkable consistency with the account that had been received in Emmor Kimber's letter, without any knowledge, on his part, so far as is known, that this had been transmitted to any of his hearers.

P. 128 includes speculation about a possible further connection with James Mott.

35. In the fall of 1832 James G. Birney probably passed within a few miles of the plantation where Williams would be enslaved two years later. Birney had lived in Madison County, Alabama, in the northern part of the state, but as an agent of the American Colonization Society, he toured out of state then traveled from Tuscaloosa to Montgomery in the fall of 1832, arriving in Mobile in southern Alabama by December of that year. The direct road from Tuscaloosa to Montgomery passed about thirty miles north of Caleb Tate's plantation at Valley Creek, Dallas County. If Birney had traveled by boat from Montgomery to Mobile, he would have come even closer, within seven or eight miles, when the Alabama River flowed past Selma. He apparently never knew any of the slave owners in the Dallas County area whom Williams mentioned, given that he failed to recognize them in the narrative and was as puzzled as any of the abolitionists about their names.

William Birney, *James G. Birney and His Times* (New York: D. Appleton & Co., 1890), 117–19, 266; *The North American Tourist* (New York: A. T. Goodrich, 1839), 464; Larimer in Birney and Tappan, "Alabama Beacon versus James Williams"; Thomas Curry, "Slatter vs. Holton," *Reports of Cases Argued and Determined in the Supreme Court of the State of Louisiana* (New Orleans: E. Johns, 1842), 19:40.

36. As John B. Rittenhouse of Alabama discovered, the man whom Williams called "Larrimore" was a reference to real-life George Thacker Fauntleroy Larimer (also often spelled *Lorimer*).

37. The phrase came from William Cowper's antislavery poem "Charity," published in 1782:

> But ah! what wish can prosper, or what pray'r,
> For merchants rich in cargoes of despair,
> Who drive a loathsome traffic, gage and span,
> And buy the muscles and the bones of man?
> —from "Charity," in *Poems* (London: J. Johnson, 1782), 187.

38. See pp. 36, 38, 42.

39. See pp. 45–46, 51.

40. See p. 46.

41. See pp. 41, 44–46, 52.

42. See p. 41.

43. See p. 50.

44. Most of the abolitionists involved in the production of the book had indeed suffered for their beliefs. James Birney, Lewis Tappan, and John Greenleaf Whittier had all endured attacks by mobs and death threats during the previous few years, particularly in Cincinnati, New York, and New Hampshire, respectively.

Whittier was perhaps speaking against those who focused more on their own martyrdom than the suffering of the enslaved people they claimed to help, a problem that Catharine Beecher also pointed out:

> It is a fact, that Abolitionists have taken the course most calculated to awaken illegal acts of violence, and that when they have ensued, they have seemed to rejoice in them, as calculated to advance and strengthen their cause. The violence of mobs, the denunciations and unreasonable requirements of the South, the denial of the right of petition, the restrictions attempt to be laid upon freedom of speech, and freedom of the press, are generally spoken of with exultation by Abolitionists, as what are among the chief means of promoting their cause. It is not so much by exciting feelings of pity and humanity, and Christian love, towards the oppressed, as it is by awakening indignation at the treatment of Abolitionists themselves, that their cause has prospered.
>
> —*An Essay on Slavery and Abolitionism* (Philadelphia: Henry Perkins, 1837), 35–36.

45. The phrase gained popularity among abolitionists after the 1833 publication of the Declaration of the National Anti-Slavery Convention in Philadelphia. (Whittier served as secretary of the convention, along with Lewis Tappan.) The statement included the promise: "We shall enlist the PULPIT and the PRESS in the cause of the suffering and the dumb." In this context *dumb* meant "unable to speak." The phrase carried biblical overtones, evoking passages such as Isaiah 53:7: "He was oppressed, and he was afflicted, yet he opened not his mouth: he is brought as a lamb to the slaughter, and as a sheep before her shearers is dumb, so he openeth not his mouth." "American Anti-Slavery Society," *Abolitionist* (December 1833): 177, 179.

46. Whittier dated the introduction in Quaker style, using *1st. mo.*, for "first month," rather than *January*.

NARRATIVE

I was born in Powhatan County, Virginia,[1] on the plantation of George Larrimore, sen.,[2] at a place called Mount Pleasant,[3] on the 16th of May, 1805.[4] My father was the slave of an orphan family whose name I have forgotten, and was under the care of a Mr. Brooks, guardian of the family.[5] He was a native of Africa, and was brought over when a mere child, with his mother. My mother was the slave of George Larrimore, sen. She was nearly white, and is well known to have been the daughter of Mr. Larrimore himself.[6] She died when myself and my twin brother Meshech were five years of age.[7] I can scarcely remember her. She had in all eight children, of whom only five are now living. One, a brother, belongs to the heirs of the late Mr. Brockenbrough, of Charlottesville;[8] of whom he hires his time, and pays annually $120 for it.[9] He is a member of the Baptist church, and used to preach occasionally.[10] His wife is a free woman from Philadelphia and being able to read and write, taught her husband.[11] The whites do not know that he can write, and have often wondered that he could preach so well without learning.[12] It is the practice when a church is crowded to turn the blacks out of their seats.[13] My brother did not like this, and on one occasion preached a sermon from a text, showing that all are of one blood. Some of the whites who heard it said that such preaching would raise an insurrection among the negroes. Two of them told him that if he would prove his doctrine by Scripture, they would let him go, but if he did not, he should have nine and thirty lashes.[14] He accordingly preached another sermon, and spoke with a great deal of boldness. The two men who were in favor of having him whipped left before the sermon was over, those who remained acknowledged that he had proved his doctrine, and preached a good sermon, and many of them came up and shook hands with him. The two opposers, Scott and Brockley,[15] forbid my brother, after this, to come upon their estates. They were both Baptists, and my brother had before preached to their people.[16] During the cholera at Richmond,[17] my brother preached a sermon, in which he compared the pestilence to the plagues which afflicted the Egyptian slave-holders, because they would not let the people go. After the sermon some of the whites threatened to whip him. Mr. Valentine,[18] a merchant on Shocko Hill, prevented them; and a young lawyer named Brooks said it was wrong to threaten a man for preaching the truth.[19] Since the insurrection of Nat. Turner he has not been allowed to preach at all.[20]

My twin brother was for some time the property of Mr. John Griggs, of Richmond,[21] who sold him, about three years since, to an Alabama cotton planter, with whom he staid one year, and then ran away; and in all probability escaped into the free states or Canada, as he was seen near the Maryland line.[22] My other brother lives in Fredericksburg, and belongs to a Mr. Scott, a merchant, formerly of Richmond.[23] He was sold from Mr. Larrimore's plantation because his wife was a slave of Mr. Scott. My only sister is the slave of John Smith, of King William.[24] Her husband was the slave of Mr. Smith, when the latter lived in Powhatan County, and when he removed to King William she was taken with her husband.

My old master, George Larrimore, married Jane Roane, the sister of a gentleman named John Roane, one of the most distinguished men in Virginia, who in turn married a sister of my master.[25] One of his sisters married a Judge Scott,[26] and another married Mr. Brockenbrough, of Charlottesville.[27] Mr. Larrimore had three children; George, Jane, and Elizabeth.[28] The former was just ten days older than myself;[29] and I was his playmate and constant associate in childhood. I used to go with him to his school, and carry his books for him as far as the door, and meet him there when the school was dismissed.[30] We were very fond of each other, and frequently slept together. He taught me the letters of the alphabet, and I should soon have acquired a knowledge of reading, had not George's mother discovered her son in the act of teaching me. She took him aside and severely reprimanded him. When I asked him, not long after, to tell me more of what he had learned at school, he said that his mother had forbidden him to do so any more, as her father had a slave who was instructed in reading and writing, and on that account proved very troublesome. He could imitate the hand-writing of all the neighboring planters, and used to write passes and certificates of freedom for the slaves, and finally wrote one for himself, and went off to Philadelphia, from whence her father received from him a saucy letter, thanking him for his education.[31]

The early years of my life went by pleasantly. The bitterness of my lot I had not yet realized. Comfortably clothed and fed, kindly treated by my old master and mistress and the young ladies, and the playmate and confidant of any young master, I did not dream of the dark reality of evil before me.[32]

When he was fourteen years of age, master George went to his uncle Brockenbrough's, at Charlottesville, as a student of the University.[33] After his return from college, he went to Paris and other parts of Europe, and spent three or four years in study and travelling. In the mean time I was a waiter in the house, dining-room servant, &c.[34] My old master visited and received visits from a great number of the principal families in Virginia. Each summer, with his family, he visited the sulphur springs and the mountains.[35] While George was absent, I went with him to New Orleans, in the winter season, on account of his failing health.[36] We spent three days in Charleston, at Mr. McDuffie's, with whom my master was on intimate terms. Mr. McDuffie spent several days on one occasion at Mt. Pleasant.[37] He took a fancy to me, and offered my master the servant whom he brought with him, and $500 beside, for me. My master considered it almost an insult, and said, after he was gone, that Mr. McDuffie needed money, to say the least, as much as he did.[38]

He had a fine house in Richmond,[39] and used to spend his winters there with his family, taking me with him. He was not there much at other times, except when the Convention of 1829, for amending the State Constitution, was held in that city. He had a quarrel with Mr. Neal, of Richmond Co., in consequence of some remarks upon the subject of slavery. It came near terminating in a duel.[40] I recollect that during the sitting of the Convention my master asked me, before several other gentlemen, if I wished to be free and go back to my own country. I looked at him with surprise, and inquired what country.

"Africa, to be sure," said he, laughing.

I told him that was not my country—that I was born in Virginia.

"Oh yes," said he, "but your father was born in Africa." He then said that there was a place on the African coast called Liberia, where a great many free blacks were going;[41] and asked me to tell him honestly whether I would prefer to be set free on condition of going to Africa, or live with him and remain a slave. I replied that I had rather be as I was.

I have frequently heard him speak against slavery to his visitors. I heard him say on one occasion, when some gentlemen were arguing in favor of sending the free colored people to Africa, that this was as really the black man's country as the white's, and that it would be as humane to knock the free Negroes, at once, on the head, as to send them to Liberia. He was a kind man to his slaves. He was proud of them, and of the reputation he enjoyed of feeding and clothing them well. They were, as near as I can judge, about

300 in number.[42] He never to my knowledge sold a slave, unless to go with a wife or husband, and at the slave's own request.[43] But all except the very wealthiest planters in his neighborhood sold them frequently. John Smoot, of Powhatan Co., has sold a great number.[44] Bacon Tait* used to be one of the principal purchasers.[45] He had a jail at Richmond where he kept them. There were many others who made a business of buying and selling slaves. I saw on one occasion, while travelling with my master, a gang of nearly two hundred men fastened to a single chain.[46] The women followed unchained and the children in wagons. It was a sorrowful sight. Some were praying, some crying, and they all had a look of extreme wretchedness. It is an awful thing to a Virginia slave to be sold for the Alabama and Mississippi country.[47] I have known some of them to die of grief, and others to commit suicide, on account of it. Sometimes, when slaves are to be sold, they go to the rich planters in their vicinity and beseech them to purchase them. It is no uncommon thing for those planters to whom they thus apply, to give orders for their concealment somewhere on the plantation, and, after they are advertised as runaways, to offer to buy them, and run the risk of finding them. In this way they get them for a fourth part of their value. After the bargain is made, the slaves come back to their old masters, ask pardon for running away, and are turned over to their new owners.[48] Mr. Larrimore employed his overseer in obtaining six slaves in this way,[49] of Stephen Ransdell, of Caroline County.[50]

[*Footnote in original narrative:* *Bacon Tait's advertisement of "new and commodious buildings" for the keeping of negroes, situated at the corner of 15th and Carey streets, appears in the Richmond Whig of Sept. 1835.—EDITOR.][51]

In my seventeenth year, I was married to a girl named Harriet, belonging to John Gatewood, a planter, living about four miles from Mt. Pleasant.[52] She was about a year younger than myself[53]—was a tailoress, and used to cut out clothes for the hands.

We were married by a white clergyman named Jones; and were allowed two or three weeks to ourselves, which we spent in visiting and other amusements.

The field hands are seldom married by a clergyman. They simply invite their friends together, and have a wedding party.[54]

Our two eldest children died in their infancy; two are now living. The youngest was only two months old when I saw him for the last time.[55] I used to visit my wife on Saturday and Sunday evenings.[56]

My young master came back from Europe in delicate health. He was advised by his physicians to spend the winter in New Orleans, whither he accordingly went, taking me with him. Here he became acquainted with a French lady of one of the first families in the city. The next winter he also spent in New Orleans, and on his third visit, three years after his return from Europe, he was married to the lady above mentioned.[57] In May he returned to Mt. Pleasant, and found the elder Larrimore on his sick bed, from which he never rose again. He died on the 14th of July. There was a great and splendid funeral, as his relatives and friends were numerous.[58]

His large property was left principally in the hands of his widow until her decease, after which it was to be divided among the three children. In February, Mrs. Larrimore also died.[59] The administrators upon the estate were John Green, Esq.,[60] and Benjamin Temple.[61]

My young mistresses, Jane and Elizabeth, were very kind to the servants.[62] They seemed to feel under obligations to afford them every comfort and gratification, consistent with the dreadful relation of ownership which they sustained towards them. Whipping was scarcely known on the estate; and, whenever it did take place, it was invariably against the wishes of the young ladies.

But the wife of master George was of a disposition entirely the reverse.[63] Feeble, languid, and inert, sitting motionless for hours at her window, or moving her small fingers over the strings of her guitar, to some soft and languishing air, she would have seemed to a stranger incapable of rousing herself from that indolent repose, in which mind as well as body participated. But, the slightest disregard of her commands, and sometimes even the neglect to anticipate her wishes, on the part of the servants, was sufficient to awake her. The inanimate and delicate beauty then changed into a stormy virago. Her black eyes glowed and sparkled with a snaky fierceness, her full lips compressed, and her brows bent and darkened. Her very voice, soft and sweet when speaking to her husband, and exquisitely fine and melodious when accompanying her guitar, was at such times shrill, keen, and loud. She would order the servants of my young mistresses upon her errands, and if they pleaded their prior duty to obey the calls of another would demand that they should be forthwith whipped for their insolence. If the young ladies remonstrated with her, she met them with a perfect torrent of invective and abuse. In these paroxysms of fury she always spoke in French,[64] with a vehemence and volubility which strongly contrasted with the calmness and firmness of the young ladies. She would boast of what she had done in New Orleans, and of the excellent discipline of her father's slaves. She said she had gone down in the night to the cell under her father's house, and whipped the slaves confined there with her own hands.[65] I had heard the same thing from her father's servants at New Orleans when I was there with my master.[66] She brought with her from New Orleans a girl named Frances.[67] I have seen her take her by the ear, lead her up to the side of the room, and beat her head against it. At other times she would snatch off her slipper and strike the girl on her face and head with it.

She seldom manifested her evil temper before master George. When she did, he was greatly troubled, and he used to speak to his sisters about it. Her manner towards him was invariably that of extreme fondness. She was dark complexioned, but very beautiful; and the smile of welcome with which she used to meet him was peculiarly fascinating. I did not marvel that he loved her; while at the same time, in common with all the house servants, I regarded her as a being possessed with an evil spirit,—half woman, and half fiend.[68]

Soon after the settlement of the estate, I heard my master speak of going out to Alabama.[69] His wife had 1500 acres of wild land in Greene County, in that State, and he had been negotiating for 500 more.[70] Early in the summer of 1833, he commenced making preparations for removing to that place a sufficient number of hands to cultivate it.[71] He took great pains to buy up the wives and husbands of those of his own slaves who had married out of the estate, in order, as he said, that his hands might be contented in Alabama, and not need chaining together while on their journey.[72] It is always found necessary by the regular slave-traders, in travelling with their slaves to the far South, to handcuff and chain their wretched victims, who have been bought up as the interest of the trader and the luxury or necessities of the planter may chance to require, without regard to the ties sundered or the affections made desolate by these infernal bargains.[73] About the 1st of September, after the slaves destined for Alabama had taken a final farewell of their old home, and of the friends they were leaving behind, our party started on their long journey. There were in all 214 slaves, men, women, and children.[74] The men and women travelled on foot—the small children in the wagons, containing the baggage, &c.[75] Previous to my departure, I visited my wife and children, at Mr. Gatewood's.[76] I took leave of them with the belief that I should return with my master, as soon as he had seen his hands established on his new plantation. I took my children in my arms and embraced them; my wife, who was a member of the Methodist church,[77] implored the blessing of God upon me during my absence, and I turned away to follow my master.

Our journey was a long and tedious one, especially to those who were compelled to walk the whole distance.[78] My master rode in a sulky, and I, as his body servant, on horseback.[79] When we crossed over the Roanoke, and were entering upon North Carolina, I remember with what sorrowful countenances and language the poor slaves looked back for the last time upon the land of their nativity. It was their last farewell to Old Virginia. We passed through Georgia, and, crossing the Chattahooche, entered Alabama.[80] Our way for many days was through a sandy tract of country, covered with pine woods, with here and there the plantation of an Indian or a half-breed.[81] After crossing what is called Line Creek, we found large plantations along the road, at intervals of four or five miles.[82] The aspect of the whole country was wild and forbidding, save to the eye of a cotton planter. The clearings were all new, and the houses rudely constructed of logs. The cotton fields were skirted with an enormous growth of oak, pine, and bass wood. Charred stumps stood thickly in the clearings, with here and there a large tree girdled by the axe and left to decay.[83] We reached at last the place of our destination. It was a fine tract of land, with a deep rich soil.[84] We halted on a small knoll, where the tents were pitched, and the wagons unladen.[85] I spent the night with my master at a neighboring plantation, which was under the care of an overseer named Flincher.[86]

The next morning my master received a visit from a man named Huckstep,[87] who had undertaken the management of his plantation as an overseer. He had been an overseer on cotton plantations many years in Georgia and North Carolina.[88] He was apparently about forty years of age, with a sunburnt and sallow countenance. His thick shock of black hair was marked in several places with streaks of white, occasioned, as he afterwards told me, by blows received from slaves whom he was chastising.[89]

After remaining in the vicinity for about a week, my master took me aside one morning, told me he was going to Selma, in Dallas County, and wished me to be in readiness, on his return the next day, to start for Virginia.[90] This was to me cheering news. I spent that day and the next among my old fellow-servants who had lived with me in Virginia.[91] Some of them had messages to send by me to their friends and acquaintances. In the afternoon of the second day after my master's departure, I distributed among them all the money which I had about me, viz., fifteen dollars.[92] I noticed that the overseer Huckstep laughed at this and called me a fool; and that whenever I spoke of going home with my master, his countenance indicated something between a smile and a sneer.

Night came; but, contrary to his promise, my master did not come. I still, however, expected him the next day. But another night came, and he had not returned. I grew uneasy, and inquired of Huckstep where he thought my master was.

"On his way to old Virginia," said he, with a malicious laugh.

"But," said I, "master George told me that he should come back and take me with him to Virginia."

"Well, boy," said the overseer, "I'll now tell ye what master George, as you call him, told me.[93] You are to stay here and act as driver of the field hands. That was the order. So you may as well submit to it at once."

I stood silent and horror-struck. Could it be that the man whom I had served faithfully from our mutual boyhood, whose slightest wish had been my law, to serve whom I would have laid down my life, while I had confidence in his integrity—could it be that he had so cruelly and wickedly deceived me? I looked at the overseer. He stood laughing at me in my agony.

"Master George gave you no such orders," I exclaimed, maddened by the overseer's look and manner.

The overseer looked at me with a fiendish grin. "None of your insolence," said he, with a dreadful oath. "I never saw a Virginia nigger that I couldn't manage, proud as they are. Your master has left you in my hands, and you must obey my orders. If you don't, why, I shall have to make you '*hug the widow there*,'" pointing to a tree, to which I afterwards found the slaves were tied when they were whipped.[94]

That night was one of sleepless agony. Virginia, the hills and the streams of my birth-place; the kind and hospitable home; the gentle-hearted sisters, sweetening with their sympathy the sorrows of the slave; my wife, my children—all that had thus far made up my happiness, rose in contrast with my present condition. Deeply as he has wronged me, may my master himself never endure such a night of misery![95]

At daybreak, Huckstep told me to dress myself and attend to his directions. I rose, subdued and wretched, and at his orders handed the horn to the headman of the gang, who summoned the hands to the field.[96] They were employed in clearing land for cultivation, cutting trees, and burning. I was with them through the day, and at night returned once more to my lodgings to be laughed at by the overseer. He told me that I should do well, he did not doubt, by and by, but that a Virginia driver generally had to be whipped a few times himself before he could be learned to do justice to the slaves under his charge. They were not equal to those raised in North Carolina, for keeping the lazy hell-hounds,[97] as he called the slaves, at work.

And this was my condition! a driver set over more than one hundred and sixty of my kindred and friends,[98] with orders to apply the whip unsparingly to every one, whether man or woman, who faltered in the task, or was careless in the execution of it, myself subject at any moment to feel the accursed lash upon my own back, if feelings of humanity should perchance overcome the selfishness of misery, and induce me to spare and pity.[99]

I lived in the same house with Huckstep;[100] a large log house, roughly finished, where we were waited upon by an old woman, whom we used to call aunt Polly.[101] Huckstep was, I soon found, inordinately fond of peach brandy; and once or twice in the course of a month he had a drunken debauch, which usually lasted from two to four days. He was then full of talk, laughed immoderately at his own nonsense, and would keep me up until late at night listening to him. He was at these periods terribly severe to his hands, and would order me to use up the cracker of my whip every day upon the poor creatures who were toiling in the field;[102] and in order to satisfy him, I used to tear it off when returning home at night. He would then praise me for a good fellow, and invite me to drink with him. He used to tell me at such times that if I would only drink as he did I should be worth a thousand dollars more for it.[103] He would sit for hours with his peach brandy, cursing and swearing, laughing and telling stories full of obscenity and blasphemy. He would sometimes start up, take my whip, and rush out to the slave quarters, flourish it about and frighten their inmates, and often cruelly beat them. He would order the women to pull up their clothes, in Alabama style, as he called it, and then whip them for not complying.[104] He would then come back roaring and shouting to the house, and tell me what he had done; if I did not laugh with him, he would get angry and demand what the matter was. Oh! how often have I laughed, at such times, when my heart ached within me; and how often, when permitted to retire to my bed, I found relief in tears!

He had no wife,[105] but kept a colored mistress in a house situated on a gore of land between the plantation and that of Mr. Goldsby's.[106] He brought her with him from North Carolina, and had three children by her.[107]

Sometimes, in his fits of intoxication, he would come riding into the field, swinging his whip, and crying out to the hands to strip off their shirts and be ready to take a whipping; and this too when they were all busily at work. At another time, he would gather the hands around him and fall to cursing and swearing about the neighboring overseers. They were, he said, cruel to their hands, whipped them unmercifully, and in addition starved them.[108] As for himself, he was the kindest and best fellow within forty miles; and the hands ought to be thankful that they had such a good man for their overseer.

He would frequently be very familiar with me, and call me his child; he would tell me that our people were going to get Texas, a fine cotton country, and that he meant to go out there and have a plantation of his own, and I should go with him and be his overseer.[109]

The houses in the "negro quarters" were constructed of logs, and from twelve to fifteen feet square; they had no glass, but there were holes to let in the light and air. The furniture consisted of a table, a few stools, and dishes made of wood, and an iron pot, and some other cooking utensils. The houses were placed about three or four rods apart, with a piece of ground attached to each of them for a garden, where the occupant could raise a few vegetables. The "quarters" were about three hundred yards from the dwelling of the overseer.

The hands were occupied in clearing land and burning brush, and in constructing their houses, through the winter.[110] In March we commenced ploughing, and on the first of April began planting seed for cotton.[111] The hoeing season commenced about the last of May. At the earliest dawn of day, and frequently before that time, the laborers were roused from their sleep by the blowing of the horn.[112] It was blown by the headman of the gang, who led the rest in the work and acted under my direction, as my assistant.[113]

Previous to the blowing of the horn the hands generally rose and eat what was called the "morning's bit," consisting of ham and bread.[114] If exhaustion and fatigue prevented their rising before the dreaded sound of the horn broke upon their slumbers, they had no time to snatch a mouthful, but were hurried out at once.[115]

It was my business to give over to each of the hands his or her appropriate implement of labor, from the tool-house, where they were deposited at night.[116] After all had been supplied, they were taken to the field, and set at work as soon as it was sufficiently light to distinguish the plants from the grass and weeds. I was employed in passing from row to row, in order to see that the work was well done, and to urge forward the laborers.[117] At 12 o'clock the horn was blown from the overseer's house, calling the hands to dinner, each to his own cabin. The intermission of labor was one hour and a half to hoers and pickers, and two hours to the ploughmen. At the expiration of this interval the horn again summoned them to their labor. They were kept in the field until dark, when they were called home to supper.[118]

There was little leisure for any of the hands on the plantation. In the evenings, after it was too dark for work in the field, the men were frequently employed in burning brush, and in other labors, until late at night. The women, after toiling in the field by day, were compelled to card, spin, and weave cotton for their clothing, in the evening. Even on Sundays there was little or no respite from toil.[119] Those who had not been able to work out all their task during the week were allowed by the overseer to finish it on the Sabbath, and thus save themselves from a whipping on Monday morning. Those whose tasks were finished frequently employed most of that day in cultivating their gardens.

Many of the female hands were delicate young women, who in Virginia had never been accustomed to field labor.[120] They suffered greatly from the extreme heat and the severity of the toil. Oh! how often have I seen them drawing their weary limbs frown the cotton field at nightfall, faint and exhausted. The overseer used to laugh at their sufferings. They were, he said, Virginia ladies, and altogether too delicate for Alabama use; but they must be made to do their tasks notwithstanding.[121] The recollection of these things even now is dreadful. I used to tell the poor creatures, when compelled by the overseer to urge them forward with the whip, that I would much rather take their places and endure the stripes than inflict them.

When but three months old, the children born on the estate were given up to the care of the old women who were not able to work out of doors. Their mothers were kept at work in the field.[122]

It was the object of the overseer to separate me in feeling and interest as widely as possible from my suffering brethren and sisters. I had relations among the field hands, and used to call them my cousins.[123] He forbid my doing so, and told me if I acknowledged relationship with any of the bands I should be flogged for it. He used to speak of them as devils and hell-hounds,[124] and ridicule them in every possible way; and endeavored to make me speak of them and regard them in the same manner. He would tell long stories about hunting and shooting "runaway niggers," and detail with great apparent satisfaction the cruel and horrid punishments which he had inflicted.[125] One thing he said troubled him. He had once whipped a slave so severely that he died in consequence of it, and it was soon after ascertained that he was wholly innocent of the offence charged against him. That slave, he said, had haunted him ever since.

Soon after we commenced weeding our cotton, some of the hands, who were threatened with a whipping for not finishing their tasks, ran away. The overseer and myself went out after them, taking with us five bloodhounds, which were kept on the estate for the sole purpose of catching runaways. There were no other hounds in the vicinity, and the overseers of the neighboring plantations used to borrow them to hunt their runaways. A Mr. Crop,[126] who lived about ten miles distant,[127] had two packs, and made it his sole business to catch slaves with them. We used to set the dogs upon the track of the fugitives, and they would follow them until, to save themselves from being torn in pieces, they would cling into a tree, where the dogs kept them until we came up and secured them.

These hounds, when young, are taught to run after the negro boys; and being always kept confined except when let out in pursuit of runaways, they seldom fail of overtaking the fugitive, and seem to enjoy the sport of hunting men as much as other dogs do that of chasing a fox or a deer. My master gave the sum of $500 for his five dogs, a slut and her four puppies.[128]

While going over our cotton picking for the last time, one of our hands, named Little John, ran away.[129] The next evening the dogs were started on his track. We followed them awhile, until we knew by their ceasing to bark that they had found him. We soon met the dogs returning. Their jaws, heads, and feet, were bloody. The overseer looked at them and said "he was afraid the dogs had killed the nigger." It being dark, we could not find him that night. Earlier the next morning we started off with our neighbors, Sturtivant[130] and Flincher,[131] and after searching about for some time, we found the body of Little John lying in the midst of a thicket of cane. It was nearly naked, and dreadfully mangled and gashed by the teeth of the dogs. They had evidently dragged it some yards through the thicket: blood, tatters of clothes, and even the entrails of the unfortunate man, were clinging to the stubs of the old and broken cane. Huckstep stooped over his saddle, looked at the body, and muttered an oath. Sturtivant swore it was no more than the fellow deserved.[132] We dug a hole in the cane-brake, where he lay, buried him, and returned home.

The murdered young man had a mother and two sisters on the plantation, by whom he was dearly loved. When I told the old woman of what had befallen her son, she only said that it was better for poor John than to live in slavery.

Late in the fall of this year, a young man, who had already run away several times, was missing from his task. It was four days before we found him. The dogs drove him at last up a tree, where he was caught, and brought home. He was then fastened down to the ground by means of forked sticks of wood selected for the purpose, the longest fork being driven into the ground until the other closed down upon the neck, ankles, and wrists. The overseer then sent for two large cats belonging to the house. These he placed upon the naked shoulders of his victim, and dragged them suddenly by their tails downward. At first they did not scratch deeply. He then ordered me to strike them with a small stick after he had placed them once more upon the back of the sufferer. I did so; and the enraged animals extended their claws, and tore his back deeply and cruelly as they were dragged along it.[133] He was then whipped and placed in the stocks, where he was kept three days. On the third morning, as I passed the stocks, I stopped to look at him. His head hung down over the chain which supported his neck. I spoke, but he did not answer. *He was dead in the stocks!* The overseer on seeing him seemed surprised, and, I thought, manifested some remorse. Four of the field hands took him out of the stocks and buried him; and every thing went on as usual.

It is not in my power to give a narrative of the daily occurrences on the plantation. The history of one day was that of all. The gloomy monotony of our slavery was only broken by the overseer's periodical fits of drunkenness, at which times neither life nor limb on the estate were secure from his caprice or violence.

In the spring of 1835, the overseer brought me a letter from my wife, written for her by her young mistress, Mr. Gatewood's daughter.[134] He read it to me. It stated that herself and children were well—spoke of her sad and heavy disappointment in consequence of my not returning with my master, and of her having been told by him that I should come back the next fall.

Hope for a moment lightened my heart, and I indulged the idea of once more returning to the bosom of my family. But I recollected that my master had already cruelly deceived me, and despair again took hold on me.

Among our hands was one whom we used to call Big Harry.[135] He was a stout, athletic man, very intelligent, and an excellent workman; but he was of a high and proud spirit, which the weary and crushing weight of a life of slavery had not been able to subdue. On almost every plantation at the South you may find one or more individuals whose look and air show that they have preserved their self-respect as *men;*—that with them the power of the tyrant ends with the coercion of the body—that the soul is free, and the inner man retaining the original uprightness of the image of God. You may know them by the stern sobriety of their countenances, and the contempt with which they regard the jests and pastimes of their miserable and degraded companions, who, like Samson, make sport for the keepers of their prison-house.[136] These men are always feared as well as hated by their task-masters. Harry had never been whipped, and had always said that he would die rather than submit to it.[137] He made no secret of his detestation of the overseer. While most of the slaves took off their hats, with cowering submission, in his presence, Harry always refused to do so. He never spoke to him except in a brief answer to his questions. Master George, who knew and dreaded the indomitable spirit of the man, told the overseer, before he left the plantation, to beware how he attempted to punish him. But the habits of tyranny in which Huckstep had so long indulged had accustomed him to abject submission on the part of his subjects, and he could not endure this upright and unbroken manliness. He used frequently to curse and swear about him, and devise plans for punishing him on account of his impudence, as he called it.

A pretext was at last afforded him. Some time in August of this year there was a large quantity of yellow unpicked cotton lying in the gin house.[138] Harry was employed at night in removing the cotton seed, which had been thrown out by the gin. The rest of the male hands were engaged during the day in weeding the cotton for the last time, and in the night in burning brush on the new lands clearing for the next year's crop.[139] Harry was told one evening to go with the others and assist in burning the brush. He accordingly went; and the next night a double quantity of seed had accumulated in the gin house; and, although he worked until nearly two o'clock in the morning, he could not remove it all.

The next morning the overseer came into the field, and demanded of me why I had not whipped Harry for not removing all the cotton seed. He then called aloud to Harry to come forward and be whipped. Harry answered somewhat sternly that he would neither be struck by overseer nor driver; that he had worked nearly all night, and had scarcely fallen asleep when the horn blew to summon him to his toil in the field. The overseer raved and threatened, but Harry paid no farther attention to him. He [the overseer] then turned to me and asked me for my pistols, with a pair of which he had furnished me.[140] I told him they were not with me. He growled an oath, threw himself on his horse, and left us. In the evening I found him half drunk and raving like a madman.

He said he would no longer bear with that nigger's insolence, but would whip him if it cost him his life. He at length fixed upon a plan for seizing him, and told me that he would go out in the morning, ride along by the side of Harry and talk pleasantly to him, and then, while Harry was attending to him, I was to steal upon him and knock him down, by a blow on the head from the loaded and heavy handle of my whip. I was compelled to promise to obey his directions.

The next morning, when we got to the field, I told Harry of the overseer's plan, and advised him by all means to be on his guard and watch my motions. His eye glistened with gratitude. "Thank you, James," said he; "I'll take care that you don't touch me."

Huckstep came into the field about ten o'clock. He rode along by the side of Harry, talking and laughing. I was walking on the other side. When I saw that Harry's eye was upon me, I aimed a blow at him, intending, however, to miss him. He evaded the blow and turned fiercely round with his hoe uplifted, threatening to cut down any one who again attempted to strike him. Huckstep cursed my awkwardness, and told Harry to put down his hoe and come to him. He refused to do so, and swore he would kill the first man who tried to lay hands on him. The cowardly tyrant shrunk away from his enraged bondman, and for two weeks Harry was not again molested.

About the first of September the overseer had one of his drunken fits. He made the house literally an earthly hell. He urged me to drink, quarrelled and swore at me for declining, and chased the old woman round the house with his bottle of peach brandy. He then told me that Harry had forgotten the attempt to seize him, and that in the morning we must try our old game over again.

On the following morning, as I was handing to each of the hands their hoes from the tool-house, I caught Harry's eye. "Look out," said I to him; "Huckstep will be after you again to-day." He uttered a deep curse against the overseer and passed on to his work. After breakfast Huckstep came riding out to the cotton field. He tied his horse to a tree and came towards us. His sallow and haggard countenance was flushed, and his step unsteady. He came up by the side of Harry and began talking about the crops and the weather. I came at the same time on the other side, and in striking at him beat off his hat. He sprang aside and stepped backwards. Huckstep, with a dreadful oath, commanded him to stop, saying that he had determined to whip him, and neither earth nor hell should prevent him. Harry defied him, and said he had had always done the work allotted to him, and that was enough; he would sooner die than have the accursed lash touch him. The overseer staggered to his horse, mounted him and rode furiously to the house, and soon made his appearance, returning, with his gun in his hand.

"Yonder comes the devil!" said one of the women whose row was near Harry's.

"Yes," said another, "he's trying to scare Harry with his gun."

"Let him try as he pleases," said Harry, in his low, deep, determined tones. "He may shoot me, but he can't whip me."

Huckstep came swearing on. When within a few yards of Harry he stopped, looked at him with a stare of mingled rage and drunken imbecility, and bid him throw down his hoe and come forward. The undaunted slave refused to comply, and, continuing his work, told the drunken demon to shoot if he pleased. Huckstep advanced within a few steps of him when Harry raised his hoe and told him to stand back. He stepped back a few paces, levelled his gun, and fired. Harry received the charge in his breast, and fell instantly across a cotton row. He threw up his hands wildly and groaned, "Oh Lord!"

The hands instantly dropped their hoes. The women shrieked aloud. For my own part, I stood silent with horror. The cries of the women enraged the overseer. He dropped his gun, and snatching the whip from my hand, with horrid oaths and imprecations, fell to whipping them, laying about him like a maniac. Upon Harry's sister he bestowed his blows without mercy, commanding her to quit her screaming and go to work. The poor girl, whose brother had thus been murdered before her eyes, could not wrestle down the awful agony of her feelings, and the brutal tormentor left her without effecting his object. He then, without going to look of his victim, told four of the hands to carry him to the house, and, taking up his gun, left the field. When we got to the poor fellow, he was alive, and groaning faintly. The hands took him up, but before they reached the house he was dead. Huckstep came out and looked at him, and, finding him dead, ordered the hands to bury him. The burial of a slave in Alabama is that of a brute: no coffin, no decent shroud, no prayer. A hole is dug, and the body thrown in without further ceremony.[141]

From this time the overseer was regarded by the whole gang with detestation and fear—as a being to whose rage and cruelty there were no limits. Yet he was constantly telling us that he was the kindest of overseers—that he was formerly somewhat severe in managing his hands, but that now he was, if any thing, too indulgent. Indeed he had the reputation of being a good overseer and an excellent manager when sober. The slaves on some of the neighboring plantations were certainly worse clothed and fed, and more frequently and cruelly whipped, than ours. Whenever we saw them they complained of overworking and short feeding.[142] One of Flincher's and one of Sturtivant's hands ran away while I was in Alabama,[143] and, after remaining in the woods awhile, and despairing of being able to effect their escape, resolved to put an end to their existence and their slavery together. Each twisted himself a vine of the muscadine grape, and fastened one end around the limb of an oak, and made a noose in the other. Jacob, Flincher's man, swung himself off first, and expired after a long struggle. The other, horrified by the contortions and agony of his comrade, dropped his noose, and was retaken. When discovered two or three days afterwards, the body of Jacob was dreadfully torn and mangled by the obscene buzzards, those winged hyenas and goules of the Southwest.[144]

Among the slaves who were brought from Virginia, were two young and bright mulatto women, who were always understood throughout the plantation to have been the daughters of the elder Larrimore, by one of his slaves.[145] One was named Sarah and the other Hannah.[146] Sarah, being in a state of pregnancy, failed of executing her daily allotted task of hoeing cotton. I was ordered to whip her, and on my remonstrating with the overseer, and representing the condition of the woman, I was told that my business was to obey orders, and that if I was told "to whip a dead nigger I must do it." I accordingly gave her fifty lashes. This was on Thursday evening. On Friday she also failed through weakness, and was compelled to lie down in the field. That night the overseer himself whipped her. On Saturday the wretched woman dragged herself once more to the cotton field. In the burning sun, and in a situation which would have called forth pity in the bosom of any one save a cotton-growing overseer, she struggled to finish her task. She failed—nature could do no more—and, sick and despairing, she sought her cabin. There the overseer met her and inflicted fifty more lashes upon her already lacerated back.

The next morning was the Sabbath. It brought no joy to that suffering woman. Instead of the tones of the church bell summoning to the house of prayer, she heard the dreadful sound of the lash falling upon the backs of her brethren and sisters in bondage. For the voice of prayer she heard curses; for the songs of Zion obscene and hateful blasphemies. No Bible was there with its consolations for the sick of heart. Faint and fevered, scarred and smarting from the effects of her cruel punishment, she lay upon her pallet of moss,[147] dreading the coming of her relentless persecutor, who, in the madness of one of his periodical fits of drunkenness, was now swearing and cursing through the quarters,—the demon of that Sabbathless hell.

Some of the poor woman's friends on the evening before had attempted to relieve her of the task which had been assigned her, but exhausted nature and the selfishness induced by their own miserable situation did not permit them to finish it; and the overseer, on examination, found that the week's work of the woman was still deficient. After breakfast, he ordered her to be tied up to the limb of a tree, by means of a rope fastened round her wrists, so as to leave her feet about six inches from the ground. She begged him to let her down for she was very sick.

"Very well!" he exclaimed, with a sneer and a laugh; "I shall bleed you then,[148] and take out some of your Virginia blood. You are too proud a miss for Alabama."

He struck her a few blows. Swinging thus by her arms, she succeeded in placing one of her feet against the body of the tree, and thus partly supported herself, and relieved in some degree the painful weight upon her wrists. He threw down his whip, took a rail from the garden fence, ordered her feet to be tied together, and thrust the rail between them. He then ordered one of the hands to sit upon it.[149] Her back at this time was bare, but the strings of the only garment which she wore passed over her shoulders and prevented the full force of the whip from acting on her flesh. These he cut off with his penknife, and thus left her entirely naked. He struck her only two blows, for the second one cut open her side and abdomen with a frightful gash. Unable to look on any longer in silence, I entreated him to stop, as I feared he had killed her. The overseer looked at the wound, dropped his whip, and ordered her to be untied. She was carried into the house in a state of insensibility, and died in three days after.

During the whole season of picking cotton, the whip was frequently and severely plied. In his seasons of intoxication, the overseer made no distinction between the stout man and the feeble and delicate woman—the sick and the well. Women in a far advanced state of pregnancy were driven out to the cotton field. At other times he seemed to have some consideration, and to manifest something like humanity. Our hands did not suffer for food—they had a good supply of ham and cornmeal; while on Flincher's plantation the slaves had meat but once a year, at Christmas.[150]

Near the commencement of the weeding season of 1835, I was ordered to whip a young woman, a light mustee,[151] for not performing her task. I told the overseer that she was sick. He said he did not care for that; she should be made to work. A day or two afterwards, I found him in the house half intoxicated. He demanded of me why I had not whipped the girl; and I gave the same reason as before. He flew into a dreadful rage, but his miserable situation made him an object of contempt rather than fear. He sat shaking his fist at me and swearing for nearly half an hour. He said he would teach the Virginia lady to sham sickness; and that the only reason I did not whip her was that she was a white woman, and I did not like to cut up her delicate skin.[152] Some time after I was ordered to give two of our women, named Hannah and Big Sarah,[153] 150 lashes each, for not performing their tasks. The overseer stood by until he saw Hannah whipped, and until Sarah had been tied up to the tree. As soon as his back was turned I struck the tree instead of the woman, who, understanding my object, shrieked as if the whip at every blow was cutting into her flesh. The overseer heard the blows and the woman's cries, and, supposing that all was going on according to his mind, left the field. Unfortunately the husband of Hannah stood looking on, and, indignant that his wife should be whipped and Sarah spared, determined to revenge himself by informing against me.

Next morning Huckstep demanded of me whether I had whipped Sarah the day before; I replied in the affirmative. Upon this he called Sarah forward and made her show her back, which bore no traces of recent whipping. He then turned upon me and told me that the blows intended for Sarah should be laid on my back. That night the overseer, with the help of three of the hands, tied me up to a large tree—my arms and legs being clasped round it, and my body drawn up hard against it by two men pulling at my arms, and one pushing against my back. The agony occasioned by this alone was almost intolerable. I felt a sense of painful suffocation, and could scarcely catch my breath.

A moment after I felt the first blow of the overseer's whip across my shoulders. It seemed to cut into my very heart. I felt the blood gush and run down my back. I fainted at length under the torture, and on being taken down my shoes were filled with the blood which ran from the gashes in my back. The skin was worn off from my breast, arms, and thighs, against the rough bark of the tree. I was sick and feverish, and in great pain, for three weeks afterwards; most of which time I was obliged to lie with my face downwards, in consequence of the extreme soreness of my sides and back.[154] Huckstep himself seemed concerned about me, and would come frequently to see me, and tell me that he should not have touched me had it not been for "the cursed peach brandy."

Almost the first person that I was compelled to whip, after I recovered, was the man who pushed at my back when I was tied up to the tree. The hands who were looking on at that time all thought he pushed me much harder than was necessary; and they expected that I would retaliate upon him the injury I had received. After he was tied up, the overseer told me to give him a severe flogging, and left me. I struck the tree instead of the man. His wife, who was looking on, almost overwhelmed me with her gratitude.

At length one morning, late in the fall of 1835, I saw Huckstep and a gentleman ride out to the field. As they approached, I saw the latter was my master.[155] The hands all ceased their labor, and crowded around him, inquiring about old Virginia. For my own part, I could not hasten to greet him. He had too cruelly deceived me. He at length came towards me, and seemed somewhat embarrassed. "Well, James," said he, "how do you stand it here?" "Badly enough," I replied. "I had no thought that you could be so cruel as to go away and leave me as you did." "Well, well, it was too bad, but it could not be helped; you must blame Huckstep for it." "But," said I, "I was not his servant; I belonged to you, and you could do as you pleased." "Well," said he, "we will talk about that by and by." He then inquired of Huckstep where Big Sarah was. "She was sick and died," was the answer.[156] He looked round among the slaves again, and inquired for Harry. The overseer told him that Harry undertook to kill him, and that, to save his life, he was obliged to fire upon him, and that he died of the wound. After some further inquiries, he requested me to go into the house with him. He then asked me to tell him how things had been managed during his absence. I gave him a full account of the overseer's cruelty. When he heard of the manner of Harry's death,[157] he seemed much affected and shed tears. He was a favorite servant of his father's. I showed him the deep scars on my back; occasioned by the whipping I had received. He was, or professed to be, highly indignant with Huckstep; and said he would see to it that he did not lay hands on me again. He told me he should be glad to take me with him to Virginia, but he did not know where he should find a driver who would be so kind to the hands as I was. If I would stay ten years, he would then give me a thousand dollars, and a piece of land to plant on my own account. "But," said I, "my wife and children." "Well," said he, "I will do my best to purchase them, and send them on to you."[158] I now saw that my destiny was fixed, and that I was to spend my days in Alabama, and I retired to my bed that evening with a heavy heart.

My master staid only three or four days on the plantation. Before he left, he cautioned Huckstep to be careful and not strike me again, as he would on no account permit it. He told him to give the hands food enough, and not over-work them, and, having thus satisfied his conscience, left us to our fate.

Out of the two hundred and fourteen slaves who were brought out from Virginia,[159] at least one-third of them were members of the Methodist and Baptist churches in that State.[160] Of this number five or six could read. They had been torn away from the care and discipline of their respective churches, and from the means of instruction, but they retained their love for the exercises of religion, and felt a mournful pleasure in speaking of the privileges and spiritual blessings which they enjoyed in Old Virginia. Three of them had been preachers, or exhorters, viz. Solomon, usually called uncle Solomon, Richard, and David.[161] Uncle Solomon was a grave, elderly man, mild and forgiving in his temper, and greatly esteemed among the more serious portion of our hands. He used to snatch every occasion to talk to the lewd and vicious about the concerns of their souls, and advise them to fix their minds upon the Savior, as their only helper. Some I have heard curse and swear in answer, and others would say that they could not keep their minds upon God and the devil (meaning Huckstep) at the same time: that it was of no use to try to be religious—they had no time—that the overseer wouldn't let them meet to pray—and that even uncle Solomon, when he prayed, had to keep one eye open all the time, to see if Huckstep was coming. Uncle Solomon could both read and write, and had brought out with him from Virginia a Bible, a hymn-book, and some other religious books, which he carefully concealed from the overseer. Huckstep was himself an open infidel as well as blasphemer. He used to tell the hands that there was no hell hereafter for white people, but that they had their punishment on earth in being obliged to take care of the negroes. As for the blacks, he was sure there was a hell for them. He used frequently to sit with his bottle by his side, and his Bible in his hand, and read passages and comment on them, and pronounce them lies.[162] Any thing like religious feeling among the slaves irritated him. He said that so much praying and singing prevented the people from doing their tasks, as it kept them up nights, when they should be asleep. He used to mock, and in every possible way interrupt the poor slaves, who, after the toil of the day, knelt in their lowly cabins to offer their prayers and supplications to Him whose ear is open to the sorrowful sighing of the prisoner, and who hath promised in his own time to come down and deliver. In his drunken seasons he would make excursions at night through the slave-quarters, enter the cabins, and frighten the inmates, especially if engaged in prayer or psalm-singing. On one of these occasions he came back rubbing his hands and laughing. He said he had found uncle Solomon in his garden, down on his knees, praying like an old owl, and had tipped him over and frightened him half out of his wits. At another time he found uncle David sitting on his stool with his face thrust up the chimney, in order that his voice might not be heard by his brutal persecutor. He was praying, giving utterance to these words, probably in reference to his bondage:—"*How long, oh Lord, how long?*" "As long as my whip!" cried the overseer, who had stolen behind him, giving him a blow. It was the sport of a demon.

Not long after my master had left us, the overseer ascertained for the first time that some of the hands could read, and that they had brought books with them from Virginia. He compelled them to give up the keys of their chests, and on searching found several Bibles and hymn-books. Uncle Solomon's chest contained quite a library, which he could read at night by the light of knots of the pitch-pine.[163] These books he collected together, and in the evening called uncle Solomon into the house. After jeering him for some time, he gave him one of the Bibles and told him to name his text and preach him a sermon. The old man was silent. He then made him get upon the table, and ordered him to pray. Uncle Solomon meekly replied that "forced prayer was not good for soul or body." The overseer then knelt down himself, and in a blasphemous manner prayed that the Lord would send his spirit into uncle Solomon, or else let the old man fall from the table and break his neck, and so have an end of "nigger" preaching. On getting up from his knees he went to the cupboard, poured out a glass of brandy for himself, and brought another to the table. "James," said he, addressing me, "uncle Solomon stands there, for all the world, like a Hickory Quaker. His spirit don't move; I'll see if another spirit won't move it." He compelled the old preacher to swallow the brandy, and then told him to preach and exhort, for the spirit was in him. He set one of the Bibles on fire, and after it was consumed mixed up the ashes of it in a glass of water, and compelled the old man to drink it,[164] telling him that as the spirit and the word were now both in him, there was no longer any excuse for not preaching. After tormenting the wearied old man in this way until nearly midnight, he permitted him to go to his quarters.

The next day I saw uncle Solomon, and talked with him about his treatment. He said it would not always be so—that slavery was to come to an end, for the Bible said so—that there would then be no more whippings and fightings, but the lion and the lamb would lie down together, and all would be love. He said he prayed for Huckstep—that it was not he, but the devil in him, who behaved so. At his request, I found means to get him a Bible and a hymn-book from the overseer's room, and the old man ever afterwards kept them concealed in the hen-house.

The weeding season of 1836 was marked by repeated acts of cruelty on the part of Huckstep.[165] One of the hands, Priscilla,[166] was, owing to her delicate situation, unable to perform her daily task. He ordered her to be tied up against a tree, in the same manner that I had been. In this situation she was whipped until *she was delivered of a dead infant at the foot of the tree!* Our men took her upon a sheet and carried her to the house, where she lay sick for several months, but finally recovered. I have heard him repeatedly laugh at the circumstance.

Not long after this, we were surprised, one morning about ten o'clock, by hearing the horn blown at the house. Presently aunt Polly came screaming into the field. "What is the matter, Aunty?" I inquired. "Oh Lor!" said she, "old Huckstep's pitched off his horse and broke his head, and is e'en about dead."

"Thank God!" said Little Simon;[167] "the devil will have him at last."

"God-amighty be praised!" exclaimed half a dozen others.

The hands, with one accord, dropped their hoes, and crowded round the old woman, asking questions: "Is he dead?" "Will he die?" "Did you feel of him—was he cold?"

Aunt Polly explained, as well as she could, that Huckstep, in a state of partial intoxication, had attempted to leap his horse over a fence, had fallen and cut a deep gash in his head, and that he was now lying insensible.

It is impossible to describe the effect produced by this news among the hands. Men, women, and children shouted, clapped their hands, and laughed aloud. Some cursed the overseer, and others thanked the Lord for taking him away. Little Simon got down on his knees, and called loudly upon God to finish his work, and never let the overseer again enter a cotton field. "Let him die, Lord," said he, "let him die; he's killed enough of us. Oh, good Lord, let him die and not live."[168]

"Peace, peace! it is a bad spirit," said uncle Solomon; "God himself willeth not the death of a sinner."[169]

I followed the old woman to the house, and found Huckstep at the foot of one of those trees, so common at the South, called the Pride of China.[170] His face was black, and there was a frightful contusion on the side of his head. He was carried into the house, where, on my bleeding him, he revived.[171] He lay in great pain for several days, and it was nearly three weeks before he was able to come out to the cotton fields.

On returning to the field, after Huckstep had revived, I found the hands sadly disappointed to hear that he was still living. Some of them fell to cursing and swearing, and were enraged with me for trying to save his life. Little Simon said I was a fool; if he had bled him he would have done it to some purpose. He would, at least, have so disabled his arm that he would never again try to swing a whip.[172] Uncle Solomon remonstrated with Simon, and told me that I had done right.

The neighboring overseers used frequently to visit Huckstep, and he, in turn, visited them. I was sometimes present during their interviews, and heard them tell each other stories of horseracing, negro huntings, &c. Some time during this season, Ludlow, who was overseer of a plantation about eight miles from ours,[173] told of a slave of his, named Thornton, who had twice attempted to escape with his wife and one child.[174] The first time he was caught without much difficulty, chained to the overseer's horse, and in that way brought back. The poor man, to save his wife from a beating, laid all the blame upon himself, and said that his wife had no wish to escape, and tried to prevent him from attempting it. He was severely whipped; but soon ran away again, and was again arrested. The overseer, Ludlow, said he was determined to put a stop to the runaway, and accordingly had resort to a somewhat unusual method of punishment.

There is a great scarcity of good water in that section of Alabama; and you will generally see a large cistern attached to the corners of the houses to catch water for washing, &c. Underneath this cistern is frequently a tank from eight to ten feet deep, into which, when the former is full, the water is permitted to run.[175] From this tank the water is pumped out for use. Into one of these tanks the unfortunate slave was placed, and confined by one of his ankles to the bottom of it, and the water was suffered to flow in from above. He was compelled to pump out the water as fast as it came in, by means of a long rod or handle connected with the pump above ground. He was not allowed to begin until the water had risen to his middle. Any pause or delay after this, from weakness and exhaustion, would have been fatal, as the water would have risen above his head. In this horrible dungeon, toiling for his life, he was kept for twenty-four hours without any sustenance. Even Huckstep said that this was too bad; that he had himself formerly punished runaways in that way, but should not do it again.[176]

I rejoice to be able to say that this sufferer has at last escaped, with his wife and child, into a free State. He was assisted by some white men, but I do not know all the particulars of his escape.

Our overseer had not been long able to ride about the plantation, after his accident, before his life was again endangered. He found two of the hands, Little Jarret and Simon,[177] fighting with each other, and attempted to chastise both of them. Jarret bore it patiently, but Simon turned upon him, seized a stake or pin from a cart near by, and felled him to the ground.[178] The overseer got up, went to the house, and told aunt Polly that he had nearly been killed by the "niggers," and requested her to tie up his head, from which the blood was streaming. As soon as this was done, he took down his gun, and went out in pursuit of Simon, who had fled to his cabin, to get some things which he supposed necessary previous to attempting to escape from the plantation. He was just stepping out of the door when he met the enraged overseer with his gun in his hand. Not a word was spoken by either. Huckstep raised his gun and fired. The man fell without a groan across the door-still. He rose up twice on his hands and knees, but died in as few minutes. He was dragged off and buried. The overseer told me that there was no other way to deal with such a fellow. It was Alabama law, if a slave resisted, to shoot him at once.[179] He told me of a case which occurred in 1834, on a plantation about ten miles distant, and adjoining that where Crop, the negro hunter, boarded with his hounds.[180] The overseer had bought some slaves at Selma, from a drove or coffle passing through that place. They proved very refractory. He whipped three of them, and undertook to whip a fourth, who was from Maryland. The man raised his hoe in a threatening manner, and the overseer fired upon him. The slave fell, but instantly rose up on his hands and knees, and was beaten down again by the stock of the overseer's gun. The wounded wretch raised himself once more, drew a knife from the waistband of his pantaloons, and, catching hold of the overseer's coat, raised himself high enough to inflict a fatal wound upon the latter. Both fell together, and died immediately after.

Nothing more of special importance occurred until July, of last year,[181] when one of our men, named John, was whipped three times for not performing his task. On the last day of the month, after his third whipping, he ran away. On the following morning, I found that he was missing at his row. The overseer said we must hunt him up; and he blew the "nigger horn," as it is called, for the dogs. This horn was only used when we went in pursuit of fugitives. It is a cow's horn, and makes a short, loud sound. We crossed Flincher's and Goldsby's plantations,[182] as the dogs had got upon John's track, and went off barking in that direction, and the two overseers joined us in the chase.[183] The dogs soon caught sight of the runaway, and compelled him to climb a tree. We came up; Huckstep ordered him down, and secured him upon my horse by tying him to my back. On reaching home he was stripped entirely naked and lashed to a tree. Flincher then volunteered to whip him on one side of his legs and Goldsby on the other.[184] I had, in the mean time, been ordered to prepare a wash of salt and pepper, and wash his wounds with it. The poor fellow groaned, and his flesh shrunk and quivered as the burning solution was applied to it. This wash, while it adds to the immediate torment of the sufferer, facilitates the cure of the wounded parts.[185] Huckstep then whipped him from his neck down to his thighs, making the cuts lengthwise of his back. He was very expert with the whip, and could strike, at any time, within an inch of his mark. He then gave the whip to me and told me to strike directly across his back. When I had finished, the miserable sufferer, from his neck to his heels, was covered with blood and bruises. Goldsby and Flincher now turned to Huckstep, and told him that I deserved a whipping as much as John did; that they had known me frequently disobey his orders, and that I was partial to the "Virginia ladies," and didn't whip them as I did the men. They said that if I was a driver of theirs they would know what to do with me. Huckstep agreed with them; and after directing me to go to the house and prepare more of the wash for John's back, he called after me, with an oath, to see to it that I had some for myself, for he meant to give me, at least, two hundred and fifty lashes. I returned to the house, and, scarcely conscious of what I was doing, filled an iron vessel with water, put in the salt and pepper, and placed it over the embers.

As I stood by the fire watching the boiling of the mixture, and reflecting upon the dreadful torture to which I was about to be subjected, the thought of *escape* flashed upon my mind.[186] The chance was a desperate one, but I resolved to attempt it. I ran up stairs, tied my shirt in a handkerchief,[187] and stepped out of the back door of the house, telling aunt Polly to take care of the wash at the fire until I returned. The sun was about one hour high,[188] but, luckily for me, the hands, as well as the three overseers, were on the other side of the house. I kept the house between them and myself, and ran as fast as I could for the woods. On reaching them I found myself obliged to proceed slowly, as there was a thick undergrowth of cane and reeds. Night came on; I straggled forward by a dim starlight, amidst vines and reedbeds. About midnight the horizon began to be overcast, and the darkness increased, until, in the thick forest, I could scarcely see a yard before me. Fearing that I might lose my way and wander towards the plantation, instead of from it, I resolved to wait until day. I laid down upon a little hillock and fell asleep.

When I awoke it was broad day. The clouds had vanished, and the hot sunshine fell through the trees upon my face. I started up, realizing my situation, and darted onward. My object was to reach the great road by which we travelled when we came out from Virginia.[189] I had, however, very little hope of escape. I knew that a hot pursuit would be made after me, and what I most dreaded was that the overseer would procure Crop's bloodhounds to follow my track. If only the hounds of our plantation were sent after me, I had hopes of being able to make friends of them, as they were always good-natured and obedient to me. I travelled until, as near as I could judge, about ten o'clock,[190] when a distant sound startled me. I stopped and listened. It was the deep bay of the bloodhound, apparently at a great distance. I hurried on until I came to a creek about fifteen yards wide, skirted by an almost impenetrable growth of reeds and cane.[191] Plunging into it, I swam across and ran down by the side of it a short distance, and, in order to baffle the dogs, swam back to the other side again. I stopped in the reed-bed and listened. The dogs seemed close at hand, and by the loud barking I felt persuaded that Crop's hounds were with them. I thought of the fate of Little John,[192] who had been torn in pieces by the hounds, and of the scarcely less dreadful condition of those who had escaped the dogs only to fall into the hands of the overseer. The yell of the dogs grew louder. Escape seemed impossible. I ran down the creek with a determination to drown myself. I plunged into the water and went down to the bottom, but the dreadful strangling sensation compelled me to struggle up to the surface. Again I heard the yell of the bloodhounds, and again desperately plunged down into the water. As I went down I opened my mouth, and, choked and gasping, found myself once more struggling upward. As I rose to the top of the water and caught a glimpse of the sunshine and the trees, the love of life revived in me. I swam to the other side of the creek, and forced my way through the reeds to a large bass-wood tree, and stood under one of its lowest limbs, ready, in case of necessity, to spring up into it. Here, panting and exhausted, I stood waiting for the dogs. The woods seemed full of them. I heard a bell tinkle, and, a moment after, our old hound Venus came bounding through the cane,[193] dripping wet from the creek. As the old hound came towards me, I called to her as I used to do when out hunting with her.

She stopped suddenly, looked up at me, and then came wagging her tail and fawning around me. A moment after the other dogs came up hot in the chase, and with their noses to the ground. I called to them, but they did not look up, just came yelling on. I was just about to spring into the tree to avoid them, when Venus, the old hound, met them, and stopped them. They then all came fawning and playing and jumping about me.[194] The very creatures whom a moment before I had feared would tear me limb from limb, were now leaping and licking my hands, and rolling on the leaves around me. I listened awhile in the fear of hearing the voices of men following the dogs, but there was no sound in the forest save the gurgling of the sluggish waters of the creek, and the chirp of black squirrels in the trees. I took courage and started onward once again, taking the dogs with me. The bell on the neck of the old dog I feared might betray me, and, unable to get it off her neck, I twisted some of the long moss of the trees around it, so as to prevent its ringing. At night I halted once more with the dogs by my side. Harassed with fear, and tormented with hunger, I laid down and tried to sleep. But the dogs were uneasy, and would start up and bark at the cries or the footsteps of wild animals, and I was obliged to use my utmost exertions to keep them quiet, fearing that their barking would draw my pursuers upon me. I slept but little, and as soon as daylight started forward again. The next day towards evening I reached a great road, which, I rejoiced to find, was the same one my master and myself had travelled on our way to Greene County.[195] I now thought it best to get rid of the dogs, and accordingly started them in pursuit of a deer. They went off, yelling on the track, and I never saw them again.[196] I remembered that my master told me, near this place, that we were in the Creek country, and that there were some Indian settlements not far distant.[197] In the course of the evening I crossed the road, and, striking into a path through the woods, soon came to a number of Indian cabins.[198] I went into one of them and begged for some food. The Indian women received me with a great deal of kindness, and gave me a good supper of venison, corn-bread, and stewed pumpkin.[199] I remained with them till the evening of the next day, when I started afresh on my journey. I kept on the road leading to Georgia. In the latter part of the night I entered into a long low bottom, heavily timbered, sometimes called Wolf Valley. It was a dreary and frightful place. As I walked on, I heard on all sides the howling of the wolves, and the quick patter of their feet on the leaves and sticks, as they ran through the woods. At daylight I laid down, but had scarcely closed my eyes when I was roused up by the wolves snarling and howling around me. I started on my feet and saw several of them running by me. I did not again close my eyes during the whole day.[200] In the afternoon, a bear with her two cubs came to a large chestnut tree near where I lay.[201] She crept up the tree, went out on one of the limbs, and broke off several twigs trying to shake down the nuts. They were not ripe enough to fall, and, after several vain attempts to procure some of them, she crawled down the tree again and went off with her young.

The day was long and tedious. As soon as it was dark I once more resumed my journey; but fatigue and the want of food and sleep rendered me almost incapable of further effort. It was not long before I fell asleep, while walking, and wandered out of the road. I was wakened by a bunch of moss which hung down from the limb of a tree and met my face. I looked up and saw, as I thought, a large man standing just before me. My first idea was that some one had struck me over the face, and that I had been at last overtaken by Huckstep. Rubbing my eyes once more, I saw the figure before me sink down upon its hands and knees; another glance assured me that it was a bear, and not a man. He passed across the road and disappeared. This adventure kept me awake for the remainder of the night. Towards morning I passed by a plantation, on which was a fine growth of peach-trees, full of ripe fruit.[202] I took as many of them as I could conveniently carry in my hands and pockets, and, retiring a little distance into the woods, laid down and slept till evening, when I again went forward.

Sleeping thus by day and travelling by night, in a direction towards the North star,[203] I entered Georgia. As I only travelled in the night-time, I was unable to recognise rivers and places which I had seen before, until I reached Columbus, where I recollected I had been with my master.[204] From this place I took the road leading to Washington, and passed directly through that village.[205] On leaving the village, I found myself, contrary to my expectation, in an open country, with no woods in view. I walked on until day broke in the east. At a considerable distance ahead, I saw a group of trees, and hurried on towards it. Large and beautiful plantations were on each side of me, from which I could hear dogs bark, and the driver's horn sounding. On reaching the trees, I found that they afforded but a poor place of concealment; on either hand, through its openings, I could see the men turning out to the cotton fields. I found a place to lie down between two oak stumps, around which the new shoots had sprung up thickly, forming a comparatively close shelter. After eating some peaches, which since leaving the Indian settlement had constituted my sole food, I fell asleep. I was waked by the barking of a dog. Raising my head and looking through the bushes, I found that the dog was barking at a black squirrel who was chattering on a limb almost directly above me. A moment after, I heard a voice speaking to the dog, and soon saw a man, with a gun in his hand, stealing through the wood. He passed close to the stumps, where I lay trembling with terror lest he should discover me. He kept his eye, however, upon the tree, and, raising his gun, fired. The squirrel dropped dead close by my side. I saw that any further attempt at concealment would be in vain, and sprang upon my feet. The man started forward on seeing me, struck at me with his gun, and beat my hat off.[206] I leaped into the road, and he followed after, swearing he would shoot me if I didn't stop. Knowing that his gun was not loaded,[207] I paid no attention to him, but ran across the road into a cotton field where there was a great gang of slaves working. The man with the gun followed, and called to the two colored drivers, who were on horseback, to ride after me and stop me. I saw a large piece of woodland at some distance ahead, and directed my course towards it. Just as I reached it, I looked back and saw my pursuer far behind me, and found, to my great joy, that the two drivers had not followed me. I got behind a tree, and soon heard the man enter the woods and pass me. After all had been still for more than an hour, I crept into a low place in the depth of the woods, and laid down amidst a bed of reeds, where I again fell asleep. Towards evening, on awaking, I found the sky beginning to be cloudy, and before night set in it was completely overcast. Having lost my hat, I tied an old handkerchief over my head, and prepared to resume my journey. It was foggy and very dark, and, involved as I was in the mazes of the forest, I did not know in what direction I was going. I wandered on until I reached a road, which I supposed to be the same one which I had left. The next day the weather was still dark and rainy, and continued so for several days. During this time I slept only by leaning against the body of a tree, as the ground was soaked with rain. On the fifth night after my adventure near Washington, the clouds broke away, and the clear moonlight and the stars shone down upon me.

I looked up to see the North star, which I supposed still before me. But I sought it in vain in all that quarter of the heavens. A dreadful thought came over me that I had been travelling out of my way. I turned round and saw the North star, which had been shining directly upon my back. I then knew that I had been travelling away from freedom, and towards the place of my captivity, ever since I left the woods into which I had been pursued on the 21st, five day before.[208] Oh, the keen and bitter agony of that moment! I sat down on the decaying trunk of a fallen tree, and wept like a child. Exhausted in mind and body, nature came at last to my relief, and I fell asleep upon the log. When I awoke it was still dark. I rose and nerved myself for another effort at freedom. Taking the North star for my guide, I turned upon my track, and left once more the dreaded frontiers of Alabama behind me. The next night, after crossing a considerable river, I came to a large road crossing the one on which I travelled, and which seemed to lead more directly towards the North. I took this road, and the next night after I came to a large village. Passing through the main street, I saw a large hotel which I at once recollected. I was in Augusta, and this was the hotel at which my master had spent several days when I was with him on one of his southern visits.[209] I heard the guards patrolling the town cry the hour of twelve; and, fearful of being taken up, I turned out of the main street, and got upon the road leading to Petersburg.[210] On reaching the latter place, I swam over the Savannah river into South Carolina, and from thence passed into North Carolina.[211]

Hitherto I had lived mainly upon peaches, which were plenty on almost all the plantations in Alabama and Georgia; but the season was now too far advanced for them, and I was obliged to resort to apples. These I obtained without much difficulty until within two or three days' journey of the Virginia line. At this time I had had nothing to eat but two or three small and sour apples for twenty-four hours, and I waited impatiently for night, in the hope of obtaining fruit from the orchards along the road. I passed by several plantations, but found no apples. After midnight, I passed near a large house, with fruit-trees around it. I searched under and climbed up and shook several of them to no purpose. At last I found a tree on which there were a few apples. On shaking it, half a dozen fell. I got down, and went groping and feeling about for them in the grass, but could find only two; the rest were devoured by several hogs, who were there on the same errand with myself. I pursued my way until day was about breaking, when I passed another house. The feeling of extreme hunger was here so intense, that it required all the resolution I was master of to keep myself from going up to the house and breaking into it in search of food. But the thought of being again made a slave, and of suffering the horrible punishment of a runaway, restrained me. I lay in the woods all that day without food. The next evening, I soon found a large pile of excellent apples, from which I supplied myself.

The next evening I reached Halifax Court House, and I then knew that I was near Virginia.[212] On the 7th of October, I came to the Roanoke, and crossed it in the midst of a violent storm of rain and thunder. The current ran so furiously that I was carried down with it, and with great difficulty, and in a state of complete exhaustion, reached the opposite shore.

At about 2 o'clock, on the night of the 15th, I approached Richmond;[213] but not daring to go into the city at that hour, on account of the patrols, I lay in the woods near Manchester,[214] until the next evening, when I started in the twilight, in order to enter before the setting of the watch. I passed over the bridge unmolested, although in great fear, as my tattered clothes and naked head were well calculated to excite suspicion;[215] and, being well acquainted with the localities of the city, made my way to the house of a friend.[216] I was received with the utmost kindness, and welcomed as one risen from the dead. Oh, how inexpressibly sweet were the tones of human sympathy, after the dreadful trials to which I had been subjected, the wrongs and outrages which I witnessed and suffered! For between two and three months I had not spoken with a human being, and the sound even of my own voice now seemed strange to my ears. During this time, save in two or three instances, I had tasted of no food except peaches and apples. I was supplied with some dried meat and coffee, but the first mouthful occasioned nausea and faintness. I was compelled to take my bed, and lay sick for several days. By the assiduous attention and kindness of my friends, I was supplied with every thing which was necessary during my sickness. I was detained in Richmond nearly a month.[217] As soon as I had sufficiently recovered to be able to proceed on my journey, I bade my kind host and his wife an affectionate farewell, and set forward once more towards a land of freedom. I longed to visit my wife and children in Powhatan County,[218] but the dread of being discovered prevented me from attempting it. I had learned from my friends in Richmond that they were living and in good health, but greatly distressed on my account.

My friends had provided me with a fur cap,[219] and with as much lean ham, cake, and biscuit as I could conveniently carry. I proceeded in the same way as before, travelling by night and lying close and sleeping by day. About the last of November I reached the Shenandoah river.[220] It was very cold; ice had already formed along the margin, and in swimming the river I was chilled through; and my clothes froze about me soon after I reached the opposite side. I passed into Maryland, and on the 5th of December stepped across the line which divided the free state of Pennsylvania from the land of slavery.[221]

I had a few shillings in money, which were given me at Richmond, and after travelling nearly twenty-four hours from the time I crossed the line, I ventured to call at a tavern and buy a dinner.[222] On reaching Carlisle,[223] I inquired of the ostler in a stable if he knew of any one who wished to hire a house-servant or coachman.[224] He said he did not. Some more colored people came in, and, taking me aside, told me that they knew that I was from Virginia, by my pronunciation of certain words—that I was probably a runaway slave—but that I need not be alarmed, as they were friends, and would do all in their power to protect me. I was taken home by one of them, and treated with the utmost kindness; and at night he took me in a wagon, and carried me some distance on my way to Harrisburg, where he said I should meet with friends.[225]

He told me that I had better go directly to Philadelphia, as there would be less danger of my being discovered and retaken there than in the country, and there were a great many persons there who would exert themselves to secure me from the slave-holders. In parting he cautioned me against conversing or stopping with any man on the road, unless he wore a plain, straight collar on a round coat, and said "thee" and "thou."[226] By following his directions I arrived safely in Philadelphia, having been kindly entertained and assisted on my journey by several benevolent gentlemen and ladies, whose compassion for the wayworn and hunted stranger I shall never forget, and whose names will always be dear to me. On reaching Philadelphia, I was visited by a large number of the Abolitionists, and friends of the colored people, who, after hearing my story, thought it would not be safe for me to remain in any part of the United States. I remained in Philadelphia a few days, and then a gentleman came on to New York with me, I being considered on board the steam-boat, and in the cars, as his servant.[227] I arrived at New York on the 1st of January.[228] The sympathy and kindness which I have every where met with since leaving the slave states, has been the more grateful to me because it was in a great measure unexpected. The slaves are always told that if they escape into a free state they will be seized and put in prison until their masters send for them.[229] I had heard Huckstep and the other overseers occasionally speak of the Abolitionists, but I did not know or dream that they were the friends of the slave.[230] Oh, if the miserable men and women, now toiling on the plantations of Alabama, could know that thousands in the free states are praying and striving for their deliverance, how would the glad tidings be whispered from cabin to cabin, and how would the slave-mother, as she watches over her infant, bless God, on her knees, for the hope that this child of her day of sorrow might never realize, in stripes, and toil, and grief unspeakable, what it is to be a slave!

NOTES TO THE 2013 EDITION

1. Williams apparently spent most of his early life in or near Essex County, Virginia, not Powhatan. Later in the narrative he also stated the wrong county in Alabama, Greene instead of Dallas, though he named many real people in both Virginia and Alabama. See the introduction for more detail.

2. Wherever Williams was born, it was most likely not on the plantation of the man he called "George Larrimore, sen." George Larimer stated, "I did not know this Mr. Williams, as he styles himself, until the fall of 1832, nor was he ever owned by my father, nor did I ever have the management of him in any way."

Williams probably first met George Larimer (or Lorimer) when Larimer began courting Virginia Garland Collins, the daughter of Williams's owner, Adelaide Garland Janey. The mother and daughter, both widows, lived at the plantation Monte Verde in Bowler's Wharf, Essex County. George Larimer's new mother-in-law, Mrs. Janey, had owned Williams since she inherited him from her late husband, Joseph Janey, in 1832. Williams worked as her carriage driver.

George married Virginia on March 2, 1833, and moved into Monte Verde with her; he had no other family home in the area. His father, James H. T. Larimer, who would have been the same generation as the man Williams called "George Larrimore, sen.," had died in 1827, and so had George's brother, William E. L. Larimer. George's only other brother, James H. T. Larimer Jr., had moved to Florida after his father's death, taking the family slaves with him.

Eva Eubank Wilkerson, *Index to Marriages of Old Rappahannock and Essex Counties, Virginia* (1953; repr., Baltimore: Clearfield Co., 2008), 62; George T. F. Larimer, qtd. in James G. Birney and Lewis Tappan, "Alabama Beacon versus James Williams," *Emancipator*, August 30, 1838, reprinted in *Friend of Man*, September 19, 1838; Inventory of the Estate of Joseph Janey, Reel 56, Essex County Wills, no. 22, 1829–32, 475–76, Library of Virginia; Sara Ann Lindsey, "Monte Verde," pamphlet, *Essex County Historical Society* (October 1990).

3. Mount Pleasant was a common plantation name, and one existed in Powhatan County, but neither abolitionists nor their detractors found any connection between it and Williams or his owner. At least two Mount Pleasant plantations also existed near Bowler's Wharf in Essex County, where Williams first appeared in the historical record as belonging to Joseph Janey. There is no evidence available yet to indicate which of the nearby Mount Pleasants, if either, he had a connection with before coming under Janey's ownership.

Muscoe and Grace Fenton Mercer Garnett owned Mount Pleasant near Loretto, Essex County, about thirty miles northwest of Janey's plantation. Muscoe died in 1803 and Grace in 1814. About the time Williams would have been born, James Hunter and Maria Garnett Hunter, the son-in-law and daughter of the elderly Garnetts, lived nearby, and she gave birth to a son,

Robert M. T. Hunter, at Mount Pleasant on April 21, 1809 (some sources give the year as 1801, but 1809 is based on the memoir by his daughter). Maria and her husband were apparently living across the Rappahannock River at Layton's, where he kept a store, but she returned to her mother's home to give birth. When her mother died, Mount Pleasant went to John Mercer Garnett, Maria's brother. James and Maria Hunter then settled at Hunter's Hill, James's family home, near Layton's.

This Mount Pleasant, according to a fire insurance policy, centered upon "a dwelling house, 2-stories high, the walls of brick, covered with wood. 48 x 34 feet." According to Martha Hunter, "The large brick mansion stood on the summit of the lofty range of hills overlooking the valley of the Rappahannock, and was built about 1734, on a large landed estate embracing thousands of acres." The other Mount Pleasant sat across the county line in King and Queen County, near Miller's Tavern, about fifteen miles northwest of Janey's plantation. Colonel John Hoskins inherited this Mount Pleasant and lived there until his death, on December 19, 1813, when it passed to his twenty-four-year-old son George. The two-story house, built of wood, was twenty-eight by fifty-four feet in its main section, with additions and outbuildings.

Several circumstances surrounding the Garnett/Hunter families resemble anecdotes that Williams related about his young master. More information may be found in the notes to pages where the anecdotes appear. Some incidents connected with the Brockenbrough family of Essex County also resemble incidents in the narrative and are also described in the notes. Although the Hoskins Mount Pleasant was closer to Joseph Janey's plantation, fewer circumstances about the Hoskins family match the narrative.

Williams may have related anecdotes from personal experience, or he may have heard of things happening to others and used them as inspiration for fictional experiences, or the surviving historical anecdotes may be only confirmation that similar but undocumented things were also happening elsewhere in the area. Firm evidence of Williams's birthplace and youth may be found eventually, but none is available now. A list of James Hunter's slaves in May 1811 did not include any named Shadrack or Meshech, nor did his will in 1826.

J. B. Rittenhouse, in Birney and Tappan, "Alabama Beacon versus James Williams"; James G. Birney and Lewis Tappan, "Statement Authorized by the Executive Committee," the *Emancipator*, reprinted in *The African Repository and Colonial Journal* (June 1839): 163; "The History of Mt. Pleasant, Gathered by Crystal Dingler," *Descendants of John Garnett*, http://familytreemaker.genealogy.com/users/w/a/g/Rick--Waggener/GENE3-0004.html (accessed August 31, 2011); Martha T. Hunter, *A Memoir of Robert M. T. Hunter* (Washington, D.C.: Neale Publishing Co., 1893), 13, 24–25, 32; "Genealogical Department," *Daughters of the American Revolution Magazine* (March 1918): 171; Charles Willard Hoskins Warner, *Hoskins of Virginia and Related Families* (Tappahannock, Va.: By the author, 1971), 35–37; Malcolm Hart Harris, *Old New Kent County* (1977; repr., Baltimore: Genealogical Publishing Co., 2006), 1:531; "Mount Pleasant," *Marker History*, www.markerhistory.com/mount-pleasant-marker-o-43/ (accessed August 31, 2011); Hunter family papers, Virginia Historical Society, Richmond; Will of James Hunter, February 26, 1826, Essex County Wills, Library of Virginia, Richmond.

4. Information on Williams's age comes from an ad that his Alabama master, Caleb Tate, placed when Williams ran away in the fall of 1835, which listed his age as twenty-six and his wife's as twenty-two. That would have made his birth year around 1809, though it may only

have been Tate's estimate. If he was born at the Garnetts' Mount Pleasant in 1809, he would have been born the same year as Robert M. T. Hunter, who was born April 21. William Austin Brockenbrough, a nephew of Arthur S. Brockenbrough who attended the University of Virginia, was also born that year. (See p. 30 for Williams's claim he was born the same year as his young master.)

Although the number twenty-six sounds precise, Tate may have based it on Williams's age when he purchased him the previous year then added a year. If so, the age at purchase, provided by Larimer or a trader, would have been a round number, twenty-five, and might have been estimated.

Another estimate of Williams's age came from Captain Ulysses Spalding of the steamboat *Wave*, who "suppose[d] him to be between twenty two and twenty five" when Williams worked on his boat in January 1837. Walter Cox, a steamboat passenger who saw him more briefly, estimated that he was much older, "about 30 to 35 years of age." Slatter *vs*. Holton, Docket no. 2894, Eastern District, June 1841, Supreme Court of Louisiana 19 LA 39, 00948, 00930, Earl K. Long Library, University of New Orleans, http://libweb.uno.edu/jspui/handle/123456789/12613 (accessed October 23, 2011).

5. While the name Brooks (or Brookes, Brooke, Broockes, or Broocke) was unusual in Powhatan County, it was common in Essex and the nearby counties in the early nineteenth century, as indicated by the 1810 Federal Census. Several individuals with that name appeared in the Essex County "List of Negroes Belonging to Those under a Guardian" (available on microfilm at the Library of Virginia, Richmond), including John T. Brooke, who applied to be one of the executors of Muscoe Garnett's Mount Pleasant estate in 1803 and "to be guardian of any children" (reel 104, p. 133), and R. Brooke, guardian of William Garnett Hunter's estate in the 1790s.

Without knowing more about who Williams's father was or the family he belonged to, it is impossible to tell which of the many Brookses Williams was referring to, but the situation he described was certainly plausible. When queried about it at the time, George Larimer misunderstood the question, thinking that Brooks was supposed to be *his* guardian, and answered, "A family of Brooks' lived near my father's, but they never had any thing to do with the guardianship of myself, or any one else that I know of; in fact I never had a guardian. My father never owned a native born African to my knowledge." A man named Brooks did show up in the 1810 Middlesex County Federal Census, where Larimer lived in his youth, as "Brooks, Wm. (guardian)" in a household with no white persons and four slaves. This Brooks appeared on census p. 394, while Larimer's father appeared as J.H.T. Lorimer with forty-eight slaves on p. 396.

George T. F. Larimer, qtd. in Birney and Tappan, "Alabama Beacon versus James Williams"; Garnett Family Papers, 1789–1846, Accession no. 28488, Personal Papers Collection, Library of Virginia, Richmond.

6. George Larimer denied this claim in his letter after the narrative was published: "There was but one mulatto on my father's estate, and he was about his age . . . there was not a mulatto child born on my father's estate from 1804 till 1830; when the slaves were sent to Florida."

Other plantation owners were less faithful. James Hunter fathered a son with one of his female slaves when he was about twenty-five years old, three years after his marriage to Maria Garnett of Mount Pleasant. The son, Samuel Troy, was born in 1799 and was enslaved at Hunter's Hill across the river from Mount Pleasant. His ownership passed to Hunter's daughter Jane in

1826, when Hunter died. He eventually hired his time and worked as a shoemaker in the nearby village of Loretto, then purchased his freedom.

Samuel Troy's son, Rev. William Troy, later moved to Canada and wrote about his experiences as his master's grandson in Essex County. Although James Hunter was born in 1774, too young to have fathered Williams's grandfather, and Williams did not appear among the slaves in Hunter's will, Reverend Troy's description of his father echoes Williams's own description of his early life, including the likable heiress Jane (p. 33): "My father was the son of his master, and, during a portion of his master's life, his domestic servant. His master died, and left him still a slave, to be, with the rest of the property, divided among several lawful children. When the estate was divided, my father was fortunate enough to fall into the hands of one of the daughters, named Jane. Jane had taken a liking to my father."

George T. F. Larimer, qtd. in Birney and Tappan, "Alabama Beacon versus James Williams"; Rev. William Troy, *Hair-Breadth Escapes from Slavery to Freedom* (Manchester: W. Bremner, 1861), 2; Benjamin Drew, *Narratives of Fugitive Slaves in Canada* (Boston: John P. Jewett, 1856), 353–57; J. A. Troy, "Troy Family—Rev. William Troy," AfriGeneas Slave Research Forum Archive, www.afrigeneas.com/forumdarchive/index.cgi/md/read/id/7770/sbj/troy-family-rev-william-troy/ (accessed September 1, 2011).

7. After his final escape from Alabama in 1835, Williams changed his name from Shadrach Wilkins to James Williams, but here he apparently reported his twin brother's actual name, Meshech, without adjusting it to fit his own new alias. When Larimer claimed he recognized the narrator as Shadrach Wilkins, no one seemed to notice that Larimer's story meant the twins had biblically matched names, Shadrach and Meshech, instead of James and Meshech.

Evidence in Alabama, Maryland, and Virginia corroborates the fact that Shadrach and James Williams were the same person. Larimer recognized him from the narrative and drawing as the man he knew called Shadrach. His Alabama owner advertised for him as "Shadrick" when he ran away, but when he was captured in Maryland as James, he admitted his real name was Shadrach to the officials. His owner's deposition, taken in Montgomery County, Alabama, June 1, 1836, referred to him as "~~James~~ Shadrach," and the arresting officer's deposition, taken in Baltimore May 17, 1836, referred to him as "James alias Shadrick."

Not surprisingly, Larimer denied in a letter that his father had "ever own[ed] a negro by the name of Meespec [Meshech]." Both the twins had presumably been born on another plantation, probably in or near Essex County.

George T. F. Larimer, qtd. in Birney and Tappan, "Alabama Beacon versus James Williams"; Caleb Tate, "Forty Dollars Reward," *Selma Free Press*, October 24, 1835; Alabama Governor (1835–37: Clay), Extraditions and requisitions file, SG24782 Reel 11, Alabama Department of Archives and History.

8. Perhaps the only Brockenbrough of Charlottesville at that time, and certainly the most famous, was Arthur Spicer Brockenbrough, proctor of the University of Virginia, who died on April 27, 1832. He was the only person with that last name in the 1830 Federal Census of Albemarle County, Virginia, which included Charlottesville, appearing as A. S. Brockenborough in a household that included himself, his wife, eight white children or teenagers, and sixteen enslaved people.

Brockenbrough's heirs were his brothers. He wrote in his April 23, 1832, will, "I bequeath

& divide to my two brothers John and Thomas Brockenbrough of Richmond . . . all the rest & residue of my estate real and personal in Richmond Albimarle or elsewhere in trust to dispose of . . . as they may think proper and from the proceeds to pay all my just debts, and the remainder either of property or money to divide among my wife and children."

Williams's later description of the First Baptist Church indicated that his brother lived in Richmond, not Charlottesville, but Brockenbrough did not itemize his Richmond property, and there is no evidence available to show whether he owned a slave who lived there. Will Book 11, p. 28, Albemarle County Courthouse.

9. Owners who had more enslaved people than they needed for work—not uncommon in Virginia—solved the problem by allowing trustworthy slaves to hire their own time. A resident of nearby King and Queen County recalled a similar enslaved man named Washington Lewis: "He was a tall, well formed mulatto, a mechanic by trade. He paid his master so much per month and pocketed all that remained over his earnings, his master consenting to this arrangement. He was sincerely religious and a leader among his people. Washington was a gifted speaker, being fluent, sensible, self-possessed; and being naturally graceful, frequently spoke in their meetings for worship." Alfred Bagby, *King and Queen County Virginia* (New York: Neale Publishing Co., 1908), 278–79.

10. The mention later of "Shocko Hill" implied the church was in Richmond rather than Charlottesville. The rapidly growing First Baptist Church of Richmond, located at H and Broad Streets, had a membership in the early nineteenth century about one-third white and two-thirds black, both enslaved and free, until it split into separate black and white congregations in 1841. White preacher Rev. John Kerr presided over the congregation with the help of white deacons as well as black ones who were appointed to minister to the black members. He served from 1825 to 1832, staying active with the church through 1833, so he would have been the pastor during both the cholera epidemic and Nat Turner's revolt, which Williams mentioned on the following page.

On July 11, 1826, a church committee appointed to "ascertain the number and names of the coloured brethren permitted to speak in pulpit" reported that "Ned Cary, Joe Abraham, Bartlett Lewis, Owen Dickerson, and Saml Clear" were permitted to preach, while "George Montague, Richard Vaughan, Martin Jenkins, Robert Dandridge, Thomas Johnson, John Craig, and Ceasar Hawkins" could exhort in public but not "take texts." Three years later, on July 9, 1829, the church required all black members to obtain new certificates because, it claimed, "many complaints have been made to the church of the irregular and improper conduct of coloured persons, stating themselves authorized by the church to preach or exhort." New approvals trickled in, but none of the earlier or new names can be linked to Williams without knowing more about his brother.

Whether or not Williams was describing his actual brother, the situation he depicted—an enslaved man who was a member of the First Baptist Church in Richmond and preached occasionally—would not have been unusual. Two other enslaved men, Lott Carey and Collin Teague, had already risen to prominence in the First Baptist Church, bought their freedom, and in 1821 left for the new colony of Liberia in Africa.

Robert Ryland, "Origin and History of the First African Church," in First Baptist Church, *The*

First Century of the First Baptist Church of Richmond, Virginia: 1780–1880 (Richmond: C. McCarthy, 1880), 86, 248, 249; J. B. Jeter, D.D., "Reminiscences of Rev. John Kerr," *Christian Repository* (August 1857): 478; J. L. Burrows, "History of the Church," in First Baptist Church, *First Century of the First Baptist Church of Richmond,* 69, 74–75; W. D. Thomas, "Deceased Pastors," in First Baptist Church, *First Century of the First Baptist Church of Richmond,* 126; Midori Takagi, *Rearing Wolves to Our Own Destruction: Slavery in Richmond, Virginia, 1782–1865* (Charlottesville: University of Virginia Press, 2002), 55–57; First Baptist Church, Richmond, Minute Book, January 8, 1825 to December 23, 1830, Library of Virginia, Richmond; Christopher Richardson, "The Lionization of Lott Cary," 1995, http://srnels.people.wm.edu/antrichf95/richardsn.html (accessed February 21, 2011).

11. Philadelphia's Quaker abolitionist population helped make it a common destination for runaway or manumitted slaves from Richmond and the South in general, so a free black woman *from* Philadelphia, living in Richmond, might have aroused suspicion that she had connections to abolitionists. By secretly teaching her husband to read and write, and probably supporting his outspoken views, she would have been fulfilling slave owners' worst fears of the disruptive influence of free black persons. Gregg D. Kimball, *American City, Southern Place: A Cultural History of Antebellum Richmond* (Athens: University of Georgia Press, 2003), 127.

12. Williams himself claimed not to be able to read or write (p. 30), but his surprising knowledge of geographic and historic details also caused doubt that an illiterate person dictated the story (p. 81). If he was indeed illiterate, his observation skills and memory were excellent. Evidence that he may not have been illiterate includes the fact that he wrote a letter from New York to his enslaved sister in Virginia, apparently at the same time he was giving different information verbally to the abolitionists.

13. The practice of allowing whites to be seated at the First Baptist Church, while turning away blacks, was implied in a list of reasons for constructing a new building in 1841: "Their old house was becoming too small for the congregation . . . The colored element was so large, that only a small part of it could be furnished with sittings," though apparently all of the white element could find seats. Ryland, "Origin and History of the First African Church," 247.

14. Thirty-nine lashes was a common punishment for lesser offenses, but the actual sentence for a slave who "shall, at any time, consult, advise or conspire to rebel, or make insurrection," was death. The threat of "nine and thirty lashes" and the fear of raising an insurrection may have been an allusion to the newly instituted penalty for black preachers after Nat Turner's rebellion because it included the punishment of "stripes . . . not exceeding thirty-nine lashes," for any slave who would "undertake to preach, exhort or conduct, or hold any assembly or meeting," whether or not he had been ordained. If so, it places this scene at least after the law was passed in March 1832 and probably after it went into effect in July.

The leniency of allowing a second chance to preach was not unknown. Even after the laws changed, "there were several [black] ministers of respectable gifts in the [First Baptist Church of Richmond], who, at the request of private families and by the connivance of the officers of the law, often attended funerals in the city and the adjacent country."

The usual way of dealing with the law was to allow blacks to assemble and be preached to, as long as a white person was present. Former slave Beverly Jones recalled in another Virginia county, "'Couse they wouldn' let us have no services lessen a white man was present. Most times the white preacher would preach, then he would set dere listenin' while the colored preacher preached. That was the law at that time."

Supplement to the Revised Code of the Laws of Virginia (Richmond: Samuel Shepherd, 1833), 246; *The Revised Code of the Laws of Virginia* (Richmond: Thomas Ritchie, 1819), 1:427; Ryland, "Origin and History of the First African Church," 258; Beverly Jones (b. 1848), Gloucester Court House, Va., interviewed by William T. Lee, qtd. in Charles L. Perdue Jr., Thomas E. Barden, and Robert K. Phillips, *Weevils in the Wheat: Interviews with Virginia Ex-Slaves* (1976; repr., Charlottesville: University of Virginia Press, 1992), 183.

15. There were numerous Scotts in Richmond, but no Brockleys appeared in the 1830 census. David *Barclay*, however, was a tobacco dealer and owner of sixty-seven slaves in the 1830 Richmond census.

The Scott with the largest number of slaves would have been Robert G. Scott, with eleven in the 1830 census. He was a lawyer born in Georgia who practiced for many years in Richmond and then later moved to Alabama. He was active in the Colonization Society, whose goal was "to restore to the land of their forefathers [Africa] a degraded and hopeless population, and to civilize and christianize a new continent, while our own loved land is relieved from its heaviest curse," according to a statement he undersigned in 1833. Williams expressed his less favorable sentiments about the colonization movement on p. 31. "Intelligence," *African Repository and Colonial Journal* (July 1833): 152.

16. "Their people" refers to Scott and Brockley's slaves. Especially before the Nat Turner scare, talented enslaved preachers might be invited to speak on other plantations. An overseer recorded several instances, including one involving a slave of Arthur S. Brockenbrough's father, a generation earlier: "August 12, 1786. Negro Lewis Belonging to Mr. Brockenbrough in Essex. Spake Aug. 12, Sunday, to about 300 people at Mr. Jno Coates, on Jude. He read the latter part of the ch. to the astonishment of the auditory. His gift exceeded many white preachers." Later he wrote: "Lewis, belonging to Dr. Brockenbrough [preached at] Mrs. Allison's Nov. 2, [1794] Sunday Ps. 49:15. A funeral of a child. See the power of God,—a poor Ethiopian. Abt. 150 people." Richard Dozier, qtd. in Mechal Sobel, *The World They Made Together: Black and White Values in Eighteenth-Century Virginia* (Princeton: Princeton University Press, 1987), 211.

17. "The cholera at Richmond" refers to the great epidemic of late summer and early fall 1832. The disease began among African Americans but spread to all races and classes, causing panic and hundreds of deaths over a few weeks. See further discussion comparing the date with Nat Turner's rebellion in n. 20. William Asbury Christian, *Richmond, Her Past and Present* (Richmond: L. H. Jenkins, 1912), 120, 121.

18. This was probably Mann S. Valentine. He had been in business in the Shockoe Hill area of Richmond for a couple of decades and regularly advertised his store in the White Buildings, at the corner of Fourth and H Streets, Shockoe Hill, in the late 1820s and early 1830s. *Richmond Enquirer*, October 20, 1829, and numerous other advertisements.

19. Henry S. Brooke of Richmond denied the incident in a letter dated June 15, 1838, stating that both he and Valentine were out of town at the time of the cholera. J. B. Rittenhouse, editor of the *Alabama Beacon*, had written Valentine to inquire about the incident but received the following response from Brooke instead:

Richmond, June 15th, 1838.

Dear Sir—Mr. M. S. Valentine of this place handed me on yesterday, your letter to him asking to be informed "whether during the prevalence of the cholera at Richmond, a negro preached a sermon in Richmond in which he compared the cholera to the pestilence that afflicted the Egyptian slaveholders because they would not let the people go, whether the whites were about to flog him for the sentiments advanced, and were prevented by him (you) or any other merchant, or any other person residing on Shockoe Hill or elewhere [*sic*] by his (your) name, and if yes, whether a young lawyer by the name of Brooks interfered and said it was wrong?" and requesting him to enquire of me if I have any recollection of the circumstance, &c. I have only to say in answer to your inquiry, that I have not only no recollection of any such occurrence, but am satisfied that none such ever did take place. I was the only lawyer of my name residing here at the period, to which you refer, and still am, and as there was not then and has not been since, any lawyer by the name of *Brooks* in this place, I am forced to conclude that I am the person alluded to in the pamphlet, to the statements of which your inquiries refer. Now it so happens, that both Mr. Valentine and myself were absent during the whole time of the prevalence of the cholera in this place, and did not return until late in October following, after the disease had entirely disappeared. We were both at the Virginia Springs, where, if I mistake not, we were seen by our mutual acquaintance—Mr. James L. Price, then also a resident of Richmond, but now of your state. Mr. Valentine informs me that he has no recollection of the occurrence, and says he has made inquiries of the only person of his name in the city, none of whom knew any thing of the matter. In a word, I do not doubt that the whole story is a deliberate fabrication, intended to impose on the credulity of a set of fanatics, whose passions and prejudices are too much inflamed to allow them to discriminate between truth and falsehood, far less to take the pains necessary to vindicate the one, or expose the other. Had any such occurrence taken place, and the peace of the community been likely to be disturbed by it, the laws invested the public authorities with ample powers to suppress every disorder. As a resort, then, to illegal violence, would not have been necessary, it is not likely it would have been used, in a city where love of order, and respect for the laws, is illustrated in the fact, that since its foundation to the present time, it has never been disgraced by a single mob.

Very respectfully,
Your obedient servant,
HENRY S. BROOKE.

James G. Birney and Lewis Tappan, the committee investigating the narrative for the American Anti-Slavery Society, published the letter and responded in print: "All that we have to say of this letter is, that it relates to an unimportant incident of which James Williams does not pretend to have been an eye witness—yet one that may have occurred without the knowledge of Mr. Brooke, and the *names* of persons incorrectly given in the hearsay statement of the matter on which James told his story."

While those who threatened to whip Williams's brother would have had the legal right under the 1832 law to apprehend him themselves, receive permission from the justice of the peace, and apply up to thirty-nine lashes, there also had been deacons at the First Baptist Church who supported African Americans, such as William Crane, who mentored Lott Carey. Brooke took an anti-abolitionist view but seemed more outraged at the accusation that there would be illegal violence in the city, when the laws allowed the legal silencing of outspoken enslaved preachers. Birney and Tappan, "Alabama Beacon versus James Williams"; First Baptist Church, *First Century of the First Baptist Church of Richmond*, 222–23.

20. Nat Turner's 1831 rebellion, the worst in years and less than one hundred miles from Richmond, caused Virginia legislators to consider ending slavery during their next session, but instead they chose to address the problem by passing stricter laws to prevent future communication among enslaved people. Because Turner had used his position as a preacher to organize the rebellion, all African American preachers, including Williams's brother, came under suspicion.

Turner acted in the summer of 1831, the year before the cholera epidemic. But the law restricting African American preaching, passed March 15, 1832, did not take effect until that July 1, almost a year after the rebellion and only a few weeks before the cholera hit. Therefore, the timeline is not as confused as it appears at first, though Williams's brother should still have been forced to stop preaching due to Nat Turner before the cholera epidemic, not after. The reference to nine and thirty lashes may indicate that the white congregation allowed him to preach for a while despite the new law, before stopping him altogether. *Supplement to the Revised Code of the Laws of Virginia* (Richmond: Samuel Shepherd, 1833), 246.

21. There is no available evidence of John Griggs or anyone with a similar name in Richmond. John Griggs of Jefferson County, Virginia, almost 150 miles north, owned twenty-nine slaves in the 1830 census. In the appraisal of his estate in 1836 none by the name of Meshech was listed, though if Williams described the situation accurately, Meshech would have been sold to Alabama by then. Larimer denied knowing anything about him: "nor do I know any thing of the negro belonging to Mr. Griggs."

The last name Briggs, phonetically similar, was prominent in eastern Virginia, most notably represented by John Howell Briggs, who died in 1808. David Briggs of Richmond served as secretary of the 1829 Virginia Convention (mentioned on p. 31), but there is no evidence of a John Briggs living in Richmond nor any evidence to tie Williams's brother to anyone named Briggs. Telephone call to clerk of the Jefferson County Courthouse, Jefferson County Will Book 9, pp. 144–45 (February 28, 2011); *Proceedings and Debates of the Virginia State Convention of 1829–1830* (Richmond: Samuel Shepherd & Co., 1830), 576.

22. The puzzle is how Williams knew this. "About three years since" would be early 1835, remarkably consistent with a statement on p. 41: "In the spring of 1835 the overseer brought me a letter from my wife [back in Virginia]," presumably telling Williams the news that his twin brother had been sold to Alabama. Williams did not mention further correspondence to explain how he learned his brother had escaped a year later or was seen near Maryland, though one might assume the news came in another letter from his wife.

Williams's wife, however, had actually been sold to Alabama with him, and from the fall of 1835 to January 1838 Williams himself was enslaved in various other places or on the run. He wrote to his enslaved sister in Essex County, Virginia, probably very early in 1838, according to George Larimer, so it is possible that Williams may have received a letter from her, rather than his wife, when he was in Alabama. George T. F. Larimer, qtd. in Birney and Tappan, "Alabama Beacon versus James Williams."

23. The abolitionist committee concluded that "Mr. Scott" was John Scott, "long one of the most respectable merchants in Fredericksburg." He was indeed the only Scott on Fredericksburg's merchant license lists in the period, named individually or as part of "Scott & Richards," his partnership with George B. Richards. Scott owned eighteen or nineteen enslaved people in the 1820 through 1840 censuses, both male and female and of ages that might match those of Williams's brother and his wife.

The abolitionists also learned, correctly, that Scott had never lived in Richmond. He had resided elsewhere, however, before establishing himself in Fredericksburg. When he first emigrated from Scotland, in 1786, at the age of sixteen, he worked for the Brooke family of Brooke's Bank in Essex County "for several years," until Mr. Brooke died in 1788. The main home of the Brooke's Bank property still stands and is on the National Register of Historic Places. It is located on the Rappahannock River, in the Loretto area of Essex County, about two miles from the Garnett-Hunter family's Mount Pleasant plantation and also from the home of Dr. John Brockenbrough, the father of Arthur S. Brockenbrough, whom Williams said was the owner of his other brother. The Brooke's Bank family may also have been connected to the "Brooks" who was a guardian of Williams's father's owners (p. 29). After Brooke died, in 1788, Scott moved to Fredericksburg and began his long career there, residing in Fredericksburg until his death in 1848.

Dora C. Jett, *Minor Sketches of Major Folk and Where They Sleep* (1928; repr., Whitefish, Mont.: Kessinger Publishing, 2003), 102–4; "A Guide to the Scott and Richards Mercantile Firm Papers," Accession no. 5541, Special Collections Department, University of Virginia Library, Charlottesville, http://ead.lib.virginia.edu/vivaead/published/uva-sc/viu03385.document (accessed February 27, 2011); Merchant Licenses in Fredericksburg, 1810, 1811, 1812, 1813, 1817, and 1820, Fredericksburg Research Resources, http://resources.umwhisp.org/fredburg.htm (accessed February 27, 2011); 1820, 1830, and 1840 U.S. Federal Censuses, Town of Fredericksburg, Va.; Birney and Tappan, "Statement Authorized by the Executive Committee," 163; George T. F. Larimer, qtd. in Birney and Tappan, "Alabama Beacon versus James Williams"; St. George Tucker Brooke, "The Brooke Family of Virginia," *Virginia Magazine of History and Biography* (1905): 101, 102. For a photograph of Brooke's Bank on the National Register of Historic Places, see www.dhr.virginia.gov/registers/Counties/Essex/BrookesBank_photo.htm (accessed February 28, 2011).

24. As might be expected, several slave-owning John Smiths lived in the area, though none showed up on the census in King William or Powhatan Counties with female slaves. Larimer, perhaps making a revealing slip, denied that he knew anything about a slave "belonging to Mr. Smith of King and Queen," a neighboring county where a John G. Smith, postmaster at the village of Patricks, owned one male and one female slave between the ages of twenty-four and thirty-five in the 1830 census. Another man, John H. Smith of King and Queen, had served in the Virginia House of Delegates in the 1806 and 1808 terms. Other John Smiths also owned female slaves in nearby Middlesex and Essex Counties.

More significantly, Larimer explained that Williams's sister actually "belongs to a Mr. Hundly of this county [Essex]" in 1838. The Hundleys owned Rose Hill, a plantation about two miles south of Monte Verde, the Janey family plantation where William was enslaved. (Records show the Hundley name spelled both with and without the *d* around this time.) When Thomas Hundley died, in 1814, Joseph Janey helped administer his estate. After Hundley's wife also died in 1820, the slaves passed to their children, including two sons who lived in Essex County, Larkin, at the family home of Rose Hill, and Thomas Jr. Both sons owned female slaves in the 1830 and 1840 censuses who would be the right age range to be Williams's sister. (Larkin Hundley served as one of the gentlemen justices at the poisoning trial of Dr. Roy's slaves, in which the commonwealth's attorney chose not to prosecute Williams.)

The names listed on the January 31, 1815, appraisal of Thomas Hundley's estate were Marlow, James, John, Phill, Jerry, Daphney, Anaky, Moses, Dennis, Eady, Hannah, Isaac, Elijah, John, and Spencer, but without more information there is no way to know which, if any, of the female slaves was Williams's sister.

1810, 1820, 1830 and 1840 U.S. Federal Censuses of Virginia, Middlesex, King and Queen, King William, Essex and Powhatan Counties; George T. F. Larimer, qtd. in Birney and Tappan, "Alabama Beacon versus James Williams"; William A. Weaver, *Register of All Officers and Agents, Civil, Military, and Naval, in the Service of the United States* (Washington, D.C.: Blair & Rives, 1835), 148; *Table of the Post Offices in the United States* (Washington, D.C.: Duff Green, 1831), 127; Bagby, *King and Queen County Virginia*, 385; Essex County, Va., Will Book 18, p. 92, cited by Thomas Moore's Genealogy Site, Person Sheet, Thomas Hundley, http://homepage.mac.com/thomas_moore/genealogy/ps03/ps03_206.html (accessed March 3, 2011); Warner, *Hoskins of Virginia and Related Families*, 118, 119; Thomas Hunley estate appraisal, Reel 52, Essex County Wills, no. 18, 1814–16, 290, Library of Virginia; 1830 and 1840 U.S. Federal Censuses of Virginia, Essex County; "Captain Larkin Hundley of Rose Hill Obituary," Essex County Historical Society (May 1984), http://essexmuseum.org/archive/bulletin-vol-24.pdf (accessed September 4, 2011).

25. This tangle of relationships bore little resemblance to George Larimer's family, but it hinted more strongly toward the Brockenbrough family. It may therefore be a useful clue to who owned Williams before the Janeys or at least what families he knew when he was younger.

John Roane (1736–1805) of Uppowoc, King William County, Virginia, had only three sisters, Sarah, Mary, and Lucy. Sarah and Lucy both married Brockenbrough brothers, and John Roane's son John also married a Brockenbrough. More specifically, Dr. John Brockenbrough (1741–1801) of Essex County married Sarah (not Jane) Roane (1750–1810), who was the sister of John Roane (1736–1805). Dr. John Brockenbrough's brother Colonel Moore Fauntleroy Brockenbrough (b. 1746) married the sister of Sarah and John Roane, Lucy Roane (b. 1741). John Roane's son, also named John (1766–1838), a congressional representative, married Elizabeth Fauntleroy Brockenbrough (1771–1813), the daughter of Newman Brockenbrough (d. 1791), who was Dr. John Brockenbrough's brother.

There is no evidence that Dr. John Brockenbrough had any sisters. The wife of "Mr. [Arthur Spicer] Brockenbrough, of Charlottesville" was Lucy Gray, apparently unrelated to the families in question. Arthur Spicer Brockenbrough would have been related, however, as the nephew of Dr. John Brockenbrough. Despite the similarity in names, Moore Fauntleroy Brockenbrough, son of Elizabeth Fauntleroy, was only distantly related to the Fauntleroy branch that married with the Larimers.

Austin Brockenbrough, the brother of Arthur Spicer Brockenbrough of Charlottesville, lived in Essex County and was present at the court session at which the attorney for the commonwealth chose not to prosecute Williams for attempting to poison Dr. Roy. While investigating the claims in the narrative, abolitionists Tappan and Birney received a reply "from Dr. John

Brockenbrough, who has resided in Richmond forty years, and been long and extensively known as among the most respectable and intelligent of its citizens." This was probably Dr. John Brockenbrough Jr., born in Essex County in 1775, who died in Richmond in 1852.

This man was the son of Dr. John Brockenbrough Sr. and Sarah Roane. Yet because they were too focused on the Larrimore family, the abolitionists failed to ask the right questions or receive useful answers and concluded, "There has been no intermarriage between the Larrimores and Roanes, Brockenbroughs or Scotts, for the last fifty years, if ever," missing that the Roanes and Brockenbroughs were closely intermarried in a pattern similar to what Williams reported for the Larrimores.

George Larimer denied these relationships for his own family, of course. He wrote: "My father's name was James T. Larimer. He married a Miss Catherine Fauntleroy, a daughter of Samuel Fauntleroy, deceased, of the county of King and Queen . . . He had two sisters, one of whom died single, and without ever having been married; a Mr. Thomas Fauntleroy married the other. There was never any family connexion between my father's family and the Lcotto (sp?), [Scotts] or Brookenborough's, that I knew of."

When the relationships are applied to his family, the resemblance is superficial. If the real-life George Larimer was George Larrimore Jr. of the narrative, then the "old master" would refer to his father, James. James Larimer and his sister did both marry people with the same last name, but it was Fauntleroy rather than Roane, and the two Fauntleroys were first cousins once removed, not siblings. James married Catherine Todd Fauntleroy. James's sister Isabella married Thomas Waring Fauntleroy.

For a detailed discussion of the Roane family and their relationships, see Frank G. Ruffin to Paul C. Cameron, June 1, 1870, in J. G. De Roulhac Hamilton, *The Papers of Thomas Ruffin* (Raleigh: Edwards & Broughton, 1920), 4:237–45, http://books.google.com/books?id=pDcTAAAAYAAJ&pg=PA236 (accessed February 24, 2011); and Charles Henry Ambler, *Thomas Ritchie, A Study in Virginia Politics* (Richmond: Bell Book & Stationery, 1913), 303, http://books.google.com/books?id=8zt3AAAAMAAJ&pg=PA303 (accessed September 4, 2011). For similar information in family tree form, see the Dave Buchroeder family tree, Ancestry.com, at http://awt.ancestrylibrary.com/cgi-bin/igm.cgi?op=AHN&db=flakey&id=I529102565&ti=5542 (accessed February 24, 2011). A similar family tree, focusing on the Brockenbroughs, is: "Dr. John Brockenbrough," Hutchins/Chapman Family Home Page, www.bannerblue.com/users/h/u/t/Christopher-F-Hutchins/WEBSITE-0001/UHP-0074.html (accessed September 24, 2011). Sources give varying dates for Dr. John Brockenbrough's birth and death, but 1741–1801 is based on his tombstone at his Richmond County estate, Doctor's Hall, recorded in Dr. G. W. Beale, "Early Tombs in Westmoreland, Richmond and Northumberland Counties," *William and Mary College Quarterly* (October 1902): 125. Birney and Tappan, "Statement Authorized by the Executive Committee," 162–63; George T. F. Larimer, qtd. in Birney and Tappan, "Alabama Beacon versus James Williams."

26. The obvious choice for "Judge Scott" would be Judge John Scott of Richmond, who married Elizabeth Blackwell Pickett, apparently unrelated, and in fact the abolitionists received a letter from "Hon. John Scott, judge of the sixth circuit court, residing in Fauquier County" and concluded there was no connection. In this case their conclusion seems correct that there was

no marriage between the Brockenbroughs, Larrimores, and Roanes and the Scotts. Birney and Tappan, "Statement Authorized by the Executive Committee"; Robert E. Scott, "Robert Eden Scott, A Biographical Sketch," *Bulletin Fauquier Historical Society* (August 1921): 79–80.

27. See p. 65 for more discussion about this Uncle Brockenbrough.

28. The actual Larimer family consisted only of sons. George Larimer stated that his father "had three children, James H.T., William E.L. and myself . . . my father and Wm. E.L. my youngest brother died in 1827."

Only one family had daughters, Jane and Elizabeth, and a son who attended the University of Virginia as a nephew of Arthur S. Brockenbrough: the family of Judge William Brockenbrough (1778–1838). He was the father of Elizabeth (1808–93), Sarah Jane (1804–90), who often went by "Jane," and John White Brockenbrough (1806–77), who attended the University of Virginia in 1825. There were also several younger children, Mary S. (1810–87), Judith (1813–99), and William Spencer Roane (1819–80). Their father was the son of Dr. John Brockenbrough of Tappahannock, Essex County. Judge Brockenbrough represented Essex in the state legislature in 1802–3, then served as a judge, starting in 1812 for the circuit centered in Richmond, where he lived until his death in 1838.

Williams may have blended details from several families in the Tappahannock area, given that Judge William Brockenbrough's life does not match the narrative's old master any more than several other possibilities, such as Robert M. T. Hunter or Austin Brockenbrough. Hunter, who was born April 21, 1809, at Mount Pleasant and grew up near it, had a sister named Jane, among other siblings. His parents died while he was a young man. After he returned from attending the University of Virginia, he moved to Fonthill with his two maiden sisters, Jane and Martha (see pp. 62–63). Austin Brockenbrough (1782–1858) also had two sons who were nephews of Arthur S. Brockenbrough and who attended the University of Virginia in the 1820s (see p. 31). William Austin Brockenbrough (1809–58), born the same year as Hunter, attended in 1827–28. John Fauntleroy Brockenbrough (1812–65) attended in 1829–30. Their father lived at Greenfield, a plantation bordering the village of Tappahannock.

Without further information it is impossible to know which of these families owned Williams or which he was familiar with in his youth, if any. Other anecdotes from both families, noted as they appear in the narrative, echo incidents he included in the narrative.

George T. F. Larimer, qtd. in Birney and Tappan, "Alabama Beacon versus James Williams"; Lenora Higginbotham Sweeny, "The Upshaw Family of Essex" (1838) *Genealogies of Virginia Families from the William & Mary College Quarterly* (Baltimore: Genealogical Publishing Co., 2006), 281–84; *Catalogue of the Officers and Students of the University of Virginia First Session, March 7th, 1825–December 15, 1825* (Charlottesville, Va.: Chronicle Steam Book Printing House, 1880), http://xtf.lib.virginia.edu/xtf/view?docId=2005_Q4_2/uvaBook/tei/z000000102.xml (accessed September 5, 2011), and similar catalogs at the same site through 1830; "An Act to Incorporate the Town of Tappahannock," *Acts and Joint Resolutions Passed by the General Assembly of the State of Virginia during the Session of 1893–94* (Richmond: J. H. O'Bannon, 1894), 263.

29. This would make George Larrimore born on May 6, 1805, based on the birth date that Williams gives on p. 29. George Larimer was actually born sometime between late 1802 and late 1804, according to his obituary, which states he died on Monday, November 4, 1839, "in the 36th year of his age." Williams probably first met Larimer when they were adults, so they

did not grow up together, but the birthday also does not match any known birthday among the Brockenbroughs, Garnetts, or Hunters. "Died, at Mont Verde . . . ," *Virginia Enquirer*, November 15, 1839.

30. A similar little story was preserved in the family of Robert M. T. Hunter. His daughter wrote:

> Up to his eleventh year he was educated at home by his sisters [at Hunter's Hill, across the river from Mount Pleasant], but at that time his father, and his uncle, William Garnett, together employed a teacher, who was at liberty to take other scholars besides those of his two patrons. This gentleman lived a part of the year with one of his employers and a part with the other, but the schoolhouse was built at Rose Hill [owned by the Garnetts, not the Rose Hill owned by the Hundleys], a distance of about two miles and a half from Hunter's Hill. To this place little Robert walked every day, attended by a colored boy called Austin.
>
> His father gave him the choice of a riding-horse or the escort of this boy, and Robert chose the latter. Every morning the two set forth together and Austin, after accompanying his charge to school, would go home and return for him in the afternoon.

James Hunter, Robert's father, who died in 1826, listed a slave named Austin in his will. Although Austin was apparently not Williams, this may be another example of something Williams observed and fictionalized in his narrative. Hunter, *Memoir of Robert M. T. Hunter*, 29–30.

31. George Larimer stated, "I never at any period of my life taught, or attempted to teach any of my father's slaves to read or write." Although forging of free papers was not unusual, the Brockenbrough family had trouble with a similar enslaved man. Austin Brockenbrough (1738–1810) of Westmoreland, the uncle of Dr. John Brockenbrough (1775–1852), advertised in 1789 for a runaway slave named Romeo, who "reads, writes, and knows something of figures, and for some time before his departure had exercised his talents in giving passes and certificates of freedom to run-away slaves; but made his escape a few days before the detection." George T. F. Larimer, qtd. in Birney and Tappan, "Alabama Beacon versus James Williams"; *Virginia Independent Chronicle*, Davis, March 4, 1789, *The Geography of Slavery in Virginia*, www2.vcdh.virginia.edu/gos/ (accessed September 4, 2011).

32. James Birney and Lewis Tappan mentioned that after his narrative had been published, Williams told other incidents that had been left out. They described in detail only one, which would have taken place during his youth in Virginia: "For the sake of brevity, a multitude of minute particulars were omitted in the book, that gave James' personal narrative a very uncommon air of reality. Among other things he mentioned having once rode a racehorse for his master in Virginia. The horse was named Goliah, and would have won the bet, which was very large, had he not broke down on the course." Other than the horse's name, it was not an unbelievable story. Williams apparently had some experience with horses; he was a carriage driver by the 1830s, and African American boys who perhaps had never raced before were sometimes used as jockeys even in major races. A report in 1830, describing a race on the Union Course, Long Island, the same day as one in which Goliah ran, stated: "The race (like the generality of races run in our country,) was ridden by boys. This can scarcely be avoided, so long as our young horses carry

their present weights—90 for a 3, 104 for a 4, and 114 for a five year old . . . That we are not sufficiently awake to the importance of judgment in the jockey, is proved by the sort of riders that shew at the starting post. They are, usually, exercise boys, weighing from 70 to 100 lbs.; and one out of three of these, probably never rode a race before." A visitor to the same course in 1833 noted, "The jockeys were of all hues, generally coloured boys, whose black faces appeared very grotesque under their bright-coloured, ill-fitting dresses."

Several families in the area owned racehorses, including the Brockenbroughs and especially their friends the Tayloes and John Randolph. The Hoskins of Mount Pleasant in King and Queen County also raised racehorses—perhaps the only significant resemblance between that Mount Pleasant and Williams's narrative of his early life. Neither Joseph Janey nor George Larimer seems to have been connected with horseracing.

At five foot ten Williams was too large to be a jockey as an adult, but as a boy, he might have been asked to ride. That would place the event perhaps within a few years of 1820, probably no later than 1825, even if his birth date was later than he claimed. The problem is that the most famous Goliah of his lifetime was not foaled until 1827.

The chestnut colt Goliah, sired by the American Eclipse, won his maiden race on October 6, 1829, at the Union Course in Long Island, under the ownership of Walter Livingston of New York. In December 1832 the *American Turf Register* reported he had gone to the stables of Colonel William R. Johnson, the renowned owner and trainer of Petersburg, Virginia. In 1833 Johnson "sold half of his interest in Goliah to William L. White of Hanover County, Virginia, where he would begin standing stud."

It is not a stretch, then, to believe that Williams might have known of this Goliah, if he had a connection to the Brockenbrough family, who occasionally raced on the Tree Hill course in Richmond where Goliah had raced and who knew the Tayloes, who sometimes sold horses to Johnson and had horses in numerous races. It is very doubtful, however, that he was selected as a jockey for an official race with heavy betting because he was a tall, full-grown man during Goliah's career.

At the time there was no requirement for racehorses or thoroughbreds to have unique names, and in fact the Livingston Goliah was probably named after one of the two previous famous Goliahs, sired in the eighteenth century. Therefore, it is possible another unknown Goliah, named after the eighteenth-century horses, competed around 1820 but never in races significant enough to be recorded in contemporary turf reports, and the "very large" bet was only large, relatively speaking. Williams also may have ridden a horse with a different name.

It is also possible this incident was another example of Williams starting with a real name, or a real incident, and fictionalizing it into his own life, though in most cases he kept the incidents realistic unless he was unaware of a contradiction, such as not knowing that the University of Virginia had not been founded in time for his fictionalized version of George Larimer to attend. In this case, if he knew of the famous Goliah and was referring to that horse specifically, he would have known he was too old to ride him.

Among the abolitionists James G. Birney was the one most versed in contemporary racehorses, especially from fifteen or twenty years ago, when he had raised and bet on horses in Kentucky and Alabama. He might not have been as familiar with Virginia horses, however. He apparently noticed nothing untoward about Williams's anecdote because he reported it in an article generally defending the believability of the narrative.

Birney and Tappan, "Alabama Beacon versus James Williams"; "Eclipse and His Stock," *American Turf Register and Sporting Magazine* (January 1830): 219–22; Patrick Shirreff, *A Tour through North America* (Edinburgh: Oliver & Boyd, 1835), 12; "Racing Calendar," *American Turf Register* (June 1834): 530; Patrick Nisbett Edgar, *The American Race-Turf Register, Sportsman's Heralad, and General Stud Book* (New York: Henry Mason, 1833); "Principal Matches and Sweepstakes over the Union (L.I.) Course," *American Turf Register and Sporting Magazine* (September 1831): 44; "Sporting Intelligence," *American Turf Register and Sporting Magazine* (December 1832): 198; "Sales of Horses," *American Turf Register and Sporting Magazine* (June 1833): 537.

33. The obvious reference would be to Arthur S. Brockenbrough, proctor at the University of Virginia in Charlottesville. J. B. Rittenhouse, editor of the *Alabama Beacon* in Greensborough, noticed the mistake and pointed it out on April 26, 1838, amid a series of attacks on the credibility of the narrative: "The hero of this romance is made to say that he was born in 1805, that his young master George was just ten days older than himself, and that at 14 years of age, the latter was sent to Charlottesville, as a student in the University. This would make the University in operation in 1819, whereas it is notorious that it was not organized till 1825."

Abolitionists Birney and Tappan responded in the *Emancipator,* trying to defend the narrative two ways, by excusing any errors and also pointing out the date might not be an error: "In the second extract from his paper, [Rittenhouse] speaks with derision of a 'negro' being able to give accurate details of dates, geography, &c. Yet in one of the two just given he seems to place the whole merits of the controversy (as he would call it) on James' accuracy as to the particular college to which his young master George was sent at 14 years of age. And it is to be borne in mind that there was a literary institution at Charlottesville long before the organization of the University, and the University offices were several years in building, so that the mistake is not a very strange one for a slave."

Although the abolitionists did not believe George Larimer of Essex was the same person as the young master of the narrative, he confirmed in a June 22 letter, "I never was at the University of Virginia." In fact, he was probably unacquainted with Williams until later. But using only the information in the narrative itself, Birney and Tappan could have mounted a better defense. Counting backward from 1833, the year that Williams said he left for Alabama, one can see that Larimer would have returned from Europe in 1829 and spent the winter of 1829–30 in New Orleans. The "three or four years" he spent in study and travel would mean he had left for Europe in 1826 or 1825, after returning from college. The University of Virginia's first session ended in December 1825, so he could have attended one or two sessions before leaving for Europe.

A student typically entered the university in his late teens and attended for two years, so one or two years starting at age nineteen would have been common, even more so than starting at age fourteen. This would mean that Williams was only mistaken about his owner's age. Williams was disguising his real owner at this time, however, by using other details and pinning them all on Larimer, so neither Larimer's birth date nor his age upon attending the university reflected what Williams actually witnessed. Page 74 discusses likely possibilities among the young men who attended the University of Virginia in its first few years. Without more information it is impossible to know what details from the narrative apply to Williams's actual owner at this time and which he adapted and fictionalized from families around him. Rittenhouse and Larimer, qtd. in Birney and Tappan, "Alabama Beacon versus James Williams."

34. Williams was remarkable "for his neatness & activity in acting as a Waiter," despite taking on the impromptu job during his later escape from New Orleans, so he apparently had some experience serving in a dining room. *Slatter v. Holton,* Docket no. 2894, Eastern District, June 1841, Supreme Court of Louisiana 19 LA 39, 00928, Earl K. Long Library, University of New Orleans, http://libweb.uno.edu/jspui/handle/123456789/12613 (accessed October 23, 2011).

35. The situation that Williams described was common for young men of wealthy families, though it was more typical of slightly higher social classes than the Brockenbroughs, Hunters, or Larimers. There is no indication that any of their sons studied in Europe. George Larimer was surprised "that I should have been represented as being so wealthy" and stated: "I never was at the University of Virginia, in Paris, or in Europe. I never was in New Orleans—my father went many years since, say about 1804, as far south as Milledgeville, Georgia, and he carried with him a servant named James Brown, who has since died (say about two years ago)."

In this case it is difficult to find even a nearby family whose son studied in Europe at the time outside of the very wealthy, such as the Tayloes. Williams may have simply made up this part of the story, knowing his listeners would believe it as typical.

The "sulphur springs" might be White Sulphur Springs, a fashionable health resort in the mountains of Greenbrier County, now West Virginia, or any of the other springs nearby, including the Warm Springs in Bath County, which Dr. John Brockenbrough (1775–1852) had owned an interest in since 1811 and where he would reside beginning in 1844. John Randolph wrote him in 1813, "'How and where I shall pass the summer months?' To which I can only reply—as it pleases God! If I go to any watering-place, it will be to our hot springs, for the purpose of stewing the rheumatism out of my carcase."

Dr. John Brockenbrough also owned a home in Richmond (as Williams said his master did on p. 31), where he received visits from notable Virginians. Lenora Higginbotham Sweeny wrote, "It was a center of the social life of the period, its owner and his wife distinguished in family, wealthy and hospitality. Chief Justice Marshall, and many other famous men were among those entertained at this mansion. The 'caustic' John Randolph, of Roanoke, was a constant visitor . . . The beautiful nieces of Mrs. Randolph were entertained there . . . Bishop Meade was long and intimately acquainted with Dr. Brockenbrough, of whom he writes: 'His house was my house during many years whenever I visited Richmond, and we freely corresponded at other times. A more amiable man is not easily found.'" Dr. Brockenbrough also owned seventeen slaves in the 1830 census. The home today houses the Museum of the Confederacy at Twelfth and Clay Streets.

George T. F. Larimer, qtd. in Birney and Tappan, "Alabama Beacon versus James Williams"; Philip St. George Cocke's diary, cited by "Taking the Waters, 19th c. Medicinal Springs of Virginia," *Historical Collections at the Claude Moore Health Sciences Library,* www.hsl.virginia.edu/historical/exhibits/springs/warm/harvie/letter.cfm (accessed September 6, 2011); Kenneth Shorey, ed., *Collected Letters of John Randolph of Roanoke to Dr. John Brockenbrough, 1812–1833* (New Brunswick, N.J.: Transaction Publishers, 1988), 5; Sweeny, "Upshaw Family of Essex," 280–81.

36. Williams first appears in the historical record in March 1832 in the inventory of Joseph Janey's estate under the name "Shaderack," unless future research uncovers his name earlier. Although Williams was describing the late 1820s, he may have already been owned by the Janeys and accompanying them on visits to New Orleans, or he may have used other trips or other information to make up this part of the narrative.

Janey's wife, Adelaide Langourant Garland, and her daughter by her first husband, Virginia Garland, were both natives of New Orleans, though Mrs. Janey and presumably her daughter had come to Virginia in 1815. As late as 1849, Mrs. Janey had "many relatives" still living in New Orleans, and the *Richmond Whig* asked that New Orleans newspapers copy her obituary that year. There is no evidence whether Mrs. Janey or her family actually traveled to New Orleans after she moved to Virginia. George Larimer, who married Virginia Garland Collins in 1832, said he was never in New Orleans himself. His future wife was already the widow of a Virginian when he met her locally, probably when she was living at her father's home in Essex County.

There is no indication that Robert M. T. Hunter, the young slave owner born at Mount Pleasant, ever went to New Orleans either, though at about this time "an idea [was] prevailing among his friends that Mr. Hunter would do well to leave his native State and settle in New Orleans to practice law, but this was abandoned, and we find him in 1830 following his profession in his own county [of Essex]."

Williams did travel to New Orleans later, under circumstances he failed to mention in the narrative. During his final escape attempt from Alabama he was sold in 1836 to slave trader Hope H. Slatter of Baltimore, who sent him to New Orleans by ship, and from there he escaped successfully.

"Died on the 26th of March . . . ," *Richmond Whig,* May 1, 1849, 1, col. 3; Hunter, *Memoir of Robert M. T. Hunter,* 44; George T. F. Larimer, qtd. in Birney and Tappan, "Alabama Beacon versus James Williams"; C2063 Baltimore County Jail (Runaway Docket), 1831–32, C2064 Baltimore City & County Jail (Runaway Docket), 1832–36, 2/72/4/19, docket no. 928, Maryland State Archives, Annapolis.

37. Williams was surely referring to outspoken, volatile congressman George McDuffie of Charleston, South Carolina. During the encounter that Williams described, McDuffie would have been a U.S. representative from South Carolina, though he later served as governor of that state.

One biographer described him: "George McDuffie was a spare, grim-looking man, with a very long nose. He was remarkably taciturn and reserved, at times moody and sad; but on occasions he would enjoy the society of his friends and companions with as much zest as any man . . . He was clear-headed, pure-hearted, frank, bold, and determined; he had passionate convictions and was not afraid to utter them or act in accordance with them."

Not surprisingly, George Larimer said his father "never called at Mr. McDuffie's that I ever heard of, nor do I believe he ever saw Mr. McD." Also not surprisingly, Thomas Miller, a resident of Powhatan County, wrote on May 24, 1838, in answer to an inquiry, that he had never heard "of [McDuffie] visiting any person in Powhatan, or any one from Powhatan visiting him in South Carolina."

More significantly, however, Miller said that he had met McDuffie once, "in Richmond, in

March, 1827." That would have been at the close of the second session of the Nineteenth Congress, which ended March 3, 1827, when McDuffie would have been traveling from Washington, D.C., home to South Carolina. McDuffie might have visited that year in Richmond with Williams's master, either Joseph Janey or whoever his master was before Janey, perhaps a politically connected person from Essex County such as John or William Brockenbrough, who had the "fine house in Richmond" he mentioned on this page.

Edwin L. Green, ed., *Two Speeches of George McDuffie* (Columbia, S.C.: State Company, 1905), 7; George T. F. Larimer and Thomas Miller, qtd. in Birney and Tappan, "Alabama Beacon versus James Williams"; "House History," *Office of the Clerk, U.S. House of Representatives*, http://artandhistory.house.gov/house_history/Session_Dates/sessionsAll.aspx (accessed September 7, 2011).

38. This bland encounter with Mr. McDuffie is evidence that John Greenleaf Whittier "carefully abstained from comments of his own" when writing down the narrative (p. 13), despite accusations that he had authored it or influenced it.

J. B. Rittenhouse of Alabama suggested the narrative was "a foul fester of falsehood, a miserably 'weak invention of the enemy,'" written by "some peddling Yankee preacher," but if Whittier controlled the narrative, he might have chosen to portray McDuffie as an outright villain, rather than in this neutral role, because Whittier's personal focus on McDuffie was specific and intense.

McDuffie had been loudly proslavery and a special target of abolitionists for years. In 1835 Whittier wrote a long, angry poem titled "To Governor McDuffie," which he included in collections of his poetry reprinted in 1837 and 1838, bracketing the time he was writing down Williams's narrative in January 1838. The poem, which Whittier removed from later collections, attacked McDuffie's support of slavery, insinuated he had sexual relations with his slaves, and in the end condemned him to "guilt's fiery torture ever burning." In comparison, the description of McDuffie's little attempt to purchase Williams seems remarkably mild.

Concerning McDuffie's attitude toward spending money on purchases, a contemporary wrote: "The latter part of his life was devoted to agriculture and making money. It was said he became avaricious. This Judge Huger denied to me in strong terms. He said that he and McDuffie kept house together whilst they were in the Senate, and although their expenses were heavy, he never saw the slightest wish on the part of McDuffie to curtail them. He said McDuffie did not care to spend money in order to make a display, for he scorned all such vanity, but when necessary he was as willing to spend money as any one. Judge Huger said that he seemed to regard money as little as any one he ever knew . . . There was no pretension about Mr. McDuffie in anything. He was very plain in his appearance and dress, and rustic in his manners."

J. B. Rittenhouse, qtd. in Birney and Tappan, "Alabama Beacon versus James Williams"; John Greenleaf Whittier, "To Governor McDuffie," reprinted in William Sloane Kennedy, *John G. Whittier, the Poet of Freedom* (New York: Funk & Wagnalls, 1892), 122–24. The poem first appeared in *New England Magazine* (February 1835), then in *Poems* (Boston, 1837), and *Poems* (Philadelphia, 1838), according to William Peterfield Trent, ed., *The Cambridge History of American Literature* (New York: G. P. Putnam's Sons, 1918), 444; Francis H. Underwood, *John Greenleaf Whittier, A Biography* (Boston: James R. Osgood, 1884), 122; B. F. Perry, *Reminiscences of Public Men* (Philadelphia: John D. Avil, 1883), 78, 79.

39. Some plantation owners from the surrounding counties also had homes in the city, though certainly not all. George Larimer said that his father "never resided in Richmond nor did he ever own any property in that place." There is no evidence that Joseph Janey owned property there either. See p. 78 for information about Dr. John Brockenbrough's house at Twelfth and Clay Streets. Judge William Brockenbrough (1778–1838), who was the father of John White Brockenbrough and William Spencer Roane Brockenbrough (p. 74), also had a home and twenty-three slaves in Richmond, according to the 1830 Federal Census. George T. F. Larimer, qtd. in Birney and Tappan, "Alabama Beacon versus James Williams."

40. J. B. Rittenhouse of Alabama drew attention to this passage, sarcastically implying it showed abolitionists had written or prompted much of the narrative, rather than a "negro (who gives so accurate a detail of dates, European and American geography, and the meetings of conventions for the purpose of amending State Constitutions)." Larimer also pointed out its impossibility: "[My father] was never acquainted with Mr. Neal to my knowledge, and having died [in 1827] before the setting of the Virginia Convention, could not have had the quarrel before alluded to."

The encounter with Mr. Neal (or Neale) gives circumstantial evidence, however, that Williams actually may have been present at the convention, either with his unknown former owner or with Joseph Janey, because it includes information not easily accessible to the New York abolitionists and makes more sense in relationship to his connection with Essex rather than Powhatan County.

The Virginia constitutional convention excited much interest. Almost a half-century after the framing of the U.S. Constitution, it was a chance for a new generation to see the statesmen of Virginia debating on constitutional topics again, led by the original seventy-eight-year-old James Madison.

Hugh B. Grigsby, one of the delegates, recalled that the convention "drew towards Richmond a large concourse of intelligent persons from various parts of the Union. Young men came on horseback from Kentucky, Tennessee, and other Southern States. Statesmen, men of mature years, who had already earned for themselves a title to the public regard, ministers of foreign powers, who wished to see men whose names had become historical, educated men of every profession and class, came, many of them with their families, to behold the gathering, and listen to the discussions of the body."

It would therefore not be surprising that Joseph Janey, who had fled France in 1790 in the midst of its revolution and the formation of its own constitution, and who lived only about fifty miles northeast, would be curious to attend the convention as a spectator, accompanied by his carriage driver or servant, if Williams already belonged to him by then. Any of the politically connected families of Essex County might have attended as well, including the Garnetts and Hunters, because James M. Garnett was a delegate from Essex County, or the Roanes and Brockenbroughs, because John Roane was a delegate from King William, and Dr. John Brockenbrough (1775–1852) of Richmond was a friend of John Randolph, representing Charlotte.

Of all the people to mention specifically at the convention, Mr. Neale seems an odd choice if abolitionists were constructing a fictional narrative. The lawyer Augustine Neale represented Richmond County, but his name did not appear on the list of delegates published before the convention because he had only been proclaimed in September, a month before it started, as a replacement for Ellyson Currie, who had recently died.

But if Williams was describing his experiences as Janey's servant, an encounter with Neale makes more sense. Larimer stated that his own father "was never acquainted with Mr. Neale" but failed to mention that Joseph Janey surely was because Janey and Neale were neighbors. Despite being in different counties, their plantations faced each other diagonally across the Rappahannock River, Janey at Bowler's Wharf (the address Larimer used on his letter) and Neale at Shandy Hall just to the northeast.

A lawyer as well as planter, Neale owned forty-six slaves in 1830, according to the census. Neale had served in the Virginia House of Delegates and was an attorney, and his home was less than ten miles southeast of Tappahannock, so he also probably would have been known by the members of the Brockenbrough, Garnett, and Hunter families who lived in that area or were in the legal profession.

The claim that the quarrel "came near terminating in a duel" is supported by the fact that it would not have been the first time for Neale. When he served in the Virginia House of Delegates from Richmond County in 1826, Neale had to swear an oath that he had not challenged anyone in violation of the "act to suppress duelling." He took the oath, admitting he had challenged someone to a duel in 1810 but justifying it to his peers:

> I gave a challenge in the year 1810, which was refused; since that period to the present, I have never taken the test oath of the act to suppress duelling, and have now conscientiously taken it, because I consider the plain reading of the said act applies to the revision of the laws of 1818–19; and at all events, that the test oath prior to the year 1818, was at that time repealed, and was operative only subsequent to the last mentioned period. I make this statement, in order that every member of the House of Delegates may know the construction which I have put upon the said laws, and to know precisely the time to which I meant the oath aforesaid should extend; protesting against all intention to be misunderstood, by any person whomsoever. Aug. Neale.

After taking the oath, he was allowed to remain a delegate.

Thomas Miller of Powhatan County, Virginia, when asked about the incident between Williams's owner and Neale, wrote: "I am pretty certain [Neale] had no quarrel with any person, about slavery or any thing else. I never heard such a report." He was being asked about an argument in connection with Powhatan County residents, however, and was unaware that Williams's owner probably lived in Essex instead.

J. B. Rittenhouse and George T. F. Larimer, qtd. in Birney and Tappan, "Alabama Beacon versus James Williams"; Ritchie and Cook, preface to *Proceedings and Debates of the Virginia State Convention of 1829–1830* (Richmond: Samuel Shepherd & Co., 1830), iii; Hugh B. Grigsby, *The Virginia Convention of 1829–30* (Richmond: MacFarlane & Fergusson, 1854), 6–10; *Thirteenth Annual Report of the Library Board of the Virginia State Library* (Richmond: Davis Bottom, 1917), 246; "A Guide to the Governor William B. Giles Executive Papers, 1827–1830," Accession no. 42310, Library of Virginia, Richmond, ead.lib.virginia.edu/vivaead/published/lva/vi00886.document (5

March 2011). For Neale's votes and participation at the convention, see *Proceedings and Debates of the Virginia State Convention of 1829–1830*; 1830 U.S. Federal Census, Virginia, Richmond and Essex Counties; "Augustine Neale (1777–1852) Find a Grave Memorial," www.findagrave.com/cgi-bin/fg.cgi?page=gr&GRid=31373754 (accessed March 4, 2011); William McCarty, M.D., "An Early 1800s Soap Opera," *Virginia Genealogical Society Newsletter* (June 2004): 1–5; *Journal of the House of Delegates of the Commonwealth of Virginia* (Richmond: Thomas Ritchie, 1826), 43; Th. [Thomas] Miller, qtd. in Birney and Tappan, "Alabama Beacon versus James Williams."

41. This incident involved the plan to relocate free blacks to a self-governing community in Liberia, Africa, led by the American Colonization Society. It was one of the few times that abolitionists and slave owners cooperated, abolitionists viewing it as a chance for blacks to govern themselves without white racism and slave owners seeing it as a way to solve the problem of free blacks mingling with and instigating insurrection among their enslaved people. Both supporters and detractors of the Colonization Society attended the 1829 Virginia convention. William F. Gordon, delegate from Albemarle County, expressed a view similar to the one reported by Williams: "The Colonization Society has failed to remove [the free blacks]. You cannot get them to go out of Virginia; and I think they would be blockheads if they did, living as comfortably as they do."

There is no available evidence for Joseph Janey's or George Larimer's views on colonization. Among the other Essex families discussed, the Brockenbroughs were more likely to hold the view indicated by Williams, while the Hunters and Garnetts were more likely to support colonization.

John Randolph, friend of Dr. John Brockenbrough (1775–1852) and a representative to the convention from Charlotte County, was pro-colonization in 1816, but by January 30, 1826, he wrote to Brockenbrough, "I am against all Colonization, &c., societies—am for the good old plan of making the negroes work, and thereby enabling the master to feed and clothe them well, and take care of them in sickness and old age." He repeated the view on February 20, decrying "false indulgence," which made plantations unprofitable and forced slaves into "the hand-cuffs, and the Alabama negro trader's slave-chain." Although he preferred that free blacks be removed, he felt the Colonization Society could not remove enough of them without a miracle, "while their proceedings and talks disturbed the rest of the slaves." Ambivalent about slavery, in his will he directed that his slaves be freed. There is no evidence that Brockenbrough disapproved of Randolph's views on colonization.

James Mercer Garnett, representing Essex County, was a longtime supporter of colonization. Charles Fenton Mercer, his brother-in-law and cousin, represented Loudoun County and was also a longtime proponent of colonization. Garnett had been born at Mount Pleasant plantation and was the brother of Robert M. T. Hunter's father. Both would be vice presidents of the Virginia Colonization Society in 1836.

Williams's negative response to returning to Africa was all too familiar to colonization advocates, including abolitionist James Birney. A former slaveholder from Alabama, Birney was appointed an American Colonization Society agent in 1832 for the district that included Alabama as well as Arkansas, Louisiana, Mississippi, and Tennessee, but he found the work disappointing. Slave owners of the Deep South never accepted the society as well as their more northern counterparts. In New Orleans he complained, "The blacks, both free and slave, were permitted to be present [at a meeting]. But I could not rouse the society into action."

Birney eventually became frustrated, resigned from the Colonization Society, and joined the American Anti-Slavery Society instead, advocating immediate emancipation. In his resignation letter he explained the problems he had faced, including the fact that slave owners complained their slaves did not want to go to Africa when they were asked. Although Birney suspected the slaveholders were describing Liberia negatively and thus biasing their slaves against it, he felt it was an unsolvable problem. Some blacks did choose to go to Liberia, such as Lott Carey, a former member of the First Baptist Church of Richmond, who was named acting governor of Liberia in 1828 (p. 66). But acceptance was not universal.

Whether Williams realized the New York abolitionists wanted to hear that colonization was a poor plan and tailored his story to match or whether he was simply reporting what happened or what was typical, the discussion of colonization and his reaction would have been reasonable for the time and place.

Proceedings and Debates of the Virginia State Convention of 1829–1830, 144; Kenneth Shorey, ed., *Collected Letters of John Randolph of Roanoke to Dr. John Brockenbrough, 1812–1833*, 62, 66–67; James Mercer Garnett, *Biographical Sketch of Charles Fenton Mercer, 1778–1858* (Richmond: Whittet & Shepperson, 1911), 17, 43; Birney, *James G. Birney and His Times*, 111, 121; James G. Birney, *Letter on Colonization* (New York: Office of the Anti-Slavery Reporter, 1834), 23.

42. The estimate of three hundred slaves was unrealistically high, regardless whose household Williams belonged to, though it was internally consistent with the large number of slaves he said Larrimore had sent to Alabama (pp. 34, 37, 49).

Larimer expressed surprise at having "been represented as being so wealthy" and reported a more realistic number: "My father owned between 80 and 90 slaves, and all of them except two or three were sent to Florida." Even that estimate may have been high, given that his father appeared on both the 1810 and 1820 censuses of Urbanna, Middlesex County, with only 48 slaves, though he purchased more between 1820 and his death in 1827, probably bringing the number up to that range (p. 85). Nonetheless, only a handful of Urbanna residents owned more. The largest single owner, a cousin, had 122.

In Essex County the Janey family expanded from 38 to 74 slaves between 1820 and 1830, still well below 300. Robert M. T. Hunter also owned 74 slaves in the 1830 census, while Austin Brockenbrough owned 64. The largest number of slaves reported for an Essex household by far was on Robert P. Waring's plantation, with 491 in the 1830 census. The Warings were related to most of the families in the area, at least distantly.

Among the very wealthiest families in the area, the Tayloes fit the broadest outline of Larrimore's life better than most: a young master who traveled in Europe, attended the University of Virginia, inherited his father's Virginia estate, established an absentee-owner plantation in Alabama operated by an unmarried overseer with a black mistress, and removed many of his slaves there but only visited personally once or twice. There is no indication that Williams himself had any connection to the Tayloe family, other than perhaps using his general awareness of them and similar families as he rewrote the Larimer family into a household wealthier than they were.

Henry A. Tayloe, who would later manage the Tayloe brothers' Alabama plantation, was listed on the 1830 Essex County census with sixty-nine slaves, probably at his plantation, Oakley, about ten miles from Tappahannock. The Garland family had been neighbors and employees of the Tayloe family, so Williams's owner Mrs. Janey (the former Mrs. William Griffin Garland) may have continued to keep in touch with them, although her first husband had died in 1816. Other possible Tayloe links: William Brockenbrough (1715–78), father of Dr. John Brockenbrough (1741–1801) of Tappahannock, Essex County, had been raised by Colonel John Tayloe of Mount Airy plantation. John Tayloe III purchased Dr. John Brockenbrough's Richmond County estate, Doctor's Hall, in 1801.

Williams may have known some of the Tayloe slaves or seen them start on their trek to Alabama in 1833, though the Tayloe slaves took a different route than he described in the narrative. Even so, far fewer than three hundred made the journey in the first group. Although Williams claimed he left Virginia in 1833, court records show he was still present in Virginia in August 1834 and was probably sold south soon after.

George T. F. Larimer, qtd. in Birney and Tappan, "Alabama Beacon versus James Williams"; 1810, 1820, and 1830 U.S. Federal Censuses, Middlesex County and Essex County; Laura Croghan Kamoie, *Irons in the Fire: The Business History of the Tayloe Family and Virginia's Gentry, 1700–1860* (Charlottesville: University of Virginia Press, 2007), 43, 96, 104; Essex County Court Orders, Reel 97, no. 48, 1833–36, 127, Library of Virginia, Richmond; Warner, *Hoskins of Virginia and Related Families*, 273–84.

43. George Larimer reported that his father James never purchased any slaves from anyone "except of Mr. Fauntleroy, and they were a portion of the slaves belonging to the estate of his father," in other words, George's grandfather, who was also named George.

Grandfather George Lorimer (Larimer) died in 1784 in Middlesex County, Virginia, leaving a son and daughter, James and Isabella. Isabella married Thomas Fauntleroy. On her death her share of the slaves passed to her husband, then to their children upon her husband's death. By 1820 their oldest son, John Fauntleroy, only twenty-one, was the largest slave owner in Middlesex County with 122 slaves consolidated from various inheritances, but he was destined to live only three more years. James Larimer probably purchased the slaves in question either from Thomas or, more likely, John Fauntleroy, to reunite them after they had been split between him and his sister and were now headed for his cousins.

After James Larimer died, his son James Jr., brother of George Larimer, moved to Florida, settling his share of the family slaves on a plantation there. George reported that the slaves went to Florida in 1830 and that he "disposed of [his own] portion of the slaves to Mr. Craig of Florida after having hired them out until the 1st of January, 1834." The slaves appeared neither with George nor James in the 1830 census; perhaps they were being transported down to Florida at the time. In 1830 George was listed alone in King and Queen County, and James, as "J H T Laramore," had three slaves in Gadsden County, Florida Territory. By 1840 George was dead, and James appeared in the 1840 census of Leon, Florida Territory, as Jas. F. T. Lorimer with eighty-four slaves. "Mr. Craig" referred to William P. Craig, formerly of Maryland, who used both brothers to help finance his plantation investments after he moved to Leon County, Florida.

George T. F. Larimer, qtd. in Birney and Tappan, "Alabama Beacon versus James Williams"; Malcolm Hart Harris, M.D., *Old New Kent County* (1977; repr., Baltimore: Genealogical Publishing Co., 2006), 514; Robert K. Headley Jr., *Genealogical Abstracts from 18th Century Virginia Newspapers* (Baltimore: Genealogical Publishing Co., 1987), 212; "Our Research," Chris Kraft, http://worldconnect.rootsweb.ancestry.com/cgi-bin/igm.cgi?op=GET&db=adgedge&id=I72372

(accessed March 6, 2011); Robert H. Fauntleroy, *The Fauntleroy Family* (1952); 1820 U.S. Federal Census, Middlesex County, Va.; Edward E. Baptist, *Creating an Old South: Middle Florida's Plantation Frontier before the Civil War* (Chapel Hill: University of North Carolina Press, 2002), 32; 1830 U.S. Federal Census, King and Queen County, Va.; 1830 U.S. Federal Census, Gadsden County, Fla.; 1840 U.S. Federal Census, Leon County, Fla.

44. The abolitionist committee that investigated the narrative reported that "John Smoot, described in the narrative as a planter of Powhattan," was not "known as having at any time resided in said county or elsewhere." While none of the people in the book resided in Powhatan County, John Weems Smoot was a resident of Charles County, Maryland, about seventy-five miles north of where Williams's owner lived in Virginia, and he may possibly have been who Williams was referring to, though he lived a significant distance away. "At the census of 1840 John Weems Smoot was one of the largest slave owners in Charles County, being the master of 62 negroes," according to a family genealogist.

Smoot and his wife had inherited many of their slaves and sent some to Alabama with Smoot's father-in-law. A few years before Williams himself was sold to Alabama, Smoot's father-in-law died, and the family petitioned to bring the slaves back to Virginia again. Such shipping around of enslaved people may have seemed like gratuitous buying and selling, or Williams may have been referring to some other unknown incident that caused him to single out Smoot in particular, or "John Smoot" may not have referred to John Weems Smoot at all.

Birney and Tappan, "Statement Authorized by the Executive Committee," 163; Harry Wright Newman, *The Smoots of Maryland and Virginia* (Washington, D.C., 1936), 73; "Chapter 226, An Act to Authorize the Persons Therein Named, to Bring into This State, Certain Slaves," *Laws Made and Passed by the General Assembly of the State of Maryland* (Annapolis: Jonas Green, 1829).

45. It is possible that Williams himself was sold to Alabama through Bacon Tait or another trader. George Larimer, Mrs. Janey's son-in-law, reported that Williams "was sold by her, in consequence of his having been detected in connexion with others in attempting to poison Dr. Roy and his family . . . He was sold to a Mr. Tate of South Alabama." Mrs. Janey also sold his wife, Harriet, to Tate "rather than separate her from her husband."

The trial, and the ownership of Williams and his wife by both Mrs. Janey and Caleb Tate, can be documented through court records, Joseph Janey's will, and Tate's runaway ads and legal requests to regain ownership, but there is no evidence yet why Williams wound up being owned by Tate in particular.

Caleb Tate of Alabama was born in Lynchburg, Virginia, as was his cousin Bacon Tait. Caleb's father, Jesse, and Bacon's father, also named Caleb, were both sons of Henry Tate and Sarah Netherland. Caleb moved to Georgia and then, before 1830, to Alabama, while Bacon adopted an alternate spelling of the family name and relocated to Richmond, where he entered the slave-trading business, but there is no available evidence that Bacon stayed in contact with his cousin.

George T. F. Larimer, qtd. in Birney and Tappan, "Alabama Beacon versus James Williams"; Tate, Taylor, and Southern Families, http://wc.rootsweb.ancestry.com/cgi-bin/igm.cgi?op=DESC&db=ann_blomquist&id=I01662 (accessed May 6, 2012).

46. Two hundred men on a chain would be a large number, but Williams seemed to remark on it as if it were unusual. One observer in southern Virginia reported "a drove of upwards of a hundred, between 40 and 50 of them were fastened to one chain, the links being made of iron

rods, as thick in diameter as a man's little finger . . . I have seen in the course of five years, on the road near where I reside, 12 or 15 droves at least, passing to the south. They would average 40 in each drove." Theodore Dwight Weld, *American Slavery as It Is: Testimony of a Thousand Witnesses* (New York: American Anti-Slavery Society, 1839), 70.

47. In the narrative Williams claimed he was merely moved to his owner's other plantation in Alabama, but in actuality he and his wife were sold to a new owner in Alabama, so he may have been describing his own fear here.

The opening of valuable cotton land for settlement in Alabama and the surrounding states created a demand for Virginia slaves. Estimates in the early to mid-1830s ranged from thousands to tens of thousands of slaves exported from Virginia each year, with less than one-third sold and the remainder taken with their owners, making people realize, "Virginia is, in fact, a negro-raising state for other states." Ibid., 182–84.

48. There is no specific evidence that any of Williams's Virginia owners did this, though a lawsuit filed around 1823 involving Tate's extended family in Georgia hints at neighborly problems. From the abstract at the Digital Library on American Slavery: "John Upshaw sues William Tate for $2,000 in damages. Upshaw was the owner of five slaves, valued at $2,100, collectively. He claims that he 'casually lost' the slaves, and that they came into the possession of William Tate. Upshaw claims that Tate knew that the Negroes belonged to him, but with intent to deceive, 'converted and disposed of said negro slaves to his own use.'"

Even when slaves were sold south, they might prefer one trader over another, or at least it was common for traders to claim so. Hope H. Slatter, the Baltimore trader who would briefly own Williams in 1836, said "that slaves would often come to him and ask him to purchase them, and that he was the means of transferring them from worse masters to better."

Petition 20682302 Details, Elbert County Courthouse, Elberton, Ga., Records of the Superior Court, Records, 1823–28, 154–55, Digital Library on American Slavery, http://library.uncg.edu/slavery_petitions/details.aspx?pid=5052 (accessed July 22, 2011); E. A. Andrews, *Slavery and the Domestic Slave-Trade in the United States* (Boston: Light & Stearns, 1836), 150; Joseph Sturge, *A Visit to the United States in 1841* (London: Hamilton, Adams & Co., 1842), 31; John Hope Franklin and Loren Schweninger, *Runaway Slaves: Rebels on the Plantation* (New York: Oxford University Press, 2000), 106, 108–9.

49. George Larimer stated, "I was the only overseer of my father." In 1832, when Williams and his wife were mentioned in Joseph Janey's will, James Dyke was his overseer. James Dyke (c. 1786–1853) married Betsy Hundley of the Rose Hill Hundleys, who probably owned Williams's sister (pp. 71—72).

George T. F. Larimer, qtd. in Birney and Tappan, "Alabama Beacon versus James Williams"; Will of Joseph Janey, February 16, 1832, Reel 56, Essex County Wills, no. 22, 1829–32, 417, Library of Virginia, Richmond; Eva Eubank Wilkerson, *Index to Marriages of Old Rappahannock and Essex Counties, Virginia*, 137; "A Guide to the Hundley Family Papers, 1817–1895," Library of Virginia, Richmond.

50. There is no evidence of a Stephen Ransdell in either Caroline County, Virginia, about forty miles from where Williams lived, or Caroline County, Maryland, across the Chesapeake Bay. The Ransdell family lived in Westmoreland County in the eighteenth century, drifting to Fauquier County in the years that Williams would remember. Although Westmoreland County

was close enough to make the story believable, Fauquier County was nearly one hundred miles away.

Stephen Ransdell, in particular, has been a puzzle to Ransdell family researchers. He was alive in 1765, when Major Thomas Chilton mentioned him in a will. He (or another Stephen Ransdell) and Margaret Ransdell had a son, John, in 1798, according to John's marriage certificate, and he was dead at least by 1839, according to testimony in a court case concerning Captain Thomas Ransdell's will. There is no indication that he owned any significant number of slaves or that he even survived into Williams's lifetime. The most that one can conclude from the available evidence is that members of the Ransdell family were significant slave owners in Fauquier County during Williams's lifetime. By the 1840 census Horace C. Ransdell owned fifty-five slaves, in the same range as the Larimers and Janeys.

Virginia Marriages, 1785–1940, for Stephen C. Ransdell, Family Search, https://www.familysearch.org/search/collection/show#uri=http://www.familysearch.org/searchapi/search/collection/1708698 (accessed July 15, 2011); Ronald Ray Turner, *Prince William County Virginia, Clerk's Loose Papers*, vol. 4: *Selected Transcripts, 1811–1899, Miscellaneous Records*, 74, www.pwcvabooks.com/documents/PWCClerksLoosePapersVolIV.doc (accessed July 15, 2011); William Keith Ransdell, *Sifted from the Ashes: Thirteen Generations of One Line of the Ransdell Family in America*, http://familytreemaker.genealogy.com/users/d/e/u/John-Deutsch-Dexter/FILE/0002page.html (accessed July 15, 2011); *Ransdell Family*, http://dickdfox.tripod.com/index-ransdell.html (accessed July 15, 2011); 1840 Federal Census, Fauquier County, Va., http://ftp.us-census.org/pub/usgenweb/census/va/fauquier/1840/pg0250.txt (accessed July 15, 2011); Fauquier County, Va., 1800 Tax List, http://files.usgwarchives.net/va/fauquier/taxlists/1800tax.txt (accessed July 15, 2011).

51. Bacon Tait had recently constructed a new private jail to confine enslaved people who were being sold. His name was apparently one of the few in the narrative that the abolitionists recognized immediately from scouring ads in southern papers. He announced the opening in the December 10, 1834, *Richmond Whig:*

> NOTICE.
>
> The commodious buildings which I have recently had erected in the city of Richmond, are now ready for the accommodation of all persons who may wish their NEGROES safely and comfortably taken care of.
>
> The buildings were erected upon an extensive scale, without regard to cost, my main object being to insure the safe keeping, and, at the same time, the health and comfort of the negroes who may be placed thereat.
>
> The rooms and yards for the females are separate from those for the males, and genteel house servants will have rooms to themselves . . .
>
> These buildings are situationed on the lot corner of 15th and Cary streets, between Mayo's bridge and the Bell Tavern.

Before the new accommodations opened, Tait operated a jail in the same area, though not in the same building.

Although he did not mention them in the narrative, Williams was personally familiar with traders' private jails, whether or not he was held in Tait's, because he had been held by slave dealers James Franklin Purvis and Hope H. Slatter of Baltimore and Shadrach F. Slatter of New Orleans.

The Slave Trade as a Commercial Enterprise in Richmond, Virginia, National Register of Historic Places Multiple Property Documentation Form, www.dhr.virginia.gov/registers/Counties/MultipleCounty/127-6196_Slave_Trade_In_Richmond_MPS_2008_Final.pdf (accessed May 6, 2012); advertisement quoted in the *Friend*, January 3, 1835, 104; and "The Accursed Traffic," *Anti-Slavery Record* (October 1835): 116–17.

52. The abolitionists claimed that this one sentence—in which Williams stated that his wife's name was Harriet—was the only resemblance between George Larimer's version of events and Williams's narrative, missing the fact that Larimer's letter was in fact almost entirely accurate. George Larimer wrote, "This James Williams alias Shadrack Wilkins took as a wife a mulatto girl by the name of Harriet, belonging to Mrs. Janey, who sold her likewise to Mr. Tate rather than separate her from her husband."

"Shaderack" and Harriet appeared in Joseph Janey's 1832 estate inventory, and Caleb Tate advertised that "Shadrick" and "Harriet, the wife of Shadrick" ran from his plantation in Alabama, so Larimer's statement is most likely correct. It is less clear who owned Harriet before the Janeys. Larimer wrote that he first became acquainted with Williams in the fall of 1832, so he may not have been aware who owned her at the time Williams married her, in 1822, if Williams stated his birth date and marriage age correctly, or probably at least by 1832.

A John Gatewood had settled in Essex County in the seventeenth century, leaving many descendants. The closest John Gatewoods in the 1820s appeared on the census in neighboring King and Queen, and Caroline Counties. John Gatewood of Caroline County increased his slaveholdings from twenty in 1820 to sixty-seven slaves by 1830.

Another possibility, however, is William Kemp Gatewood (c. 1780–1836), known as "Kemp." He inherited the Essex County plantation Bellevue from his father, William Gatewood, and lived there until 1828, when he purchased nearby Ben Lomond and moved to it. He owned twenty-six slaves in 1820 and thirty-five in 1830. Ben Lomond and Bellevue were both about four miles north of Janey's Monte Verde plantation, the same distance Williams stated. It is possible Williams misremembered Gatewood's first name or Whittier misheard the unusual name Kemp as "John."

If Williams married Harriet when she was living at Gatewood's plantation, that would mean Gatewood sold Harriet to Janey sometime between their marriage and Janey's 1832 estate inventory, and it may imply that Williams had lived on Janey's plantation, four miles away, since the time of his marriage, including during the 1829 constitutional convention (p. 31). Williams also may have used Gatewood's name falsely, as part of his effort not to name actual owners.

Alabama newspaper editor J. B. Rittenhouse, looking in the wrong county like everyone else, stated, "The hero of this profligate romance tells us that he married a slave of John Gatewood, a planter living about 4 miles from Mount Pleasant.—This is also a fabulous character, no such person, our informant assures us, ever having resided in Powhatan." George T. F. Larimer and J. B. Rittenhouse, qtd. in Birney and Tappan, "Alabama Beacon versus James Williams"; Warner, *Hoskins of Virginia and Related Families*, 231.

53. The only evidence for the age of Williams's wife comes from the runaway ad that Caleb

Tate placed in 1835, in which he stated she was "a bright mulatto, low in statue [*sic*] and heavy built, wears her hair long and about 22 years old." Caleb Tate, "Fifty Dollars Reward," *Alabama Intelligencer and State Rights Expositor*, August 29, 1835, and other newspapers.

54. No evidence is available to identify the man named Jones, though it was not unusual for favored slaves to be married by white clergymen. Lorenzo L. Ivy of Virginia said, for example, "When de slaves git married, de leadin' colored men dat had learned to read an' write could marry 'em . . . Sometimes a white preacher'ud marry 'em."

Charles L. Perdue Jr., Thomas E. Barden, and Robert K. Phillips, eds., *Weevils in the Wheat: Interviews with Virginia Ex-Slaves* (Charlottesville: University Press of Virginia, 1976), 153. For other examples, see Clayton E. Jewett and John O. Allen, *Slavery in the South: A State-by-State History* (Westport, Conn.: Green wood Press, 2004), 196; Albert J. Raboteau, *Slave Religion: The "Invisible Institution" in the Antebellum South* (New York: Oxford University Press, 2004), 229; George P. Rawick, *The American Slave* (1941; repr., Westport, Conn.: Greenwood Publishing Co., 1972), 149.

55. Williams did have a son named Ben, who was only a few months old when Williams was sent south, but they were sold as a family to Alabama. When Williams and his wife ran away from Alabama, they "took with them their child, a boy named BEN, about 15 months old," on August 23, 1835. That would mean Ben was born in late May 1834.

Williams claimed in the narrative that he left Virginia about September 1, 1833 (p. 34), but he was still in Virginia on August 18, 1834, when he appeared in court, and was probably sold to Alabama soon after, so Ben would have been about three months old at the time. Williams would have last seen him before escaping alone from Alabama on October 16, 1835, when Ben was about a year and a half old.

Evidence for other children is less obvious. Joseph Janey's estate inventory in 1832 listed the women and children he owned in small groups, including "Kitty, Harriet, Priscilla & Francis." If this Harriet was Williams's wife, it is unclear whether Kitty was her mother and Priscilla and Francis were her children, her siblings, or there was some other relationship among the group.

When Williams and James B. White, the abolitionist who was helping him escape, were caught in Baltimore in 1836, the arresting officer testified that White had said "he was on his way to Alabama for the purpose of liberating said James alias Shadrick's wife and children to take them likewise to Buffalow, which belonged to Caleb Tate of said State." The word *children* may have been merely a mistake in memory because it would mean that Williams and his wife left behind at least one child when they first tried to run away with Ben, or it may be evidence that Williams had more than one child with him in Alabama.

The inventory of Caleb Tate's estate, taken in 1841, also listed slaves in small groups, including "Harriet—Benjamin & Chastine." Chastine may be the other child whom the abolitionist hoped to rescue as well as the other child of the two that Williams said were still living. Chastine may also have been born to Harriet by another father between 1835 and 1841.

Caleb Tate, "Fifty Dollars Reward," *Alabama Intelligencer and State Rights Expositor*, August 29, 1835, and other newspapers; Reel 97, Essex County Court Orders, no. 48, 1833–36, 127, Library of Virginia, Richmond; Inventory of the Estate of Joseph Janey, Reel 56, Essex County Wills, no. 22, 1829–32, 475, Library of Virginia, Richmond; Alabama Governor (1835–37: Clay), Extraditions and requisitions file, SG24782, Reel 11, Alabama Department of Archives and History; Orphan's Court February Term, 1843, Petition for Dower, Book E, 327, Dallas County Courthouse, Selma, Ala.

56. From at least 1832 until his final escape from Alabama, Williams lived at the same plantation as his wife. Slaves did visit spouses on other plantations and would have needed passes from their masters to do so legally, according to Virginia law. *The Revised Code of the Laws of Virginia* (Richmond: Thomas Ritchie, 1819), 1:422.

57. George Larimer accurately stated, "I never was in New Orleans," but he failed to mention that he did in fact marry a woman who grew up in the French Quarter of New Orleans and who had a French mother and stepfather. On being questioned after the narrative was published, he explained that Williams belonged to his mother-in-law, Mrs. Janey. Mrs. Janey and her daughter were his connection to New Orleans.

Mrs. Janey was born Adelaide Langourant, the daughter of Jean Langourant and Marianne (or Marie Anne) Fortier of New Orleans. Saying that Larimer's wife was one of the "first families" of New Orleans was no exaggeration; she traced her line to the Fortier and Langlois families through her maternal grandmother. In 1801 the future Mrs. Janey married William Griffin Garland, a native of Virginia, at the St. Louis Cathedral, New Orleans. He came from an old, wealthy Richmond County family but moved to New Orleans and invested there in land, businesses, and slaves. The Garlands lived at 74 Rue de Chartres in the heart of the French Quarter in 1805, with their three-year-old daughter, Virginia, sixteen house slaves, and probably Mrs. Garland's widowed mother.

Mr. Garland's extensive business dealings led him into numerous lawsuits, both as plaintiff and defendant, including some alleging that he mortgaged the same slaves several times under false names as he dealt with insolvency in 1807, but his wife protected her interest in her own property. Under Louisiana law a wife could "administer personally her paraphernal property, without the assistance of her husband" (sec. 3, art. 2361, 1825 Louisiana Code) and could "exonerate [herself] from the debts contracted during the marriage, by renouncing the partnership or community of gains" (sec. 4, art. 2379). Similar rights appeared in the Civil Laws of the Territory of Orleans, 1803.

Mrs. Garland moved to her husband's home state of Virginia in 1815, according to her obituary. When Mr. Garland died, in 1816, she remarried a few months later, on January 20, 1817, choosing again a wealthy merchant. Although her new husband, Joseph Janey, lived in Essex County, near where the Garland family also had business dealings, his French heritage matched her own. Born in France in 1767, he had immigrated to the United States in 1790. Earlier in the century he had made his money with a mercantile business, but in December 1815, not long before Mrs. Garland married him, he purchased 793 acres from William and Sarah Smith and had finished building a plantation home on the land. He would eventually expand the plantation to 2,400 acres. The house, which he named Monte Verde, still stands overlooking the Rappahannock River near Bowlers Wharf in Essex County and is now on the National Register of Historic Places.

Although Janey needed few slaves as a merchant, his ownership increased when he shifted his interests to planting, beginning with thirty-eight slaves in the 1820 census and rising to seventy-four by the 1830 census, along with seven free colored people. He died on March 2, 1832, leaving his estate to his widow, who continued to manage the property. Sixty slaves were named in his estate inventory, so some of those in the census may have been in his wife's name.

Meanwhile, Mrs. Janey's daughter by her first husband, Virginia Garland, who had spent her youth in the New Orleans French Quarter, had moved to Virginia with her mother and married Thomas Collins on May 25, 1819. He died in 1826, and she moved back to Monte Verde with her mother and stepfather, bringing with her the two young children from her marriage, Elizabeth and Thomas.

This was the situation when George Larimer met and married her. They were wed on March 2, 1833, after she had mourned exactly one year for her father's death. Larimer moved into Monte Verde with her, where Williams was enslaved as his mother-in-law's carriage driver. Although Larimer admitted he first met Williams in the fall of 1832, presumably while he was courting Virginia Garland Collins, he emphasized that he did not "have the management of him in any way."

From Williams's viewpoint the young Frenchwoman from New Orleans had already been living in the household, perhaps since soon after she was widowed in 1826. Because he changed his story to omit the Janeys and claimed instead that he had always been owned by the Larimer family, for the sake of consistency he needed to say that the French bride from New Orleans moved into Larimer's house when Larimer married her, rather than the other way around.

George T. F. Larimer, qtd. in Birney and Tappan, "Alabama Beacon versus James Williams"; "(Marie) Anne Fortier," *Wood Family History*, http://wc.rootsweb.ancestry.com/cgi-bin/igm.cgi?op=AHN&db=beebeewood&id=I5425 (accessed July 22, 2011); Garland William Griffin Junior, Byrne Family Research, http://byrnefamily.net/genealogy/getperson.php?personID=I08201&tree=Garland (accessed July 23, 2011); "Search results for William Garland," *Louisiana Purchase: A Heritage Explored*, http://louisdl.louislibraries.org/cdm/search/collection/lapur/searchterm/william%20garland/field/all/mode/all/conn/and/cosuppress/ (accessed July 23, 2011); "Died on the 26th of March . . . ," *Richmond Whig*, May 1, 1849, 1, col. 3; "National Register of Historic Places Registration Form, Monte Verde, DHR File no. 028-0029," *Virginia Department of Historic Resources*, www.dhr.virginia.gov/registers/Counties/Essex/028-0029_Monte_Verde_2002_Final_Nomination.pdf (accessed July 23, 2011); François-Xavier Martin, *Martin's Reports of Cases Argued and Determined in the Supreme Court of the State of Louisiana* (New Orleans: J. B. Steel, 1853), 5:349–57; *1805 New Orleans City Directory by Address*, http://files.usgwarchives.org/la/orleans/history/directory/1805addr.txt (accessed July 22, 2011); "Adelaide Langourant," *Rome, St. Cyr and Early Louisiana Families*, http://wc.rootsweb.ancestry.com/cgi-bin/igm.cgi?op=GET&db=madvintner&id=I36384 (accessed July 22, 2011); Estelle Mina Fortier Cochran, *The Fortier Family and Allied Families* (San Antonio, Tex., 1963), 33; Sara Ann Lindsey, "Monte Verde," *Essex County Historical Society* (October 1990); 1810, 1820, and 1830 United States Census, Essex County, Va.; Warner, *Hoskins of Virginia and Related Families*, 183, 190; Benjamin Watkins Leigh, "Collins's adm'x &c. v. Janey and another," *Reports of Cases Argued and Determined in the Court of Appeals and the General Court of Virginia* (Richmond, 1857), 3:421–24; Eva Eubank Wilkerson, *Index to Marriages of Old Rappahannock and Essex Counties, Virginia* (1953; repr., Baltimore: Clearfield Co., 2008), 62; *Civil Code of the State of Louisiana* (Paris: E. Duverger, 1825), 511–14; *Civil Laws Now in Force in the Territory of Orleans* (New Orleans: Bradford & Anderson, 1803), 334–38.

58. This death would be on July 14, 1832. George Larimer's real father, James, died in 1827, before George married into the Janey family and therefore before Williams had any connection to him. Joseph Janey, who owned Williams at that time, "died at his residence Mt. Verde Essex County, Va., on March 2, 1832, much esteemed by his numerous friends and acquaintances," according to his gravestone, so Williams would have witnessed a funeral for his owner that year. Warner, *Hoskins of Virginia and Related Families,* 190.

59. Joseph Janey's wife, Adelaide, inherited Williams along with her husband's other slaves, but she lived until 1849. Although several of the other families who might be connected with Williams had a death and inheritance during his lifetime, none had the same pattern of the father dying followed within a few months by the mother, with the estate going to the children.

60. Thomas Gresham, a Tappahannock attorney, was the executor of Joseph Janey's estate in 1832, when Williams was left to Janey's widow. He also served as attorney for the commonwealth of Essex County in 1834, at the time the commonwealth chose not to prosecute Williams and another of Janey's slaves during Dr. Roy's poisoning trial.

John Green, Esq., may have been John Williams Green, Esq. (1781–1834), a well-known lawyer and judge, though there is no available evidence to tie him to any estate connected with Williams. He was elected to the Virginia Court of Appeals in 1822 upon the death of Judge Spencer Roane and was succeeded by William Brockenbrough in 1834, when he died. He was one of the men who licensed Robert Eden Scott, the son of Judge John Scott (p. 30), to practice law in 1830. Although he resided in Culpeper County or Fredericksburg when not required to be present for duties in Richmond and represented Culpeper at the 1829 constitutional convention (p. 31), Williams may have heard his name at the convention or through the Brockenbroughs in Richmond.

Williams correctly placed *esquire* after Green's name but not after Benjamin Temple's because this was the way the two men were commonly referred to. Green was a practicing lawyer, while Temple had been trained as a lawyer but was not practicing.

Reel 56, Essex County Wills, no. 22, 1829–32, 417, Library of Virginia, Richmond; "Some Interesting Pages of History," *Essex County Historical Society* (May 1981): 1, http://essexmuseum.org/archive/bulletin-vol-18.pdf (accessed November 6, 2011); Lyon Gardiner Tyler, ed., *Encyclopedia of Virginia Biography* (New York: Lewis Historical Publishing Co., 1915), 2:63, 64; Robert E. Scott, "Robert Eden Scott, A Biographical Sketch," *Bulletin Fauquier Historical Society* (August 1921): 80.

61. Benjamin Temple (1801–72), "while educated for the law devoted his active life to the management of his wife's estate," after marrying Lucy Lilly Robinson (1807–84) in 1825, according to *Virginia: Rebirth of the Old Dominion.* He did act as executor for several estates, primarily belonging to his relatives. There is no available evidence to tie him as an administrator to any of the families who might be connected with Williams, though it seems more than coincidence that Williams would name a man who did indeed administer estates in the general area. Temple lived first on his father's plantation, Ampthill, in Chesterfield County south of Richmond. He appeared on the 1830 census in Hanover County, Virginia, north of Richmond, where his grandfather once owned land. In 1840 he appeared in Middlesex County, just south of Essex, probably living on his wife's estate there, Locust Grove.

Benjamin Temple was the son of Robert Temple (1774–1836) and the grandson of the more well known Benjamin Temple (1734–1802) of King William County. His grandfather had been a lieutenant colonel in the Revolutionary War and a state senator and representative. If he was connected to any of the families mentioned elsewhere in the narrative or the notes, it would probably be the Brockenbroughs. Benjamin Temple's wife corresponded with Frances Blake Brockenbrough, the second wife of Dr. Austin Brockenbrough of Tappahannock, Essex County, and she was distantly related to Judith Robinson White, wife of Judge William Brockenbrough.

The abolitionists concluded after their investigation that John Green and Benjamin Temple were not "known as having at any time resided in [Powhatan] county or elsewhere," not realizing their focus should have centered on Essex County.

Kenneth M. Stampp, ed., "Records of Ante-Bellum Southern Plantations from the Revolution through the Civil War," 101, *Lexisnexis.com*, www.lexisnexis.com/documents/academic/upa_cis/2476_antebellsouthplansermpt3.pdf (accessed September 22, 2011); Lothrop Withington, *Virginia Gleanings in England* (1980; repr., Baltimore: Genealogical Publishing Co., 1998), 271; Philip Alexander Bruce, *Virginia: Rebirth of the Old Dominion* (Chicago: Lewis Publishing Co., 1929), 4:240; "Robinson Family," *William and Mary College Quarterly Historical Magazine* (January 1910): 182–86; L. Parker Temple, "Robert Temple of 'Ampthill,'" *Temple-L Archives, Rootsweb*, http://archiver.rootsweb.ancestry.com/th/read/TEMPLE/1998-02/0886390280 (accessed September 22, 2011); Mss1 H2485 b 46, Harrison family papers, sec. 5, Benjamin Temple Account book, 1833–71, and Mss1 H2485 a 606–715, Harrison family papers 1662–1915, sec. 61, Virginia Historical Society, Richmond; Birney and Tappan, "Statement Authorized by the Executive Committee," 163.

62. The two daughters, Elizabeth and Jane, do not correspond with any known family Williams might have belonged to, though there were some similarities in the Robert M. T. Hunter family, in which the kind daughter Jane inherited some of the slaves upon the old master's death, and a Brockenbrough family with daughters named Elizabeth and Jane, though their father was still alive. Williams probably blended details from several families and situations.

63. The long description that follows is perhaps the most vivid word picture of anyone in the book besides the overseer Huckstep. Abolitionist James Birney received an encouraging testimonial to the truth of the narrative, based upon it: "It will suffice now, to state, that a gentleman and lady, from Virginia, who were recently in this city, declared, after reading the Narrative, that they believed it to be substantially true; that they knew the parties mentioned generally; that the lady knew the wife of George Larrimore Jr. (supposed to be Lorimer) and declared that such was the accuracy of the delineation of her character, that she would have recognized it without her name being mentioned."

Abolitionist Sarah Grimké, formerly of Charleston, South Carolina, also endorsed Williams's description of Mrs. Larrimore as believable, although she did not actually know her, saying that she knew a similar *type* of woman who had starved a slave to death in Charleston and "that the character of young Larrimore's wife is an exact description of this [other] female tyrant, whose countenance was ever dressed in smiles when in the presence of strangers, but whose heart was as the nether millstone toward her slaves." For more information on Larimer's wife, see p. 92.

JB [James Birney], "Narrative of James Williams," *Liberator*, September 28, 1838, http://

docsouth.unc.edu/fpn/williams/support2.html (accessed September 25, 2011); "Narrative and Testimony of Sarah M. Grimké," in Weld, *American Slavery as It Is,* 23.

64. Mrs. Larimer was born in New Orleans to a French mother, grew up in the French Quarter, and her stepfather, Joseph Janey, was also born in France, so she was surely bilingual.

65. The motif of a cultured New Orleans Frenchwoman who mistreated the slaves confined to a cell in her house would have sounded familiar to Whittier and anyone who read the news, after the story of Madame Lalaurie appeared in newspapers in 1834, four years earlier. In fact, at the end of a report on their ongoing investigation of Williams's story, Birney and Tappan reprinted a news report of the Lalaurie incident as one of several examples of slave owners' cruelty.

Madame Lalaurie, a wealthy New Orleans woman, chained and tortured her slaves in a prison room upstairs in her home. The discovery of her slaves during a fire caused citizens to riot in anger, destroying the house and forcing her to flee the city. The story showed up in newspapers nationwide, which decried Lalaurie as a "monster" who committed "barbarous and fiendish atrocities." Although Mrs. Larimer's treatment was within the bounds of normal for the time and place, Madame Lalaurie's gratuitous torture was well outside what even Deep South slave owners would tolerate. The allusion to Madame Lalaurie may have been a deliberate attempt by Williams to present Mrs. Larimer in the most negative light.

"The cell under her father's house" probably referred to an above-ground or mostly above-ground area below the main house, rather than a true cellar, as found in less low-lying areas. An 1823 gazetteer described the architecture of New Orleans: "The buildings have no cellars, except the vacancy formed between the ground and the lower floors; which are raised 5 or 6 feet from the earth."

Coincidentally, Mrs. Larimer's mother had married her father at St. Louis Cathedral in 1801, the same church where Madame Lalaurie had married her first husband the previous year, so the two families may actually have been acquainted.

"Horrible Cruelty to Slaves," *Religious Intelligencer* (May 1834): 795; Stanley Clisby Arthur, *Old New Orleans, a History of the Vieux Carre* (1936; repr., Westminster, Md.: Heritage Books, 2007), 148; Jedidiah Morse and Richard C. Morse, *A New Universal Gazetteer* (New Haven, Conn.: S. Converse, 1823), 523; Birney and Tappan, "Alabama Beacon versus James Williams."

66. George Larimer stated that he was never in New Orleans, but it is possible that Mrs. Janey visited family in New Orleans and took Williams with her as her carriage driver, perhaps even before Larimer married into the family, though there is no evidence that she did. Mrs. Janey also may have brought some of her New Orleans slaves into the household when she married Joseph Janey in Virginia, and they may have told stories of the city. Williams was in New Orleans himself under different circumstances, after he was recaptured in 1836 and wound up owned by trader Shadrach F. Slatter of New Orleans. George T. F. Larimer, qtd. in Birney and Tappan, "Alabama Beacon versus James Williams."

67. Mrs. Larimer's mother, Adelaide Garland, purchased a black woman named Francoise in New Orleans on August 10, 1808, though there is no evidence to indicate whether she was the same person as Frances. Because Francoise was an adult in 1808, she would have been at least near forty at the time Williams described her. If Frances belonged to Mrs. Larimer or her

daughter, she probably would not have been included in Joseph Janey's 1832 estate inventory. An enslaved person named Francis with an *i*, the male spelling, appeared in the list of women and children in Janey's inventory, in a group with Kitty, Harriet (probably Williams's wife), and Priscilla, but was most likely a boy. Francoise, *Afro-Louisiana History and Genealogy 1718–1820*, www.ibiblio.org/laslave/individ.php?sid=41895 (accessed November 9, 2011).

68. Williams's sexually charged description of his master's wife seems a mirror image of the Jezebel archetype of a black woman who is seductive to white men. In this case she was a white woman whom a black man found sexually alluring. Almost dark-complexioned enough to be tempting as a socially acceptable partner, she nonetheless personified the dangers and evils of the white race.

Williams's mixture of adjectives resembled those that Frederick Law Olmsted used, as noted in Deborah Gray White's chapter on the Jezebel archetype in *Aren't I a Woman?* The slave women that Olmsted watched were both sly and sensual, clumsy and gross, resulting in an overall scene that was "revolting" to Olmsted, despite its sexual overtones. Mrs. Larimer was both beautiful and fascinating as well as fiendish and abusive and therefore overall evil to Williams. The result was what psychologists would classify as a typical approach-avoidance conflict. Deborah Gray White, *Aren't I a Woman? Female Slaves in the Plantation South* (New York: Norton, 1999), 33; Frederick Law Olmsted, *A Journey in the Seaboard Slave States* (New York: Dix & Edwards, 1856), 388.

69. Planters from Virginia and the older slave states saw Alabama as a destination for investment and the creation of new wealth. A British writer explained:

> The influx of planters to Alabama is clearing the cane-brake with a rapidity unprecedented even in this country: the Indian reserves are all coming into cultivation as fast as they are vacated; and, in fact, Alabama at this day may be said to present a spectacle of successful energy and industry not to be surpassed . . . The grounds on which the vast and seemingly extravagant increase of the cotton crop of this State of Alabama may be justified, are to be found, not only in the great fertility of the virgin soil yearly brought under cultivation, but in the unprecedented increase of population. This very year, it is calculated, not less than twenty-five thousand slaves have been brought into this country from the older States on the Atlantic; this amount will, in all probability, be exceeded by the increase of next season. The great cause of emigration from the Atlantic States is to be looked for in the temptation offered the planter by a soil of vastly superior fertility.

The population had more than doubled between 1820 and 1830 and would almost double again before 1840. Tyrone Power, *Impressions of America during the Years 1833, 1834, and 1835* (Philadelphia: Carey, Lea & Blanchard, 1836), 2:123–24.

70. There is no evidence that Mrs. Larimer or any of her family owned land in Alabama. Williams probably made up the story because he needed to hide the real reason he was sent to Alabama: his involvement in the attempted murder of a couple living nearby, as described in the editor's introduction. As a consequence, Mrs. Janey sold him to Caleb Tate of Dallas County, Alabama. It is unknown whether Mrs. Janey sold him through a trader or directly to Tate or how

they knew Tate, if at all, nor is there any evidence whether Tate knew the reason that Williams was on the market.

See the editor's introduction and appendix B for more information on the trial. Birney and Tappan, "Alabama Beacon versus James Williams"; Bob Roy, "Re: [ROY] Augustus G. Roy of Essex Co. Va.," *Rootsweb* http://newsarch.rootsweb.com/th/read/ROY/2008-01/1201282489 (accessed September 28, 2011); Will of Beverly Roy of King & Queen County, Va., 1819, qtd. in Beverly Fleet, *Virginia Colonial Abstracts*, vols. 1–3 (Baltimore: Genealogical Publishing Co., 1988), 171; Bagby, *King and Queen County, Virginia*, 355; Warner, *Hoskins of Virginia and Related Families*, 205.

71. Williams made the trip to Alabama in 1834, not 1833, given that he was accused in August 1834 and presumably sold soon after. There is no evidence that Mrs. Janey sold anyone other than Williams and his immediate family; her plantation was in fact expanding its number of slaves between 1830 and 1840, according to the census. Caleb Tate already owned fifty enslaved people in 1830, which he increased only to sixty-four by 1840, indicating that he did not buy the bulk of Mrs. Janey's enslaved people.

72. Larimer stated that Mrs. Janey sold Williams's wife along with him, "rather than separate her from her husband." Their infant son, Ben, must also have been included in the sale because when they ran away, on August 23, 1835, Tate advertised that they took with them their son, Ben, "about 15 months old." That would mean Ben was about three months old when Mrs. Janey sold Williams and his wife to Alabama. Caleb Tate, "Fifty Dollars Reward," *Alabama Intelligencer and State Rights Expositor*, August 29, 1835, and other newspapers; George T. F. Larimer, qtd. in Birney and Tappan, "Alabama Beacon versus James Williams."

73. An example of this situation would be the coffle recalled by a former slave who was sent south with men separated from their families. The trader did indeed feel the need to handcuff them: "Before we had proceeded far, Mr. Denton [the slave trader] gave orders for us to stop, for the purpose of handcuffing some of the men, which, he said in a loud voice, 'had the devil in them.' The men belonging to this drove were all married men, and all leaving their wives and children behind; he, judging from their tears that they were unwilling to go, had them made secure." Henry Watson, *Narrative of Henry Watson, a Fugitive Slave* (Boston: Bela Marsh, 1848), 10.

74. This would be a large number, even if Williams and his family were combined with others in a slave trader's gang going south. The nearby Tayloe family transported down less than fifty slaves in 1833 to start their Alabama cotton venture. Both Larimer in Virginia and J. B. Rittenhouse in Alabama commented on the large number that Williams had given. Rittenhouse wrote in the *Alabama Beacon*, published in Greene County, "George brought out his slaves, 214 in number, to Alabama. When and where do our readers ask? Why to Green county, but the other day, in 1833! How admirable the audacity of the knaves. The oldest residers of our county never heard of such a person."

See p. 84 for more information on the number of slaves. J. B. Rittenhouse and George T. F. Larimer, qtd. in Birney and Tappan, "Alabama Beacon, versus James Williams."

75. An English visitor described a typical family emigrating with their slaves: "The caravan usually consists of from two to four tilt wagons, long and low-roofed; each laden, first with the needful provisions and such household gear as may be considered indispensable; next, over this

portion of the freight is stowed the family of the emigrant planter, his wife, and commonly a round squad of white-haired children, with their attendants: on the march these vehicles are preceded and surrounded by the field slaves, varying in numbers from half a dozen to fifty or sixty, according to the wealth of the proprietor; a couple of mounted travellers commonly complete the cavalcade, which moves over these roads at the rate of twelve or fifteen miles a day." Tyrone Power, *Impressions of America during the Years 1833, 1834, and 1835,* (Philadelphia: Carey, Lea & Blanchard, 1836), 2:72–73.

76. This is internally consistent with Williams's claim that he had two living children and a wife who was owned by John Gatewood, though his wife and at least one child actually accompanied him to Alabama.

77. The Methodist Episcopal Church was gaining enough membership in Virginia that Essex County was enumerated separately within the Richmond District for the first time in the 1835 report from the Virginia Conference. Nevertheless, that year there were still only 15 colored members listed in the county, compared with 720 whites. Other enslaved people may have attended without being formally listed as members by the conference. Contemporary accounts indicated that Methodists had influenced the slave population second only to Baptists. The African Methodist Episcopal Church, though in existence, had more of a presence in nonslaveholding states and was probably not the church Williams referred to.

Minutes of the Annual Conferences of the Methodist Episcopal Church, for the Years 1829–1839 (New York: T. Mason & G. Lane, 1840), 2:310; Charles Spencer Smith, *A History of the African Methodist Episcopal Church* (Philadelphia: Book Concern of the A. M. E. Church, 1922), 13.

78. Williams did not specify exactly how long the journey took, though he implied they arrived before winter (p. 38). Henry A. Tayloe, who transported a gang of slaves from the same area of Virginia to nearby Marengo County in 1833, using a different route but covering a similar distance, suggested a typical trip would take forty-five days. Henry A. Tayloe to Benjamin O. Tayloe, July 29, 1839, Alderman Library, University of Virginia, Charlottesville.

79. Although George Larimer probably did not actually accompany him on this trip and there is a good chance that Williams walked, the inventory of the Janey estate in 1832 did include a carriage, a gig, a riding mare, and carriage horses. A gig was a one-horse, two-wheeled vehicle, similar to a sulky, though it might carry more than one person, while *sulky* generally referred to a vehicle that carried only one. Larimer stated that Williams was Mrs. Janey's carriage driver, but it is possible he may have also actually accompanied Larimer or Janey in the manner he described, if they drove the gig locally. Caleb Tate's estate in Alabama, inventoried in 1841, included at that time only horse and ox wagons and a four-wheeled carriage.

Noah Webster, *An American Dictionary of the English Language* (New York: S. Converse, 1830), 375, 808; Roswell Park, *Pantology; or, A Systematic Survey of Human Knowledge* (Philadelphia: Hogan & Thompson, 1842), 480; "A Southern Sulky Ride in 1837, from North Carolina to Alabama," *Publications of the Southern History Association* (November 1902): 471; Inventory of the Estate of Joseph Janey, Reel 56, Essex County Wills, no. 22, 1829–32, 475–76, Library of Virginia, Richmond; Watson, *Narrative of Henry Watson*, 10; Orphan's Court February Term, 1843, Book E, 329, Dallas County Courthouse, Selma, Ala.

80. The party probably traveled southwest to where the Roanoke River formed the border

between Virginia and North Carolina, crossed South Carolina, then followed the Federal Road from Milledgeville, Georgia, to Montgomery, Alabama, a common route for immigrants and easily recognizable from the description. Even if Williams went as part of a trader's coffle, rather than in the fictional situation he presented, the accurate details indicate this may have been the route he actually traveled. The New York abolitionists noticed the same thing: "He was interrogated by gentlemen who have lived in Alabama, and who had travelled on the route he took to the free states; his travels were traced on the maps, and remarkable accuracy was found to exist between his statements, and the names of towns and rivers."

81. In Alabama the Federal Road ran westward through Creek Indian territory between the Chattahoochee River and Line Creek (also called Oakfuskee Creek) for over fifty miles, then entered the area where whites had developed large cotton plantations on the fertile soil. About eight miles into Creek territory was "a very pretty sandy district, [with] a tolerable good road on the sand ridges. Streams, whose banks were covered with laurels, live oaks, and other evergreens, were running pleasingly at the base of graceful pine hills," according to G. W. Featherstonhaugh, an Englishman heading the opposite direction on the same road at about the same time. E. S. Abdy, who also traveled the road about that time, described the area along the Federal Road west of Fort Mitchell as "a forest of pine growing out of a sandy soil, without any undergrowth whatever,—the trees of the noblest height, and just so far apart that horsemen might have galloped in any direction without difficulty."

Featherstonhaugh noted the travelers he met coming toward him:

> In the course of the day we met a great many families of planters emigrating to Alabama and Mississippi to take up cotton plantations, their slaves tramping through the waxy ground on foot, and the heavy waggons containing the black women and children slowly dragging on, and frequently breaking down. All that were able were obliged to walk, and being wet with fording the streams were shivering with cold. The negroes suffer very much in these expeditions conducted in the winter season, and upon this occasion must have been constantly wet, for I am sure we forded from forty to fifty streams this day, which, although insignificant in dry weather, were at this time very much swollen with rain. We passed at least 1000 negro slaves, all trudging on foot, and worn down with fatigue.

He saw Indian homes ranging from "merely circular spaces covered with bark" to "miserable-looking cabins without any fences near them," and a few similar homes or taverns of whites who catered to travelers.

G. W. Featherstonhaugh, *Excursion through the Slave States* (London: John Murray, 1844), 2:311, 317, 318; E. S. Abdy, *Journal of a Residence and Tour in the United States of North America, from April, 1833, to October, 1834* (London: John Murray, 1835), 2:83; Harriet Martineau, *Society in America* (New York: Saunders & Otley, 1837), 1:216.

82. In 1839, after the homes may have been improved more, the author of a guidebook described the plantations between Creek territory and Montgomery: "we pass a number of pleasant residences of the planters in a few miles, their houses of two stories, painted white, with piazzas

and balconies: the soil of a dark rich description, well cultivated in cotton and corn; the forest trees being the lofty live oak and other oaks, magnolia, and macrophylas, wherever the moisture of the ground admits of such a growth." *North American Tourist*, 464.

83. Coming to newly settled Alabama from "old Virginia," Williams may have been as disconcerted as Philip Henry Gosse, a visiting Englishman who commented on the homes in Dallas County in 1838: "Very many of the houses, even of wealthy and respectable planters, are built of rough and unhewn logs, and to an English taste are destitute of comfort to a surprising degree." Girdling trees to clear land was a common southern practice, also mentioned by Gosse. Gosse, *Letters from Alabama* (London: Morgan & Chase, 1859), 153, 87–88.

84. The Black Belt region of Alabama had a reputation for rich soil in general, and the specific plantation where Williams arrived would have been only a little less productive than the very best in the area. It consisted mostly of Orangeburg fine sandy loam, "particularly adapted to upland cotton, being equaled in efficiency only by the Black Prairie soils. Yields of two-fifths of a bale to one bale per acre are secured, and the general average for the type is in the vicinity of one-half bale per acre." For comparison, a writer in 1835 noted that the best land in a good season would produce the equivalent of over one to one and a half bales per acre, and "highlands, where the soil is fertile, will yield under the most favourable circumstances" about one bale an acre.

Jay A. Bonsteel, "The Orangeburg Fine Sandy Loam," *U.S. Department of Agriculture Bureau of Soils—Circular No. 46* (Washington, D.C.: Government Printing Office, 1911), 18; Dallas County Soil Survey Map, U.S. Department of Agriculture, 1905, alabamamaps.ua.edu/historicalmaps/counties/dallas/dallas.html (accessed April 3, 2011); A Yankee [J. H. Ingraham], *The South-West* (New York: Harper & Brothers, 1835), 2:291.

85. Caleb Tate, Williams's new owner, lived in the tiny community of plantation owners then called Valley Creek, later renamed Summerfield. Valley Creek, named for the nearby stream, should not be confused with the area a few miles to the east still called Valley Grande today. Tate had purchased a total of twelve hundred contiguous acres at various times from the government land office over the previous fifteen years, and his estate still owned eight hundred acres when his property was itemized after his death in 1841. His plantation spread mostly south and west from the village.

Williams described the coffle's route into Alabama on the Federal Road, which would have led them to Montgomery. There they would have left the Federal Road when it angled to the southwest and continued westward into Selma, then turned north seven or eight miles to Valley Creek, where Tate's land extended on both sides of the road just south of the village. After leaving the lower land near Selma and the Alabama River, the party would have been traveling slightly uphill, until they reached the "small knoll" where the enslaved people finally camped.

Tate also owned smaller, scattered acreage several miles to the northwest of Valley Creek and in the western part of the county, though he actually lived on the Valley Creek property, according to the following evidence: the Alabama legislature in 1829 approved Valley Creek Academy's location to be "within two miles of Caleb Tate's," and the same year the Academy purchased government land adjoining Tate's Valley Creek property. Later, when Williams escaped in 1835, Tate advertised he resided "near Valley Creek Academy, Dallas county, Ala." and "in Dallas county, eight miles from Selma." He is buried at Childers Chapel Cemetery next to the Valley Creek plantation. All these descriptions point toward his residence on that land.

Various clues also point toward Williams having worked on the Valley Creek plantation, including the fact that Fincher lived closest to it and the direction that runaway John took across neighbors' property (pp. 53–54).

Government Land Office at www.glorecords.blm.gov/ and at the Dallas County Courthouse, Selma, Ala.; Orphan's Court February Term, 1843, Petition for Dower, Book E, 327, Dallas County Courthouse, Selma, Ala.; *Acts of the General Assembly of the State of Alabama* (Tuscaloosa: McGuire, Henry & McGuire, 1829), 55.

86. "Flincher" was probably Armel Fincher, not merely an overseer but the owner of a small, 166-acre plantation southwest of Tate's. Fincher's first name also appeared in records as Armor, Armil, Armiel, Arnel, and other variations. Williams may have assumed Fincher was only the overseer because he probably lived in the rougher accommodations of the Alabama frontier.

When Williams met him, Fincher would have been a Dallas County resident for almost fifteen years. Then in his mid-fifties, he and his younger wife had a household of boys and one girl, all in their teens or below. He was raised as a Quaker and had come to Alabama with no slaves, but by 1830 he owned ten, about half of them children, and the number was steadily increasing.

Fincher's Quaker ancestors left Pennsylvania in 1758 after they were chastised for "taking up arms in order to defend themselves," in violation of their religious commitment to nonviolence. They moved first to North Carolina and then settled a few years later among Quakers in South Carolina, where Fincher was born and raised. He married a Kentuckian, Satsey George, in 1816 and moved away from his family and religious community, arriving in the newly opened land of Alabama shortly before 1820.

If there was no house yet on the new plantation where the enslaved Virginians arrived, it seems logical that the owner would stay with a neighbor. In reality Tate already lived on the plantation, so even if he had accompanied his newly purchased slaves from Virginia, he merely would have returned to his own home. Williams may have been telling the story as it might have happened, if Larimer had indeed been the absentee owner, although Larimer denied knowing any of Tate's neighbors in Alabama: "I never knew Huckstep, Crop, Flincher, Stiulivant (Sturtivant) nor any of the concern."

The travelers would have passed the road to Fincher's on the way from Selma. To reach Fincher's house, Williams and his master would have left the slaves' camp, returned about a mile back down the road to the first crossroad, turned right, and gone two and a half miles.

Fincher's location and the roads are based on the 1843 dependent resurveys of Townships 17 and 18 North, Range 10 East, St. Stephens Meridian, and Fincher's 1859 will, which states the land is where "my dwelling house and outhouses are situated." The will says the land was the southeast quarter of Section 5, probably a mistake because that quarter was never owned by Fincher according to the Dallas County deed books, but they do show him owning the southwest quarter, which he originally obtained from the government land office and which his widow deeded away in 1867 (Dallas County Deed Book W, 195).

1820 Census of the State of Alabama, Dallas County, image 5; 1830 U.S. Federal Census, Alabama, Dallas County, 88; 1840 U.S. Federal Census, Alabama, Dallas County, 55; Evelyn Davis Fincher, Ann Wilson Fincher, *Fincher in the USA, 1683–1900* (Greenville, S.C.: A. Press, 1981), 324, 325, 333; F. S. Murphy, "Early Friends in South Carolina," *Friends' Intelligencer* (1876): 535;

"Fincher Family," *Literary Era* 7, no. 7 (1900): 227; Trudy Myrland, "Fincher, Marker, Baker, Holt, Emmerson, East, West, VanBenthuysen, Benson, Lewis Families," http://wc.rootsweb.ancestry.com/cgi-bin/igm.cgi?op=REG&db=:1014601&id=I00585 (accessed February 20, 2011); Armel Fincher's will, Will Book B, 200–3, Dallas County Courthouse, Selma, Ala.; George T. F. Larimer, qtd. in Birney and Tappan, "Alabama Beacon versus James Williams."

87. Huckstep may have been James W. Huckstep, illiterate, closer to thirty years than forty when Williams was in Alabama. He appeared in the 1840 census of Dallas County as J. Huckstep, in the thirty–thirty-nine age bracket (89; see also image 91 at Ancestry.com).

Although Huckaby/Huckabee was a common name in the Black Belt region of Alabama in the 1830s and 1840s, James W. Huckstep was apparently the only Huckstep head of household. Most Hucksteps originally had come to Virginia, from which they migrated to Missouri, so the name was unusual in the Deep South. Jesse Huckstep, born around 1805 in Virginia, worked as an overseer on the Virginia–North Carolina line, showing up in Northampton County, North Carolina, in the 1850 census. He was the only adult male Huckstep in North Carolina for which there is available evidence in the early to mid-nineteenth century, but he appeared in the Virginia census at the same time James W. Huckstep lived in Alabama so is not the same person.

James W. Huckstep can be tied to a member of another family mentioned in the narrative, Adam Ledlow (p. 117), because James Huckstep witnessed a deed for Ledlow in 1841. Other evidence of Huckstep's residence in Dallas County includes an 1843 deed in which James W. Huckstep borrowed two hundred dollars from William L. Dyson and pledged forty acres as security. The land was the northwest quarter of the southeast quarter, Section 11, Township 16 North, Range 7 East. He made his mark rather than signing his name in both cases, corroborating the census taker's indication of illiteracy. An unclaimed letter at the Selma post office to "J. W. Huckster [*sic*]" in 1836 also may have been for him. The location of his name in the 1840 census and the location of the land in the deeds may indicate he was living in the western part of Dallas County then.

There is no available evidence to indicate who Caleb Tate's overseer was in 1834–35, so the most that one can conclude at this time is that a man named Huckstep, of the demographic class appropriate for an overseer, lived in Dallas County at approximately the same period. Tate also had several adult sons living at home who could have acted as overseers.

Owners generally contracted for a year with overseers, who changed plantations often when their contracts ended, the worst not being rehired, the best being enticed away by neighbors. "These rich men," said an Alabaman, "were always bidding for the overseer who would make the most cotton; and a great many of the overseers did not care for any thing but to be able to say they had made so many bales in a year."

Deed Book H, 319, Dallas County Courthouse, Selma, Ala.; Deed Book J, 577–78, Dallas County Courthouse, Selma, Ala.; *Selma Free Press*, April 2, 1836; Frederick Law Olmsted, *A Journey in the Back Country* (New York: Mason Brothers, 1860), 56–57.

88. Overseers from the Carolinas were common in the area, owing to the general southward and westward migration pattern. Two in Dallas County caused trouble in the 1835–36 period. John Pegues's overseer, Thomas Curtis, was taken back to North Carolina to stand trial for murdering Thomas Cash, "an officer of justice in Anson county, while serving a civil process on him"

ten or twelve years ago. Judge Reuben Saffold's overseer from South Carolina, Richard Simmons, absconded with funds. *Selma Free Press*, December 26, 1835, and April 9, 1836.

89. White streaks in otherwise dark hair, medically called "poliosis" both in the period and today, may be caused by injury or disease or may be congenital. Huckstep might have been telling the truth or could have made up the tale to explain a less interesting cause. It would seem like a believable story, however, to anyone who had seen patches of white hair on a horse from harness or saddle sores.

For a period description under the alternate name "canities," see P. Rayer, *Treatise on Diseases of the Skin*, trans. William B. Dickinson (London: John Churchill, 1833), 361–63. The author listed a number of conditions believed to be causes in the period, including wounds.

90. The fact that Williams correctly placed Selma in Dallas County is an indication that he deliberately, rather than ignorantly, misstated the county where he lived as Greene. Selma, the nearest large town to Tate's plantation, was only eight miles to the south, so it would be believable for the master to travel there and return the following day and easy to assume the plantation was within the same county. If the plantation had actually been in Greene, two counties to the northwest, Selma would have been well over thirty miles away.

91. Although this is consistent with the rest of the narrative, there is no evidence that Williams was sold to Alabama with any other enslaved people he knew, except his immediate family.

92. Fifteen dollars was a significant sum, a couple weeks' pay for a white farmhand. Enslaved people could earn money legitimately, if their masters allowed, by performing extra labor after completing their assigned tasks, such as raising vegetables or animals in garden plots, or illegitimately by stealing and reselling items from the plantation. As a body servant to his master (in the narrative) or a carriage driver (in real life), Williams probably had various opportunities in Virginia for earning extra money.

93. Because Williams was claiming to be raised as a companion to George Larrimore Jr., he appropriately continued to refer to him as "Master George." Huckstep's sneering reference to the name emphasized that Williams was not as close to his master as he thought.

94. "Hug the widow" was not an expression unique to this plantation. It showed up in references to whipping posts both north and south, for slaves and whites, and might include a specific name for the "widow." Israel Campbell, *Bond and Free, or Yearnings for Freedom* (Philadelphia, 1861), 30–31; James H. Matheny, "The Widow Robinson," *Law* (May 1890): 233; George Teamoh, *God Made Man, Man Made the Slave* (Macon, Ga.: Mercer University Press, 1990), 74.

95. Williams's good wishes for his master, despite the wrong that his master had done him, impressed the abolitionists who heard his story. "He was there before us—the actor in the scenes he so vividly described— . . . an expressive countenance shadowing forth 'sorrow rather than anger' . . . He gave way to no denunciatory language—no resentful expressions against his master who had deceived." Birney and Tappan, "Alabama Beacon versus James Williams."

96. The positions of white overseer and black driver were common, but *headman* might also be used as a synonym for *driver* or for a slave above the driver. In this case, as Williams used the terms, Huckstep was the overseer, Williams was the driver responsible for the immediate supervision of all the slaves, and the headman was apparently the driver's assistant (p. 38).

97. Huckstep was reported as having used the same word on p. 39.

98. The number of slaves is consistent with the 214 slaves that Williams said arrived at the plantation, because presumably not all worked under him in the fields, but it was far larger than the actual number of slaves who worked on Tate's plantation. According to the 1830 census, Tate owned 50 enslaved people, and by 1840 he owned 64.

99. A writer in 1838 summarized the position of driver: "All drivers are black men, and slaves. They have to do as the overseer says, or they will get whipped themselves. They live in houses apart from the rest. Their business is to blow the horn in the morning for us to get up, and then drive us all day to get as much out of us as they can. They get praise when we do a good day's work, and that makes them drive us harder and cut and lash us, so as to make us do as much another day."

An 1836 novel described the qualifications of a driver in the least flattering terms, which nonetheless apply in Williams's case: "[He] is generally selected for his cowardly and mean-spirited subserviency, and his readiness to tyrannize over and to betray his companions. The driver is entrusted with all the unlimited and absolute authority of the master himself. He receives a double allowance; he has no task;—his sole business is to look after his gang and see that they perform the work assigned them; and for this purpose he takes his station in the midst of them, whip in hand . . . the overseer usually inducts him into office by giving him a severe castigation with the very whip which he afterwards puts into his hand to be used upon his companions." "Recollections of Slavery, by a Runaway Slave," *Emancipator*, September 13, 1838; Richard Hildreth, pseud., *The Slave; or, Memoirs of Archy Moore* (Boston: Bela Marsh, 1848), 65.

100. Even an Alabama writer trying to paint a favorable picture of the South commented on the negative reputation of overseers, who, as a class, were "very much-abused and slandered . . . owing to the drunken habits, libertinism, coarse brutalities, and general bad conduct of many of their number." If overseers were socially isolated on the plantation between the upper-class world of the owners and the lowest class of enslaved people, drivers were also isolated by having neither the freedom of the overseer nor the shared misery of fellow slaves. Huckstep and Williams thus could fall into an uneasy relationship, bonded by their isolation. D. R. Hundley, *Social Relations in Our Southern States* (New York: Henry B. Price, 1860), 203.

101. No woman named Polly appeared in the list of Tate's slaves in the 1841 inventory of his property, though she may have died or been sold by then. She may have belonged to Huckstep, but in the 1840 census J. Huckstep had only a young enslaved woman age ten to twenty-three living in his household. Orphan's Court February Term, 1843, Book E, 329, Dallas County Courthouse, Selma, Ala.

102. The cracker of a whip was the final section, several inches long, made of strips of soft buckskin, plaited horsehair, and cotton or silk twine. This section would wear faster than the braided body of the whip, so Williams could use it up and replace it. Charles Ball, *Slavery in the United States: A Narrative of the Life and Adventures of Charles Ball* (New York: John S. Taylor, 1837), 124; Ingraham, *South-West*, 2:287; Isaac D. Williams, as told to Tege, *Sunshine and Shadow of Slave Life* (East Saginaw, Mich.: Evening News Printing & Binding House, 1885), 73.

103. "A thousand dollars more" would come close to doubling Williams's value, obviously an exaggeration. In 1836 Williams was sold to a slave trader in Maryland for $700. He was sold later in the year by a trader in Louisiana for $1,600, though a lawyer noted that "$1600 for a runaway negro [who was formerly] the inmate of Baltimore prison for crime or otherwise would seem to

be an exhorbitant estimate." Alabama Governor (1835–37: Clay), Extraditions and requisitions file, SG24782 Reel 11, Alabama Department of Archives and History; Slatter *vs.* Holton, Docket no. 2894, Eastern District, June 1841, Supreme Court of Louisiana 19 LA 39, 00981, Earl K. Long Library, University of New Orleans, http://libweb.uno.edu/jspui/handle/123456789/12613 (accessed October 23, 2011).

104. Although Huckstep was surely demanding that the women pull up their clothes for his gratification, enslaved women in the Deep South did wear their skirts tucked up for ease in working. Frederick Law Olmsted described the women on a South Carolina plantation: "They were dressed in coarse gray gowns . . . which, for greater convenience of working in the mud, were reefed up with a cord drawn tightly around the body, a little above the hips—the spare amount of skirt bagging out between this and the waist-proper." Olmsted, *Journey in the Seaboard Slave States*, 387.

105. It appears that Huckstep would be married in the next few years, if he was not already, assuming the real James Huckstep of Dallas County was the same man. Williams knew him in 1835, but by the 1840 census "J. Huckstep" was living with a white woman younger than himself, possibly Mrs. Nancy Huckstep, who remarried in 1845, after his death. In that census the household included a white female in the twenty–twenty-nine age bracket, presumably his wife, as well as three white girls and an enslaved woman age ten to twenty-three. The three children were listed as under age five, five to nine, and ten to fourteen.

"Mrs. Nancy Huckstep" appeared in the marriage records for Dallas County, marrying William Roberts on January 18, 1845. The last evidence of James Huckstep was when he borrowed money in 1843; there is no evidence of another Huckstep in the county, so she may have been his widow.

106. Goldsby was probably Thornton Boykin Goldsby, a wealthy planter originally from Oglethorpe County, Georgia. The family spelled the name *Goolsby* more often in Georgia and *Goldsby* more often after coming to Dallas County. His slaveholdings increased steadily, from 12 in 1820 Georgia, to 46 in 1830 Alabama, to 142 by 1840. He owned eighty acres adjoining Caleb Tate's land in Valley Creek, but most of his extensive property, well over a thousand acres, lay in the western part of the county. He may have lived on the western plantation originally but soon moved to Valley Creek and became part of the community there. He and Robert Sturdivant (pp. 40, 45) appraised Tate's property in 1841, after Tate died, and all three are buried in Childers Chapel Cemetery just south of Valley Creek.

If Williams accurately described where Huckstep's mistress lived, the house may have been on the road leading northeast of Valley Creek (now called Summerfield Road) or anywhere along the half-mile boundary between the two eighty-acre parcels owned by Goldsby and Tate. The location would have been on the extreme northern edge of Tate's plantation, a mile or two from the main portion. There is no record of any lots divided out at the time, so the home would have been on land actually owned by either Goldsby or Tate.

The land that adjoined Tate's was the east half of the southeast quarter of Section 23, Township 18 North, Range 10 East, which he purchased from the government land office on September 20, 1833. This tract adjoined the western half of the same quarter, purchased by Caleb Tate from the land office on August 4, 1828. Goldsby's other property lay mostly in Township 17 North, Range 8 East.

"[Goldsby] first lived in Alabama at 'Meed Hall,' two and one half miles from Marion, later at Summerfield," according to the 1921 *History of Alabama and Dictionary of Alabama Biography,* but that may be an error. The town of Marion was in Perry County, but Goldsby's absentee plantation was about two and a half miles from what would later be known as Marion *Junction* in Dallas County, so the description may refer to where he lived in Dallas County before moving to Valley Creek (renamed Summerfield). According to B. M. Miller Childers, Goldsby and his wife "came to Summerfield early (ca. 1825)."

1820 U.S. Federal Census, Georgia, Oglethorpe, Thornton B Golsby; 1830 U.S. Federal Census, Alabama, Dallas County, Thornton Goolsby; 1840 U.S. Federal Census, Alabama, Dallas County, T. B. Goldsby; Dallas County Tract Book 1, Dallas County Courthouse, Selma, Ala.; October 22, 1841, Orphans Court, Book E, 84, Estate of Caleb Tate, Dallas County Courthouse, Selma, Ala.; Thomas McAdory Owen, *History of Alabama and Dictionary of Alabama Biography* (Chicago: S. J. Clarke Publishing Co., 1921), 3:672; B. M. Miller Childers, *Early Families of Summerfield,* address given at the homecoming of the Summerfield Methodist Church (May 25, 1952), 3.

107. If Huckstep had a mistress, he would not have been unusual. Goldsby, mentioned in the same paragraph, had several children by at least one free woman of color, who lived a few miles to the west in Perry County in the 1840s. John Collins, an overseer for the Tayloe family in nearby Marengo County, never married but also had relationships and children with several free or enslaved women of color.

Evidence for Goldsby's mistress comes from their son: "In a signed deposition on January 29, 1912, George Goldsby stated that he was born in Perry County, Alabama on February 22, 1843. His father was Thornton Goldsby of Selma, Alabama [his postal address] and his mother was Hester King, a mulatto, who resided on her own place west of Summerfield Road between Selma and Marion, Alabama. George also stated that he had four brothers and two sisters by the same father and mother, Crawford, Abner, Joseph, Blevens, Mary, and Susie." Bennie J. McRae Jr., "Crawford 'Cherokee Bill' Goldsby," www.coax.net/people/lwf/CHEROKEE.HTM (accessed April 3, 2011); Ben Windham, "Going from the Funeral of a Blues Legend to Freetown," *Tuscaloosa News,* posted at Thebluescorner2, March 22, 2009, http://launch.dir.groups.yahoo.com/group/thebluescorner2/message/15625 (accessed April 3, 2011).

108. See pp. 38–39 for more discussion about the slaves' meals. Huckstep may have had some cause to say his slaves were better fed. On p. 46 Williams compared his plantation's food with that of one of the neighbors, saying, "Our hands did not suffer for food—they had a good supply of ham and cornmeal; while on Flincher's plantation the slaves had meat but once a year, at Christmas." Although Huckstep's management of the slaves was brutal, he may have consoled himself by comparing it to treatments such as the cistern torture he described on page 52, which even he said was "too bad."

109. By "our people" Huckstep probably meant the United States. The growing population of U.S. immigrants to Texas had become unsatisfied with the unstable Mexican government, so Texas's future status under Mexican rule was uncertain. Rumors flew through the newspapers from state to state. A Georgia paper reported: "The New York Enquirer says, 'it is supposed by many, that there is a negotiation pending between the United States and Mexico, for the purchase of Texas.'" Although slavery had been outlawed by the Mexican government, Texas

owners avoided the prohibition by indenturing African Americans for ninety-nine years or simply ignoring the law.

It was no secret that cotton growers had their eye on Texas, despite already having gained more territory west of the original colonies. A dozen years earlier a writer had observed, "The avarice of the cotton culture craves the Texas, as possessing *the finest cotton lands in the world.*" "Texas," *Macon Weekly Telegraph*, August 28, 1834; *A Visit to Texas, Being the Journal of a Traveller* (New York: Goodrich & Wiley, 1834), 10–11, 69, 210; "On the Importance of the Cultivation of Flax and Hemp in the United States," *Portfolio* (March 1821): 118.

110. Although the actual situation did not require several hundred slaves to build their own houses on a new plantation, other families who did arrive in Alabama needed to build. Sarah L. Fountain wrote that her family had been living in Dallas County, Alabama, three weeks, after arriving with their slaves from South Carolina. "We have pretty good out-buildings except negroe-houses and Pa is making preparations to build them, the negroes are still in their tents." Sarah L. Fountain to Hannah L. Coker, February 10, 1836, qtd. in Fletcher M. Green, ed., *The Lides Go South and West, The Record of a Planter's Migration in 1835* (Columbia: University of South Carolina Press, 1952), 11.

111. Williams's description of cotton culture is similar to other contemporary accounts. See, for example, Ingraham, *South-West*, 2:281–84.

112. The horn might have been made of tin or a cow's horn.

113. See p. 103 for more discussion on the headman's position.

114. *Rose and eat* would have been pronounced "rose and et." *Eat* was a grammatically acceptable alternative to *ate*. *A New and Enlarged Dictionary of the English Language Compiled from the Best Editions of the Most Eminent Authorities, from Johnson to Webster* (London: Isaac, Tuckey, & Co., 1836), 348.

Not a phrase unique to American plantations, *morning's bit* was also English slang for "refreshments taken before breakfast." Joseph Wright, *The English Dialect Dictionary* (London: Henry Frowde, 1903), 15:162.

115. The policy of being required either to eat one's "morning's bit" before work or to do without until noon was typical, as was the blowing of a horn to mark times for work or rest. For another Alabama example, see Benjamin Drew, *The Refugee: or the Narratives of Fugitive Slaves in Canada* (Boston: John P. Jewett & Co., 1856), 139.

116. Williams mentioned this task again on p. 43. Keeping tools inaccessible in the toolhouse when they were not in use was considered good husbandry on a plantation. "Rules in the Management of a Southern Estate," *DeBow's Review* (April 1857): 378; "Rules and Regulations for the Government of a Southern Plantation," *DeBow's Review* (June 1851): 626.

117. Frederick Law Olmsted described a driver behind a hoe gang working in a field: "They are constantly and steadily driven up to their work, and the stupid, plodding, machine-like manner in which they labor, is painful to witness . . . A very tall and powerful negro walked to and fro in the rear of the line, frequently cracking his whip, and calling out, in the surliest manner, to one and another, 'Shove your hoe, there! shove your hoe!' But I never saw him strike any one with the whip." Olmsted, *Journey in the Back Country*, 81–82.

118. Williams reported the slaves eating ham and bread for their morning's bit before work,

dinner in their cabins, and supper at the end of the day. The plowmen may have been allowed a longer time at noon because they were required to tend to their horses as well as themselves during the break. Despite the grueling hours and sadistic punishment, this corroborates Williams's claim that Tate's slaves did not suffer for want of food (p. 46) and Huckstep's opinion that other overseers starved their slaves by comparison (p. 38). Plantations that allowed only two meals a day, with no meat, were not uncommon. Weld, *American Slavery as It Is*, 28–35.

119. The women probably spun and wove fabric for clothing under the direction of the owner's wife, a typical arrangement when the master lived on the estate. Mary (Polly) Middleton Tate, Caleb's wife, had grown up in a slaveholding family in Elbert County, Georgia, and would have been experienced in the duties of a plantation owner's wife. Elbert County Courthouse, Elberton, Ga., Records of the Superior Court, Record Book 1819, 17–24, Digital Library on American Slavery, http://library.uncg.edu/slavery_petitions/details.aspx?pid=4971 (accessed May 7, 2011); Olmsted, *Journey in the Back Country*, 141.

120. If Williams's description of his wife on p. 32 was accurate, she may have been included among this group because she was sold to Tate with him.

121. Henry A. Tayloe of nearby Marengo County, Alabama, reported a similar problem with enslaved people newly brought from Virginia: "Our hands pick very badly not having been accustomed to it, they improve somewhat however and another year will make good pickers." Henry A. Tayloe to William H. Tayloe, October 22, 1834, Alderman Library, University of Virginia, Charlottesville.

122. The children on the estate included Williams's own son, Ben, probably under six months old when he first arrived in Alabama.

123. Although this is consistent with the narrative, there is no evidence that Williams had relations among the other enslaved people at Caleb Tate's, other than his wife and one or possibly two young children.

124. Huckstep was reported using the same word on p. 39.

125. Others mentioned the enjoyment of hunting runaways. The topic came up as a northerner visiting Alabama was riding with a southerner, past an area where runaways were known to hide:

> "'I suppose,' said [the southerner], "t would seem kind o' barbarous to you to see a pack of hounds after a human being?'
>
> "'Yes, it would.'
>
> "'Some fellows take just as much delight in it as in runnin' a fox. Always seemed to me a kind o' barbarous sport.' (A pause.) 'It's necessary, though.'"
>
> —Olmsted, *Journey in the Back Country*, 55.

126. The name Crop is the only one among Williams's white Alabama neighbors that is not immediately recognizable as a phonetic variation of a real name in the area. The difficulty of researching the name is compounded by the fact that the name Cross, when written in the common period manner with a long *s* (ſ) followed by a regular *s*, is often transcribed incorrectly today as *Crop*, the long *s* forming the upright stroke of the *p*, at a time when the stroke of the *p*

extended above the loop in normal handwriting, and the regular *s* forming the loop. This difference in style creates many false positives when searching transcribed records. Such a mistake was rarer in the period, when typesetters were familiar with the handwriting, but it is possible even then that the typesetter misread Whittier's handwritten *Cross* as *Crop*.

Whittier did write using a long *s* for words ending in *ss*, though the original handwritten manuscript of Williams's narrative is apparently not available to show how the name Crop appeared there. He used a regular *s* in other places where some writers might have used a long *s*, such as in the middle of words, a practice that could have added to the typesetter's confusion.

If the name was Cross, there were at least three men named Cross living in the vicinity—Featherston, John, and William—though none can be linked to any specifics in the book. Featherston Cross appeared on the 1830 census in Perry County, where he had purchased government land in Township 19 North, Range 9 East, northeast of Marion and almost twenty-five miles from Tate's plantation. The January 9, 1836, *Selma Free Press* contained an ad for an unclaimed letter to him at the Selma post office. Jonathan (or John) Cross also appeared in the 1830 Perry County census and as a landowner near Featherston. William Cross at the "head of Bogue Chitto" advertised that he took up a stray horse in the July 15, 1820, *Cahawba Press and Alabama Intelligencer.* His name also appeared in a list of unclaimed letters at the Cahawba post office in the January 16, 1836, *Selma Free Press.* Bogue Chitto was the name of a community and creek in western Dallas County, within a few miles of where Adam Ledlow lived and where Thornton Goldsby and Caleb Tate owned additional property and twenty to twenty-five miles from Tate's Valley Creek plantation, where Williams worked.

The words *pass, glass, Miss,* and *Mass.* appeared with a long *s* in examples of Whittier's handwriting: John Greenleaf Whittier to Jane Addams [1873], Jane Addams Papers Project, www.janeaddamsproject.org/Jane%20Addams%20Draft_files/Page737.htm (accessed July 18, 2011); John Greenleaf Whittier, Autograph card, dated 1881, Books & Manuscripts Sale 2300, Lot 177, Skinner Auctioneers and Appraisers, www.skinnerinc.com/asp/fullCataloguese.asp?salelot=2300+++++177+&refno=++610938 (accessed July 18, 2011); John Greenleaf Whittier, Lot 369, Sale 9, Goldberg Coins and Collectibles, http://images.goldbergauctions.com/php/lot_auc.php?site=1&sale=9&lot=369 (accessed July 18, 2011).

127. Note the internal consistency concerning the distance to where Crop lived, stated as ten miles both here and on p. 180.

128. These were probably Venus and her pups, described again on pp. 55–56. The price of $100 per dog was high but not impossible. Another slave memoir gave a range of values: "A pup was worth twenty-five or thirty dollars, while a full-grown dog would easily fetch sixty or seventy dollars. One of the two dogs I killed . . . my master would not sell for one-hundred dollars." Trained bloodhounds, imported in 1840 from Cuba including transportation, "cost precisely one hundred and fifty-one dollars seventy-two cents, each, when landed in Florida." An ad in the *Fayetteville Observer* reported a sale at auction of "a pack of ten hounds, trained for hunting runaways," owned by J. L. Bryan of Moore County, North Carolina, which sold for a total of $1,540. "The highest price paid for any one dog was $301; lowest price, $75; average for the ten, $154. The terms of sale were six months' credit, with approved security, and interest from date."

According to what Philip Henry Gosse learned in Dallas County in 1838: "Bloodhounds, of high breeding and of great ferocity, are taught to follow the human trail in this manner. A negro is sent into the woods, and told to climb up into a tree; when sufficient time has been allowed him, the hound is set on the scent, and is soon at the foot of the tree, which he will not leave till the party come up and release the poor slave. If any accident prevent him from mounting the tree in time, his life will probably pay the forfeit; for these ferocious dogs not unfrequently kill their victims."

Williams, *Sunshine and Shadow of Slave Life,* 72; Joshua R. Giddings, *The Exiles of Florida* (Columbus, Ohio: Follet, Foster & Co., 1858), 266; Olmsted, *Journey in the Seaboard Slave States,* 163; Gosse, *Letters from Alabama,* 252.

129. There is no evidence of a Little John on Tate's plantation, though the first available list of his slaves is from after 1841, when Little John would have been dead. No John appeared in the list of slaves on Joseph Janey's Virginia plantation in 1832 either. Orphan's Court February Term, 1843, Book E, 329, Dallas County Courthouse, Selma, Ala; Inventory of the Estate of Joseph Janey, Reel 56, Essex County Wills, no. 22, 1829–32, 475–76, Library of Virginia, Richmond.

130. "Sturtivant" was probably Robert Sturdivant, born in 1789 in Dinwiddie County, Virginia. He had come to Alabama in 1818 after living in Georgia and originally settled in neighboring Perry County, where he owned twenty-seven slaves in 1830. He continued to buy land in both Dallas and Perry Counties and built the first gristmill in Dallas County. By 1832 he had moved to the Valley Creek area of Dallas County. His son, who died in 1832, was buried at Childers Chapel Cemetery near there, the same cemetery where Caleb Tate, Thornton Goldsby, and Sturdivant himself would be buried.

In the summer of 1835 Sturdivant advertised that he wished to sell his "plantation on which he lately resided, situated in Perry county," and asked those interested to "apply at Valley Creek Academy," the school that Caleb Tate had helped found, so Sturdivant apparently lived near there at the time. He was a trustee of the academy that year, along with Thornton Goldsby. Sturdivant continued purchasing land and increasing his slaves, to 63 by 1840 and 120 by 1850. After the sudden death of his first wife, Ann Norwood, in 1836, he remarried and two years later built a new home in Valley Creek that still stands. Sturdivant Hall museum, located in Selma, Alabama, is named after a descendant who was a benefactor, but the building was not a Sturdivant family home.

When Caleb Tate died, Sturdivant and Goldsby were among those appointed to appraise Tate's personal property, including his slaves, in 1841. The committee appraised Williams's wife, Harriet, and her two children, Ben and Chastine, at a total of $975.

When Robert Sturdivant died in 1856, the writer of his obituary in the *Dallas Gazette* stated, "We knew Mr. Sturdivant, by report and personally, for the greater portion of our life, and when we came to Selma to reside, in 1845, he gave us the warmest and heartiest welcome. He was kind, liberal and hospitable—a sincere Christian—a charitable man—a good friend of ours, and it is with profound sorrow we record his death."

Another possibility for "Sturtivant" is Ira Sturdivant, who lived five miles north of Selma, near Valley Creek, and advertised in 1835 that he could "make and repair all kinds of [cotton] Gins." Robert Sturdivant's connections with both Goldsby and Tate, however, make him a more likely choice than Ira.

Robert Sturdivant, *MKHGenealogy*, http://mkhgenealogy.com/9060/ (accessed August 11, 2011); 1830 U.S. Federal Census, Perry County, Ala.; 1840 and 1850 U.S. Federal Censuses, Dallas County, Ala.; Orphans Court Book E, Dallas County, Ala., Courthouse, 84; John Sturdivant Sledge, "Summerfield, Alabama: Historic Preservation in a Rural Context" (Master's thesis, Middle Tennessee State University, May 1982), 41–42; "Valuable Property for Sale," *Selma Free Press*, August 15, 1836; "Valley Creek Academy," *Selma Free Press*, August 8, 1835; *Dallas Gazette*, January 9, 1857, qtd. in Thomas McAdory Owen, *Dictionary of Alabama Biography*, 4:1636; "Improved Cotton Gins," *Selma Free Press*, August 29, 1835.

131. See p. 101 for possible identification of "Flincher."

132. Sturtivant's comment echoed a conversation that Harriet Martineau reported. In 1835 she spoke with a woman on a plantation about fifty miles from where Williams lived, concerning an enslaved man she saw "who had run away three times, and been re-captured. The last time he was found in the woods, with both legs frost-bitten above the knees, so as to render amputation necessary." The woman told Martineau, "I went to him when he had had his legs cut off, and I said to him, it serves you right . . . You deserve it, that you do." Martineau, *Society in America*, 1:230–31.

133. An anonymous author, writing shortly after the narrative was published, reminded Whittier of his previous skepticism: "It was at the time when the American Anti-Slavery Convention met in Philadelphia, December, 1833, if I am not mistaken. Amos A. Phelps mentioned the mode of torturing slaves by whipping them, and then tearing them with the *claws of a cat*! John G. Whittier requested Mr. Phelps not to tell that story, for nobody would believe it. When our friend Whittier afterward saw the same fact stated as undeniable on Page 130 of the *Picture of Slavery*, he doubted whereunto that thing would grow. After having heard James Williams tell the same story, and after having recorded it in his own graphical painting, in the fifty-second page of his *Narrative of James Williams*, it is worthy of inquiry, whether the poet thinks the heart-rending tale is now fit to be told and meriting belief."

The anonymous author did not misrepresent Whittier, who wrote to Phelps on January 30, 1834, suggesting "one alteration" to his speech before it was to be printed: "I allude to the description of the 5th mode of whipping. The *feline* instrument may have been made use of—but, I submit the question, whether most people will credit it?—Why not simply describe the whipping on the ladder, and the washing *with salt water*?"

"Narrative of James Williams," *Liberator*, March 9, 1838, 39, reprinted in Charles T. Davis and Henry Louis Gates, *The Slave's Narratives* (New York: Oxford University Press, 1991), 9; Whittier to Amos Augustus Phelps, January 30, 1834, reprinted in John B. Pickard, ed., *The Letters of John Greenleaf Whittier*, vol. 1: *1828–1845* (Cambridge: Harvard University Press, 1975), 140.

134. Williams's wife and son were actually living with him on the plantation in Alabama, though his statement that they still resided on John Gatewood's plantation was consistent with what he said on pp. 32 and 34.

135. A list of Joseph Janey's enslaved men in 1832 included "Harry v" and "Harry Y," but there is no indication either was sold to Alabama along with Williams. Inventory of the Estate of Joseph Janey, Reel 56, Essex County Wills, no. 22, 1829–32, 475, Library of Virginia, Richmond.

136. "And it came to pass, when their hearts were merry, that they said, Call for Samson, that

he may make us sport. And they called for Samson out of the prison house; and he made them sport." Williams may have been referring to incidents in which masters ordered enslaved people to entertain them with music or dancing. Judges 16:25, King James Version of the Bible; Solomon Northup, *Twelve Years a Slave* (Auburn: Derby & Miller, 1853), 181–82.

137. Big Harry resembled a type of person whom an overseer described to a visitor in the South: "Some negroes are determined never to let a white man whip them, and will resist you, when you attempt it; of course you must kill them in that case." Tate described Williams himself as having a "bold and impudent look" in the ads after he ran away. Olmsted, *Journey in the Back Country*, 82.

138. This would be August 1835, about the time that Williams made his second escape attempt, though in the narrative he claimed to have remained on the plantation until the fall of 1837.

139. Williams was describing three stages of cotton production occurring at the same time. The "yellow unpicked cotton" in the gin house would have been cotton picked from the fields the previous fall but still "unpicked" by the gin, so the seeds still needed to be removed. At the same time that the gin was processing the end of the past year's crop, other workers were weeding the current year's growing plants for the final time before picking would begin around the last of August or first of September. In other fields they were burning brush to prepare for planting the next year.

The gin removed the seeds from the cotton using machinery usually powered by horses. Charles Ball, another enslaved man, wrote: "One end of the cylinder and hopper being slightly elevated, the seeds as they are stripped off the [bolls], are gradually, but certainly moved toward the lower end, where they drop down into a heap . . . A good gin will clean several thousand pounds of cotton, in the seed, in a day."

Two witnesses testified in an 1827 Alabama court case that "ordinary gins would gin about 2000 pounds of seed cotton per day, and one witness said that such gins would gin from 1500 to 2000 pounds of seed cotton per day." The seeds made up as much as two-thirds of the weight of the unginned cotton, so Harry may have been hauling over a thousand pounds of seed a night.

Cotton seed soon rotted and smelled, and in fact Alabama law required "every owner or possessor of any gin, erected in, or within one quarter of a mile of any city, town, or village" to "enclose, remove, or destroy all the cotton seed which falls from said gin, so as to prevent the putrefaction thereof." Most was simply discarded, though some planters spread it on their fields as fertilizer, and others experimented with making oil or other commercial uses.

The new year's picking would begin in early September. In 1835 the *Selma Free Press* announced, "The first bale of Cotton received at this place of the present years growth, was stored on Wednesday last [Sept. 2]." This harvest time was typical of the days before the boll weevil became a pest in the United States. In the early twentieth century, to avoid damage, cotton was "not only planted earlier, but earlier maturing varieties are used. This has . . . led to fixing upon 1 August as the beginning of the commercial crop year instead of 1 September as heretofore."

Ball, *Slavery in the United States*, 108–9; George N. Stewart, *Report of Cases Argued and Determined in the Supreme Court of Alabama Embracing the Decisions Made in the Years 1827 and 1828* (Tuscaloosa, Ala.: Wiley, McGuire & Henry, Printers, 1830), 1:49; "Experiments on the American Cotton-Gin," *Civil Engineer and Architect's Journal* (September 1840): 313–14; John G. Aikin, A

Digest of the Laws of the State of Alabama (Tuscaloosa, Ala.: D. Woodruff, 1836), 97; William Darby, *The Emigrant's Guide to the Western and Southwestern States* (New York: Kirk & Mercein, 1818), 180; G. L. Cocksill, "Agriculture of North Alabama," *American Agriculturist* (January 1844): 25; "New Crop," *Selma Free Press*, September 5, 1835; "Cotton Cultivation in the United States," *The Encyclopedia Americana* (New York: Encyclopedia Americana Corp., 1918), 67.

140. Williams had evidently gained enough of Huckstep's trust to be allowed to carry pistols like a white overseer. Alabama law barred enslaved people from keeping or carrying "any gun, powder, shot, club, or other weapon whatsoever," unless they were transporting them for their master or overseer, but there was a provision for being armed with permission: "Any justice of the peace may grant, in his proper county, permission in writing to any slave, on application of his master or overseer, to carry and use a gun and ammunition within the limits of his said master's or owner's plantation, for a term not exceeding one year, and revocable at any time within such term, at the discretion of said justice." Aikin, *Digest of the Laws of the State of Alabama*, 391–92.

141. While some slaves in the Deep South received coffins and a funeral service, others were buried as Williams described. Eleazar Powell Jr. told of a similar incident near Fayette, Mississippi: "The negro took up a hoe, and none dared to take hold of him. The overseer . . . took out his pistol and shot him dead. His master ordered him to be buried in a hole without a coffin . . . No punishment was inflicted on the overseer." Weld, *American Slavery as It Is*, 45, 100.

142. Williams mentioned again on p. 46 that the slaves under Huckstep were better fed than others. He also hinted at Huckstep's lessening cruelty on p. 52, when he described a particularly inhumane treatment and then reported that Huckstep said "he had himself formerly punished runaways in that way, but should not do it again." On p. 54 the neighbors Flincher and Goldsby were the ones who convinced Huckstep that he needed to whip Williams. A possible clue to Huckstep's change can be found on pp. 39–40: "One thing he said troubled him. He had once whipped a slave so severely that he died in consequence of it, and it was soon after ascertained that he was wholly innocent of the offence charged against him. That slave, he said, had haunted him ever since."

Enslaved people in the area were generally poorly treated, so Huckstep did not need to do much to be better than the neighbors. W. L. Fagan, who came to neighboring Perry County in 1832, recalled, "I had never seen negroes work so hard, or so poorly fed." *Marion Standard*, April 9, 1909, qtd. in W. Stuart Harris, *A History of Perry County, 1814–1877* ([Summerfield, Ala.]: W. Stuart Harris, 1991), 119.

143. See p. 101 for possible identification of "Flincher." See p. 110 for possible identification of "Sturtivant."

144. *Obscene*, *hyenas*, and *goules* (ghouls) sound less like Williams's words and more like Whittier's, inspired by the metaphor of fashionable period melodrama. Whittier included a hyena as well as the word *obscene* to describe carrion birds ("Dark and obscene,—the jaguars of the air!") in his poem "The Watcher," published the same year. *Obscene* in particular was a common adjective for such birds. Charles Ball's narrative of his time in slavery, published the previous year and ghostwritten in a more dramatic style, also used it: "obscene fowls of the air."

Fortunately for the art of the story, Whittier generally left his poetic license unused, except for a few flourishes. The abolitionists realized the power of the narrative lay not only in the facts but in how Williams told them: "*His* story he must have known, needed no exaggeration [*sic*]—but rather a reduction from its realities, to secure for it the fullest confidence of those who were not fully conversant with the horrors of southern slavery."

John G. Whittier, *Poems* (Chicago: W. B. Conkey, 1900), 146–51; Trent, *Cambridge History of American Literature,* 444; Ball, *Slavery in the United States,* 336; Birney and Tappan, "Alabama Beacon versus James Williams."

145. Defending his father against this accusation of infidelity, George Larimer wrote, "There was but one mulatto on my father's estate, and he was about his age . . . there was not a mulatto child born on my father's estate from 1804 till 1830; when the slaves were sent to Florida." George T. F. Larimer, qtd. in Birney and Tappan, "Alabama Beacon versus James Williams."

146. Williams related another incident involving enslaved women named Big Sarah and Hannah on p. 47. In this incident Sarah died as the result of Huckstep's whipping. In the next incident Big Sarah avoided injury. Both incidents apparently occurred in the summer of 1835. Williams either told the stories out of order, Whittier recorded them out of order, or either Williams or Whittier mixed up the details. This is one of the few places that Williams's narrative loses its internal logic, though no one seemed to notice the duplication of names or out-of-order stories at the time. Because Williams was actually only on Tate's plantation for about a year, he may have felt pressed to create or adapt enough incidents to fill the three and a half years he claimed to have been there, and this duplication was the result.

An enslaved woman named Sarah appeared in both Joseph Janey's 1832 estate inventory in Virginia and Caleb Tate's 1841 estate inventory in Alabama, but it is unlikely that they were the same woman. There is no reason to believe that any slaves besides Williams and his family were sold from the Janey estate to Alabama. A Hannah appears in neither list.

147. The "pallet of moss" was probably a cloth sack filled with Spanish moss to make a cheap mattress. Fanny, "The South," *Ladies' Repository* (February 1841): 57; *The Americans as They Are: Described in a Tour through the Valley of the Mississippi* (London: Hurst, Chance & Co., 1828), qtd. in *London Literary Gazette,* March 8, 1828, 148.

148. Huckstep was referring sarcastically to bloodletting as a medical treatment for sickness, performed with a lancet, leeches, or a cupping glass. On p. 51 Williams described how he treated the injured Huckstep with medical bleeding, and one of the other slaves, Little Simon, made a similar sarcastic remark afterward.

149. John Rankin was quoted on p. 138 describing a similar treatment.

150. Williams also mentioned on p. 45 that the slaves under Huckstep were better fed than neighboring ones. A Dallas County visitor observed, "I believe more slaves run away from the want of food, than even from the terror of the lash. The ordinary allowance, for each adult, is a peck of corn-meal, and three pounds and a half of meat per week; sometimes a little molasses is added, and, in the fruit season, the orchard affords them a considerable help. But, when this is over, the allowance is very short for the support of robust men toiling in daily field field-labor from morn to night." Gosse, *Letters from Alabama,* 253.

151. "A light mustee" could refer either to a person with some Native American ancestry, to someone who was one-eighth black and seven-eighths white, or less precisely, to anyone whose skin was lighter than a mulatto. For a detailed discussion of the nuances of *mustee,* see Jack D.

Forbes, *Africans and Native Americans: The Language of Race and the Evolution of Red-Black Peoples* (Champaign: University of Illinois Press, 1993), 221–27.

152. Although the following story about Big Sarah and Hannah seems unconnected to Huckstep's accusation that Williams did not want to whip "white" women, Williams stated earlier that the two women were the daughters of their owner and were thus half-white (p. 45). This story about how he avoided whipping one of them, coming immediately afterward, seems to bear out Huckstep's accusation.

153. See p. 114 for a discussion of Williams's other story about Big Sarah and Hannah, ending with Sarah's death.

154. When he arrived in New York, Williams's back was scarred either from this whipping or others. The New York abolitionists reported that Williams "suffered himself much in his person from the cruelty of an overseer or master, of which his back gave shocking proof." Birney and Tappan, "Alabama Beacon versus James Williams."

155. In actuality Williams had already escaped from the plantation in September 1835. There is no evidence that Larimer visited Alabama, nor would he have had a reason to, because Williams's new owner, Caleb Tate, lived there on his own plantation.

156. He was referring to her death, described on p. 46.

157. The story of Big Harry's death begins on p. 41.

158. Although this is internally consistent with the narrative, Williams's wife, Harriet, and at least one son were already living with him in Alabama.

159. This number matches exactly what Williams said on p. 34: "There were in all 214 slaves, men, women, and children" sent to Alabama. It also sounds reasonable compared to his claim on p. 37, in which he said he was "a driver set over more than one hundred and sixty of my kindred and friends," because presumably not all the slaves worked under him. Although the numbers were internally consistent, they were unrealistically high, both for the number of slaves owned by Larimer in Virginia and by Tate in Alabama.

160. Methodist and Baptist typically would have been the most common religions among enslaved people in early-nineteenth-century Virginia, with Baptists outnumbering Methodists. Caleb Tate, Williams's Alabama owner, was a Methodist, a member of the Childers Chapel congregation in Valley Creek, which was later absorbed into the Summerfield Methodist Church when the original building burned in 1842 and the Summerfield church was built in 1845. He is buried in the Childers Chapel cemetery.

Andrews, *Slavery and the Domestic Slave-Trade in the United States*, 187; Joseph B. Earnest, *The Religious Development of the Negro in Virginia* (Charlottesville, Va.: Michie Company, 1914), 66; Henry Howe, *Historical Collections of Virginia* (Charleston, S.C.: Babcock & Co., 1845), 131; Laura C. Hood, Sara M. Hood, Hugh M. Hood, and Jack B. Hood, *Alabama Historical Association Markers* (Bloomington, Ind.: AuthorHouse, 2006), 79.

161. No enslaved men with these names appeared in either Joseph Janey's or Caleb Tate's estate inventories.

162. James W. Huckstep of Dallas County was unable to sign his name (p. 102), though it is possible he was able to read some familiar Bible passages.

163. Williams described Uncle Solomon and his books more fully on pp. 50–51.

164. This odd punishment echoed Moses's reaction to the golden calf: "And he took the calf which they had made, and burnt it in the fire, and ground it to powder, and strawed it upon the water, and made the children of Israel drink of it." Exodus 32:20, King James Version of the Bible.

165. Williams had already escaped from Tate's plantation the previous year, so the incidents he attributed to 1836 either occurred earlier, elsewhere, or were ones he made up.

166. There was a woman or girl named Priscilla listed after Williams's wife, Harriet, on the 1832 inventory of Janey's slaves in Virginia, but there is no evidence she was sold to Alabama.

167. There is no evidence that an enslaved man named Simon existed, though there is no known inventory of Caleb Tate's slaves until after his death in 1841, which would be after Simon's death.

168. Williams told a story about the death of Simon, presumably the same person as Little Simon, starting on p. 53, consistent with Little Simon's reaction here.

The conflict between Christian charity and hope for an overseer's death was an obvious one, illustrated often in literature, including, much later, *Uncle Tom's Cabin*, in which Harriet Beecher Stowe contrasted defiant George Harris with the submissively Christian Uncle Tom. Another example contemporary to Williams's narrative was Harriet Martineau's short story *Demerara*, published in 1832. The enslaved people's conflicted responses to Huckstep's injury replayed this common theme, a natural one in a society that expected acceptance of both Christianity and slavery. Harriet Martineau, *Illustrations of Political Economy, No. IV, Demerara, a Tale* (Boston: Leonard C. Bowles, 1832), 124–28, 154–57.

169. Uncle Solomon used a common quote, "God willeth not the death of a sinner," inserting the word *himself* for emphasis. Although not in the Bible, it had spread with variations from the Catholic Church into the Anglican Book of Common Prayer and from there into prayers and sermons of many Protestant denominations. From the Book of Common Prayer: "O most mighty God, and merciful Father . . . who wouldest not the death of a sinner, but that he should rather turn from his sin, and be saved."

170. Philip Henry Gosse, visiting Dallas County in 1838, commented on the prevalence of the Pride of China tree in the area: "A very great ornament, indeed a *sine qua non* in a planter's yard." Gosse, *Letters from Alabama*, 158–59.

171. Williams's treatment was only slightly different from the best recommended practice at the time, but he made a common mistake. Bleeding was not recommended while the patient was still unconscious, but "when the stupor is gone bleed him." Sir Astley Cooper described the typical mistake that Williams made:

> You are to use bleeding as a means of preventing inflammation; but you are not to resort to it as a matter of course the moment you are called to a patient under concussion. A man falls from his horse, and the instant he is picked up from the ground, some surgeons think it necessary to take the lancet from their pocket [to bleed him with it]. This conduct is quite irrational; for suppose the pulse could scarcely be felt at the wrist of the patient, and the surgeon were in such a case asked why he proceeded to bleed; what would his answer be? The probability is, that he would have no answer at all ready; or he would, perhaps, say that he bled him because the accident had brought a great quantity of blood to the brain, as if the shaking of the head could have any effect in producing a

determination of blood to the brain. It is not with this view that we bleed in concussion, but in order to prevent inflammation.

Mackenzie's Five Thousand Receipts (Philadelphia: James Kay, Jun. & Brother, 1829), 221; Sir Astley Cooper, *The Principles and Practice of Surgery* (London: E. Cox, 1836), 155.

172. Bloodletting was usually performed by tying a strip of cloth around the arm above the elbow to raise the veins, inserting a lancet or small knife into one of the veins at the bend of the arm, and allowing the blood to flow from the incision. When the operator judged enough had been removed, he untied the cloth and, if necessary, applied pressure on the incision to stop the bleeding. As Little Simon implied, an overenthusiastic amateur could choose the right arm and injure nerves or muscles when inserting the knife, if he did not remove enough blood to cause death. Samuel Cooper, *A Dictionary of Practical Surgery* (London: Longman, Hurst, Rees, Orme & Brown, 1818), 156.

173. "Ludlow" was probably a member of Adam Ledlow's family, either Adam himself, who would have been about sixty, or one of his sons, Lewis, Adam S., or Garey. The sons would have been closer to Huckstep's age, between their late twenties and forty.

Adam Sr. was originally from Georgia, where he and his family owned several hundred acres of land and slaves in Columbia, Jones, and Baldwin Counties. He came with his family to Dallas County in the 1820s and owned twenty-three slaves in the 1830 census. Like Fincher (p. 101), he would have been the owner rather than the overseer, unless one of his sons worked as his overseer. His son Lewis eventually settled in Tuscaloosa County, Alabama. A lawsuit revealed his intemperance and that his wife therefore sometimes handled his affairs. Garey (also sometimes referred to as George) moved west to Arkansas, then Texas, but either one may have been living briefly with their father in Dallas County in the 1830s before settling separately.

At the time Williams was enslaved in Dallas County, the third son, Adam S., lived in the northwest corner of the county, where he and his father were purchasing land from the government. Adam S. advertised in 1835 that those wishing to buy land he was selling in Township 17 North, Range 7 East, should "apply on the premises, to Adam S. Ledlow." The land was located about two or three miles from land that was absentee-owned by Caleb Tate and about twenty miles from Tate's plantation, where Williams worked. Although twenty miles is significantly farther than the eight miles Williams stated, it fits with the overall relationship of the other residents mentioned in the narrative, all of whom apparently lived close by, except for "Ludlow" and "Crop," who lived at a distance.

Despite the separation, the Ledlow family was connected in several ways to the Tate plantation and Huckstep. In 1841 James W. Huckstep witnessed a deed for Adam Ledlow, who was purchasing land in Township 16 North, Range 7 East, the next township to the south and one where Huckstep himself owned land in 1843. Like Huckstep, Adam Ledlow made his mark rather than signing his name.

By the 1850 census both Adam Ledlow Sr. and Caleb Tate were dead, and Tate's property had been split among his children. Two of his sons, Robert and Netherland, had moved to the northwestern part of the county near Obedience Ledlow, Adam Sr.'s widow. Another son, Charles, gave a note of ninety-five dollars to hire one or more slaves belonging to Adam and Obedience Ledlow's estate in 1856.

J. J. Ormond, reporter, *Reports of Cases Argued and Determined in the Supreme Court of Alabama during the January Term, 1848* (Tuscaloosa, Ala.: M.D.J. Slade, 1848), 13:523; "Land for Sale" advertisement, *Selma Free Press,* September 12, 1835; Deed Book H, 319, Dallas County Courthouse, Selma, Ala.; Deed Book J, 577–78, Dallas County Courthouse, Selma, Ala.; 1850 Census, Pences, Dallas County, Ala.; "Obedience, wife of Adam Ledlow," Ledlow-L Archives, http://list-searches.rootsweb.com/th/read/LEDLOW/1999-03/0922423170 (accessed July 9, 2011); "Notes on Adam Ludlow/Ledlow," Ledlow-L Archives, http://archiver.rootsweb.ancestry.com/th/read/LEDLOW/1999-03/0922370431 (accessed July 9, 2011); Estate Case File, Adam Ledlow 1855, no. 89, 29, Dallas County Courthouse, Selma, Ala.

174. The story of Thornton's escape attempts sounds surprisingly like Williams's own real life. Although he did not mention it in the narrative, Williams attempted twice to escape with his wife and son but was caught both times. Like Thornton, he succeeded in leaving Alabama on the third attempt, assisted by a white man, though in Williams's case without his wife and child, and he was recaught but never returned to Alabama.

On his final escape upriver from New Orleans, Williams himself took on the alias Jim Thornton, before reverting to the name he had used on his previous attempt, James Williams. Coincidentally, neighbor Goldsby's first name was also Thornton. *Reports of Cases Argued and Determined in the Supreme Court of the State of Louisiana* (New Orleans: E. Johns, 1842), 19:40–41.

175. A plantation owner from nearby Tuscaloosa described the difficulty of getting water in the "calcareous region called the 'Cane-brake' and 'Prairie,' according as it is timbered or destitute of timber. It is a region of great fertility, but destitute of springs, and from the peculiar character of the soil, ordinary wells cannot be obtained. Beneath the soil is a compact soft limestone of great depth, and so impervious to water that cisterns hollowed out of it retain water like a glass bottle."

Cisterns to catch rainwater were not unique to that part of the country but were adopted there as a solution to the difficulty in digging wells, the same way they came into use wherever freshwater was in short supply. The underground rainwater storage area that Williams called the "tank" was usually referred to as the cistern itself. J. J. Ormond, "Artesian Wells in Alabama—Mode and Cost of Preparing," *Plough, the Loom and the Anvil* (June 1850): 780; "Artesian Wells in Selma and Cahaba, Ala.," *American Cotton Planter* (April 1855): 117.

176. Huckstep's condemnation of the cistern torture echoes what an Englishman visiting Dallas County related: "In confidential conversation I have heard things not generally known, even here, which are truly dreadful. Instruments of torture, devised with diabolical ingenuity, are said to be secretly used by planters of the highest standing, for the punishment of refractory negroes; devices which I dare not describe by letter. It is but right, however, to say that these practices were told me with expressions of reprobation." Gosse, *Letters from Alabama,* 251.

177. There is no evidence that enslaved men named Jarret or Simon existed, though there is no available inventory of Caleb Tate's slaves at this time.

178. Simon expressed his wish for Huckstep's death on p. 51.

179. Legally, Huckstep had committed murder under Alabama law because he was no longer acting in self-defense. He may have been using the phrase *Alabama law* the way he had earlier used *Alabama style* (p. 37), to indicate how he preferred things to be, rather than how they neces-

sarily were. He also may have mistakenly believed that any slave resistance could be considered an insurrection, when the malicious killing of enslaved people *was* legally allowed.

In general, overseers had no rights in Alabama that were significantly greater than other states, though that did not stop them from overstepping their bounds. An Englishman visiting the state in 1838 commented: "Armed parties frequently go in pursuit of runaways, who are shot down relentlessly if they oppose, or refuse to surrender. The patrols are allowed this power, not indeed by law, but by public opinion."

The actual law stated: "Any person who shall maliciously dismember or deprive a slave of life, shall suffer such punishment as would be inflicted in case the like offense had been committed on a free white person, and on the like proof, except in case of insurrection of such slave." Although the law appeared to make a distinction between "insurrection" and "assault and battery on any white person with an intent to kill," an enslaved person would have difficulty providing evidence against a lone overseer, no matter how many other slaves had seen what happened, because, the law read, "No slave shall be admitted a witness against any person," except another slave.

Yet such brutality was a symptom of a greater disregard for human life, white or black. Harriet Martineau wrote, "If human life presents its fairest aspects in the retired townships of New England,—some of its very worst, perhaps, are seen in the raw settlements of Alabama and Mississippi." On her way to Alabama along the same road Williams traveled, on the Georgia line in April 1835, the members of her party "were struck with amazement at the stories that were told, and the anecdotes that were dropped, in the stage, about recent attempts on human life in the neighbourhood; and at the number of incidents of the same kind which were the news of the day along the road." Gosse, *Letters from Alabama*, 252; Aikin, *Digest of the Laws of the State of Alabama*, 114, 391; Martineau, *Society in America*, 285–86; Weld, *American Slavery as It Is*, 192–94.

180. No evidence is available to pinpoint the 1834 event Huckstep described. The story may have been a garbled retelling of an overseer's death in Edgecombe County, North Carolina, which began similarly to Huckstep's incident, with two slaves arguing, and led to a controversial state supreme court case, *The State vs. Negro Will, Slave of James S. Battle*, argued in December 1834. The North Carolina overseer shot and wounded a slave who was attempting to run away, then caught up to him and wrestled him. While on the ground, the slave stabbed the overseer, who died from loss of blood the same day. The slave survived and was convicted of murder, which on appeal the state supreme court reduced to manslaughter. The successful defense argued that overseers had no more rights than "a constable or sheriff . . . and a constable may not kill in order to prevent the escape of one guilty of [a misdemeanor]."

The verdict highlighted the limits of overseers' power, an outcome that probably would have frustrated Huckstep and may have inspired him to tell the story as part of a rant about how Alabama laws were—or should have been—different. Another assault, closer to home but less similar to Huckstep's story, occurred in 1834 about fifteen miles beyond a possible location for the Cross (Crop) residence, when a white man argued with a slave on the road. The slave took the white man's knife and beat him.

Thomas P. Devereux and William H. Battle, *Reports of Cases at Law, Argued and Determined in the Supreme Court of North Carolina* (Raleigh: Turner & Hughes, 1837), 1:121, 133; *State of Alabama vs. Negro Slave Sam*, referenced in Franklin and Schweninger, *Runaway Slaves*, 7.

181. This would be July 1837, almost two years after Williams had already fled from Tate's plantation.

182. See p. 101 for possible identification of "Flincher" and p. 105 for Goldsby.

183. John was running in a southwesterly direction. Fincher lived about three miles southwest of the plantation where Williams worked, and Goldsby's plantation was about six miles west southwest of Fincher's property. Distances and directions are based on Caleb Tate's property southwest of Valley Creek (now Summerfield), which was centered around Sections 27 and 34, Township 18 North, Range 10 East; Armel Fincher's property in Section 5, Township 17 North, Range 10 East; and Thornton B. Goldsby's property centered around Sections 1, 2 and 11, Township 17 North, Range 8 East, as recorded in the Dallas County Courthouse deed books.

184. This was the first time that a man named Goldsby actually appeared in the narrative, though Goldsby's property was mentioned previously. Thornton Goldsby owned the nearby plantation (p. 105), but Williams identified this man as an overseer, rather than owner (p. 54). He may have mistaken Thornton Goldsby for the overseer rather than the owner, as he did with Fincher/Flincher, or the overseer may have been a relative. Goldsby's sons were not even teenagers and thus were too young for the job.

185. The pepper was red pepper, rather than black. Williams's explanation for the purpose was a common one. Whittier was already familiar with the procedure because he had mentioned it in a letter to Amos Phelps in 1834. See n. 133. It was also mentioned in two testimonies in the appendix of the narrative, Stone's on p. 140 and John Rankin's, p. 138.

Lewis Clarke, *Narrative of the Sufferings of Lewis Clarke, during a Captivity of More than Twenty-Five Years among the Algerines of Kentucky* (Boston: David H. Ela, 1845), 77; *An Abstract of the Evidence Delivered before a Select Committee of the House of Commons*, 63–64; Weld, *American Slavery as It Is*, 86; George Bourne, *Picture of Slavery in the United States of America* (Middletown, Conn.: Edwin Hunt, 1834), 130; Ball, *Slavery in the United States*, 117–18.

186. Williams began attempting to escape at least as early as August 1835, about a year after he first arrived in Alabama. He succeeded in getting as far as Baltimore by the spring of the following year. For a description of his actual escape and complex journey between Alabama and Pennsylvania, see the editor's introduction and appendixes A, C, D, and E.

187. Presumably, he meant an extra shirt, tied in a bundle. Because the long tails of a man's shirt in the 1830s often served in place of underwear, he would have been taking just the minimum clothes necessary, the period equivalent of a modern change of underwear.

188. From context he meant the sun would set in an hour.

189. The "great road" would refer to the Federal Road, the main artery for immigration to Alabama from the southeastern states. It ran west from the Georgia border to Montgomery, Alabama, then dipped southwest. Williams needed to travel southeast from the plantation to reach it in the Montgomery area. See p. 123 and also 126 for a similar choice of a route eastward toward a familiar road, by runaway slave Charles Bell.

190. Because he mentioned the sunshine on the next page, this must be ten o'clock in the morning.

191. By this time Williams would have traveled less than a day from the plantation, much of it in the dark, so perhaps ten miles. The closest point of the Federal Road was over forty miles away, but to reach it, he needed to cross the Alabama River at some point. He might have trav-

eled southeast through Beech Creek Swamp, east of Selma, and the fifteen-yard creek might refer to the river at a low point of summer drought or to any of the larger creeks such as Mulberry Creek, a tributary on the north side, about ten miles from the plantation. Although there is no evidence that Williams actually fled under the circumstances he described, the details are reasonable for the area.

192. Williams describes Little John's death on p. 40.

193. Venus was a common name for a female dog in the period. Examples appeared in James Battle Avirett, *The Old Plantation: How We Lived in Great House and Cabin before the War* (New York: F. Tennyson Neely Co., 1901), 41; and numerous lists of champion dogs, especially in England.

194. On p. 40 Williams mentioned that his owner bought "five dogs, a slut and her four puppies," so the younger dogs may have been the puppies of the older one.

195. The county would have been Dallas rather than Greene. Coming from Virginia, Williams's coffle would have left the Federal Road at Montgomery and continued straight west to reach Dallas County, which he consistently identified as Greene County in the narrative. If he was traveling slightly southeast when he left the plantation, he would have run into the Federal Road again in the Montgomery area. If he encountered the Federal Road at the closest point, he would have been over forty miles from home when he sent the dogs away.

196. "The Virginian deer (Cervus Virginianus) is very abundant in these woodland regions," a naturalist visiting Dallas County reported and described how residents used dogs, including bloodhounds, to hunt them. Gosse, *Letters from Alabama,* 266–67.

197. In 1835 the Creek territory began a little less than twenty miles beyond Montgomery, where the Federal Road crossed Line Creek, also called Oakfuskee Creek. J. B. Rittenhouse of the *Alabama Beacon,* trying to discredit the story, pointed out that Williams could not possibly have traveled on foot from Greene County to the Creek territory in the time he described, a little over two days. The abolitionists, "applying the scale to a map of Alabama," concluded it was only sixty-five or seventy miles and argued that "if he had travelled in two days a distance of 90 or even 100 miles, it was not too much to be accomplished by an active young man."

An Alabaman may have understood the location of the "great road" and calculated the distance from Greene County correctly at one hundred miles or more, while the abolitionists measured merely from Greene County to the *closest* point of the Creek territory, correctly reporting that distance as a more realistic sixty-five or seventy miles.

The truth, of course, was that Williams had started from northeastern *Dallas* County. If he avoided the towns of Selma and Montgomery and swam the Alabama River, he actually needed to cover about sixty miles. The abolitionists wrote: "James represents himself as beginning his escape from Greene county, Alabama, *late in the afternoon,* in July, [a more likely interpretation of p. 53 would be August 1] as entering the limits of the Creek Indians in the evening of the second day, thus allowing himself, altogether, about 51 or 52 hours [total] for this part of his route."

According to his narrative, Williams left one hour before sundown, walked till midnight, woke at daylight, walked all day, slept, and on the next day met the Creeks in the evening, for a very roughly estimated walking time of four to six hours the first day, twelve to fifteen hours the next day, and twelve hours the following, or about thirty total hours of walking time. If he had averaged about two miles per hour during his actual reported walking time, he could have accomplished the sixty miles. Birney and Tappan, "Alabama Beacon versus James Williams"; H. S. Tanner, "A New Map of Alabama with Its Roads & Distances," *Tanner's Universal Atlas* (Philadelphia: H. S. Tanner, 1833), available online at www.n2genealogy.com/atlasmaps/1836-AL.html (accessed October 1, 2011).

198. Despite the believability of the distance, the story of Williams's escape was still fictionalized. He failed to mention the other enslaved man who escaped with him and omitted mention that at some point a white man helped him, but more important for this part of the narrative, he changed the year, unaware of another detail that he needed to alter to match.

Williams actually ran away in the fall of 1835, but because he wanted to tell a story about a steady journey from Alabama to Pennsylvania, he moved the date of his fictional escape forward to the summer of 1837, carefully adjusting seasonal details such as the ripeness of fruits and nuts (p. 57).

Creek territory had changed little since he observed it on his trip down to Alabama the previous year, so he apparently assumed it also remained unchanged between 1835 and 1837. In fact, the Creek War and subsequent forced removal of the Native American residents had dramatically reduced the Creek population, so by the summer of 1837 the chance of him finding the same settlements he expected would have been slim. The fully populated Creek territory that Williams described was more characteristic of 1835 than 1837. John T. Ellisor, *The Second Creek War: Interethnic Conflict and Collusion on a Collapsing Frontier* (Lincoln: University of Nebraska Press, 2010).

199. A traveler on the same road, entering Creek territory from Montgomery about the same time and place as Williams, described the area before the war from a white Englishman's viewpoint, which was quite different: "Everything as we advanced was Indian, the road was crooked, bad, and made without any system, and by its side occasional ragged-looking pieces of ground badly cleared up, on which were built miserable-looking cabins without any fences near them . . . Nothing could exceed the dirt and stench in these places. In one of them I stopped half an hour, and saw breakfast cooked for some Indian women by a negress who was their slave; it consisted of some rotten-looking meat, and her manner of cooking it, in a dirty pan which seemed never to have been cleaned, was something quite shocking."

A meal of "venison, corn-bread, and stewed pumpkin" would be typical of poor, frontier fare, whether among whites or Native Americans. Corn and pumpkins had long been cultivated by the Creeks. James Stuart was served venison at Fort Bainbridge on the Federal Road in Creek Territory and reported "every thing very good, but no wheaten bread," so presumably he had cornbread.

Featherstonhaugh, *Excursion through the Slave States,* 2:311–13; Robbie Ethridge, *Creek Country: The Creek Indians and Their World* (Chapel Hill: University of North Carolina Press, 2003), 146; James Stuart, *Three Years in North America* (New York: J. & J. Harper, 1833), 2:103.

200. The Federal Road was a busy thoroughfare, so Williams would need to travel it at night if he was unaccompanied by a white man, to avoid arousing suspicion as a runaway, and find an isolated location off the road to sleep in the day. In fact, by this point he may have been accompanied by James B. White.

Wolves had been common in the area a few years earlier. A traveler remembered "the hideous yells of the wolf" while passing along the same road to Georgia in 1811. In 1819 the Alabama legislature passed "an act for the encouragement of killing and destroying of Wolves and Panthers" within the state, offering a bounty of five dollars for each adult wolf killed, but repealed it the following year, when so many wolves were killed that it was impractical to pay for them. By the time Williams passed through the Creek Territory in 1835, the wolf population was surely less, but it is not unreasonable to believe that some may have remained in isolated areas. No evidence is available to locate the specific area he identified as Wolf Valley.

The Journal of Peggy Dow, reprinted in *The Dealings of God, Man, and the Devil* (Middletown, Ohio: Glazener & Marshall, 1849), 1:223; *Acts of the General Assembly of the State of Alabama* (Huntsville: John Boardman, 1820), 101; Senate Journal, December 14, 1820, www.legislature.state.al.us/misc/history/acts_and_journals/SenateJournal_1820/Dec_14.html (accessed July 12, 2011); "Chronicle," *Niles' Register,* January 27, 1821, 367.

201. Bears still roamed Alabama, though it was unusual to see one in the day. Philip Henry Gosse reported that his Dallas County neighbor was annoyed in 1838 by a bear in his cornfield and wrote that they sometimes killed pigs, though "it is very seldom that a bear is met with in the woods, for his activity is chiefly nocturnal." He also noted, "The chestnut is one of the most common, and at the same time one of the most noble, of our forest trees." On August 15 he reported that on the closely related chinquapin, "the little nuts are now ripening, and about the size of a small marble." Gosse, *Letters from Alabama,* 221, 223, 116–17, 235.

202. A visitor remarked on the abundance of peach orchards in the area, writing on July 15: "Peaches are now ripe; and beneath our sunny skies they acquire a luscious flavour that no wall can impart in a colder climate [a reference to the practice of growing fruit trees against a wall to take advantage of the radiated heat]. So highly is this fruit esteemed, that every farm has large tracts planted with it . . . There are many varieties common, differing greatly in their qualities and in the season of their maturity." Given that Williams actually escaped in October, the peach season would have been almost over, except for a few very late varieties. Gosse, *Letters from Alabama,* 194; R. Peters, "Peaches for the South," *Southern Cultivator* (October 1859): 317–18.

203. Williams's usual attention to detail failed in his description of traveling in a direction toward the North Star. Following the Federal Road from Montgomery to the Georgia line near Columbus, he was heading almost directly east. The subsequent mention of the North Star on pp. 58–59 is more believable because Williams would have been traveling north-northeast by then.

It is possible that Whittier may have added the North Star as a dramatic touch here, without Williams's approval, because the North Star had already become connected with slaves' journey to freedom. The following year Whittier would begin soliciting contributions for a book titled *The North Star: The Poetry of Freedom,* a collection of abolitionist poetry.

Alternatively, the illogical use of the North Star may indicate that Williams was already accompanied by James B. White, and therefore they could travel openly in the daytime, asking directions and reading maps and signposts as necessary. Because they would wind up far north of where they started, Williams may not have realized they were taking a *J*-shaped path which did not turn more solidly northward until later.

Escaped slave Charles Ball, fleeing through Georgia, described his direction and reasoning more clearly, explaining that he was using the North Star as a guide but not following it because he was retracing his path eastward: "I had long since learned to distinguish the north star, from all the other small luminaries of the night; and the seven pointers were familiar to me. These heavenly bodies were all the guides I had to direct me on my way, and as soon as the night had set in, I commenced my march through the woods, bearing as nearly due east as I could. I took this course for the purpose of getting down the country, as far as the road leading from Augusta to Morgan county, with the intention of pursuing the route by which I had come out from South Carolina."

Whittier may also have misunderstood a description such as Ball's to mean that Williams was actually following the star, not merely using it as a compass marker, and made the mistake as he transcribed the words. *First Editions of American Authors: The Library of Frank Maier of New York* (New York: Anderson Auction Co., 1909), 270–71; Ball, *Slavery in the United States*, 310.

204. Columbus was the first major town across the Georgia line, near the Federal Road. "An excellent bridge" crossed the Chattahoochee River, according to an English traveler, and "on the opposite bank is the pretty town of Columbus, in Georgia."

Because Williams left with another enslaved man named William and enlisted the aid of a white man to help him at some point between Dallas County and Maryland, before being recaptured in Baltimore, we know that the overall description of his escape was fictional. Most of the details of the route seem accurate, however. Williams probably actually traveled this way when he originally was brought to Alabama and possibly during his escape as well because he arrived in Baltimore instead of being recaptured along a direct route northward through Tennessee, Kentucky, and into the free states of Indiana or Ohio. Featherstonhaugh, *Excursion through the Slave States*, 2:319–20.

205. Washington, the capital of Wilkes County, Georgia, was about two hundred miles northeast of Columbus, on the other side of the state. Although it seems an insignificant town today to mention as the next goal in a cross-state trek, it was an old settlement and an early crossroads for mail and stagecoach lines. To reach it, Williams probably followed the Federal Road east-northeast to Milledgeville, the state capital, then swung north-northeast toward Washington. Passing directly through Washington would have placed him on the road to Petersburg on the South Carolina border, but he apparently chose the wrong road, either then or soon after. Writers Program of Georgia, *The Story of Washington-Wilkes* (Athens: University of Georgia Press, 1941), 41; H. S. Tanner, "A New Map of Georgia with Its Roads & Distances," *Tanner's Universal Atlas* (Philadelphia: H. S. Tanner, 1833), available online at www.n2genealogy.com/atlasmaps/1836-GA.html (accessed October 1, 2011).

206. When Williams left Alabama, he was wearing a white hat, according to Caleb Tate's runaway ad. The abolitionists did not record what kind of hat or cap he was wearing when they first met him, but Williams explained that his friends in Richmond had given him a fur cap (p. 60), which he presumably was wearing when they saw him.

Although he was under no obligation to explain the change, because the abolitionists could not connect him with Tate's advertisement under another name over two years earlier, he may have felt compelled to explain it anyway with this story, even though he probably obtained the fur cap after his escape from New Orleans. He also may have felt the need to explain why he was wearing a fur cap, having come directly from Alabama in the summer.

207. A former resident of Georgia, writing for an abolitionist publication, reported, "Should the [slave] hunters who have no dogs, start a slave from his hiding place, and the slave not stop

at the hunter's call, he will shoot at him, as soon as he would at a deer." Of course the armed man could not have in this case, even if he had wanted to, because he was carrying a single-shot weapon, which he had already discharged at the squirrel and had no time to reload—a fact Williams recognized and used to his advantage. Rev. Horace Moulton, qtd. in Weld, *American Slavery as It Is*, 21.

208. Because Williams was attempting to retrace his original route from Virginia to Alabama in the opposite direction (p. 55), the North Star would not have been before him for most of his trip until now. He had probably turned north-northeastward within the last fifty miles and therefore may have considered the star to be in front of him at this time. Traveling south at this point, however, would have led him toward Florida, not Alabama.

209. Augusta was about fifty miles southeast of Washington, Georgia. Williams was describing a walk about five days south and two days north, a reasonable length of time to place him at Augusta. The "considerable river" might have been Brier Creek, thirty feet to over fifty feet wide, depending how far south he crossed it.

Broad Street, the main street of Augusta, was "180 feet wide, and two miles long, passing nearly through the centre of the city." "The shops, the banks, the book stores and the fashionable hotels are situated upon this street, and most of the business is done upon it." The bustling city was a major trading center, with warehouses holding cotton that was bound downriver for export to the North or foreign ports. Hotels operating about this time included the Eagle and Phoenix, the Globe, the United States, and the Planter's Hotel.

Note that Williams said he remembered Augusta from "one of his [master's] southern visits," presumably not the trip to Alabama that he was retracing. This was a careful detail because if the master had taken the slaves from Washington, Georgia, directly to Columbus, Georgia, they would not have passed through Augusta, which lay out of the way to the south. Williams's journey sounds believable but may have been fictionalized at any point to compensate for the details he wanted to omit.

Adiel Sherwood, *A Gazetteer of the State of Georgia* (Washington, D.C.: P. Force, 1837), 123; "Reminiscences of a Tour to the South West, Number Two," *Southern Literary Journal and Monthly Magazine* (June 1836): 301; George White, *Statistics of the State of Georgia* (Savannah: W. Thorne Williams, 1849), 501.

210. By the 1840s Augusta's city employees had grown to include twelve watchmen. White, *Statistics of the State of Georgia*, 501.

211. Williams might have crossed a bridge over the Savannah River at Augusta, but by turning away there, he was forced to swim the river at Petersburg, which was about fifty miles upriver, northwest of Augusta. A post road ran between the two towns. Williams probably did not realize it, but at Petersburg he was in Elbert County, where his owner Caleb Tate had lived before moving to Dallas County, about fifteen years earlier. "Notes on Georgia—Augusta," *DeBow's Review* (December 1858): 724; *The Public and General Statutes Passed by the Congress of the United States of America from 1789 to 1827 Inclusive* (Boston: Wells & Lilly, 1827), 758; 1820 U.S. Federal Census, Georgia, Elbert County, Terrill Township.

212. Halifax Court House is located on the western side of the Roanoke River, a little more than fifteen miles from the Virginia line. The Roanoke runs approximately north–south beside it. Apparently, Williams did not cross the river there, because he was heading north, and instead

traveled parallel to it on the road about seven miles to Weldon, where he was forced to swim the river when it curved east-west across his path.

The river was "about one thousand feet wide at the water level" near Weldon, where construction of a railroad bridge would begin in the fall of 1836, almost a year after Williams actually traveled north on his ill-fated escape from Alabama to Baltimore, so at that time it would have been a quiet area. During the month he claimed to have crossed, in October 1837, the bridge would be almost finished and the area probably busy with workmen, since "on the 27th of November last [1837], the bridge over the Roanoke was so far completed as to allow the passage of the cars, which commenced on that day running regularly to Weldon."

"Account of the Greensville and Roanoke Railway," *American Railroad Journal, and Advocate of Internal Improvements,* May 20, 1837, 308; "Sixth Annual Report of the President and Directors of the Portsmouth and Roanoke Railroad," *Farmers' Register,* September 1, 1838, 331; H. S. Tanner, "A New Map of Nth. Carolina with Its Canals, Roads & Distances," *Tanner's Universal Atlas* (Philadelphia: H. S. Tanner, 1833), available online at www.n2genealogy.com/atlasmaps/1836-NC.html (accessed October 1, 2011).

213. Richmond is about ninety miles north of the Roanoke River, so Williams would have averaged a little over ten miles a day for eight days.

214. The city of Manchester lay just south of Richmond, across the James River. Two toll bridges connected it to Richmond, the older Mayo bridge proposed in 1785 by Colonel John Mayo, leading to Fourteenth Street in Richmond, and the newer bridge proposed in 1814 by Edward W. Trent, leading to Ninth Street.

Charles Ball, who published his escape from slavery over a year before Williams, also approached Richmond from the south and arrived about the same time of night. Also fearful of the patrols, he hid in the woods but chose to approach at noon the next day rather than at dusk. "It was only a little after midnight, when the city presented itself to my sight; but here, as well as at Petersburg, I was afraid to attempt to go through the town, under cover of the darkness, because of the patrol. Turning, therefore, back into a forest, about two miles from the small town on the south-side of the river, I lay there until after twelve o'clock in the day, when loosening the package from my back, and taking it in my hand in the form of a bundle, I advanced into the village, as if I had only come from some plantation in the neighborhood."

Williams may have passed through Richmond on his way from Alabama, before being captured in Baltimore, but probably not under the circumstances he described because he had not been alone on his journey.

Benjamin F. Hall, comp., *Official Opinions of the Attorney Generals of the United States* (Washington, D.C.: Robert Farnham, 1852), 108; *The Traveller's Guide through the Middle and Northern States, and the Provinces of Canada* (Saratoga Springs, N.Y.: G. M. Davison, 1833), 34; H. S. Tanner, *The Central Traveller, or Tourist's Guide* (New York: T. R. Tanner, 1844), 423–24; Ball, *Slavery in the United States,* 456–57.

215. He had lost his hat in his adventure with the hunter (p. 58).

216. Williams gave no clue who his friend was, other than he was a married male ("my kind host and his wife" [p. 60]). One possibility is that he visited the enslaved brother he described earlier in the narrative, who hired himself and lived in Richmond, away from his owners, with his wife, a free woman (p. 29). Williams may have either adapted an actual visit to his

brother on his way north in the winter of 1835–36 or may have made up the incident entirely.

217. In other words, he was claiming to have been in Richmond from about October 15 to about November 15, 1837, leaving him about three weeks still to account for before he met the abolitionists in Pennsylvania.

218. This detail was consistent with his story, but his family was still on the plantation in Alabama.

219. The cap would have been to replace the hat he claimed to have lost in Georgia (p. 58).

220. This is one of the few apparent geographical mistakes. Traveling approximately north in a straight line from Richmond to Carlisle, Pennsylvania, Williams would have crossed the Potomac, not the Shenandoah River, somewhere between Leesburg, Virginia, and Fredericktown (Frederick), Maryland. Even if he had veered westward and crossed the Shenandoah, he would need to cross the Potomac soon after, but he seemed to imply the Shenandoah was the major river between him and Maryland. The Maryland border would be about 140 miles north of Richmond, a reasonable distance for a journey of about two weeks, given that Williams stayed in Richmond until the middle of November and reached the river at the end of the month.

The mistake in the river's name may be due to the fact that this is one of the few parts of the route Williams did not actually travel. His first trip north took him to Baltimore, where he was recaptured in 1836, so he might have followed the route he described from Alabama to Richmond, where he would have veered northeast toward Baltimore, rather than north straight to Pennsylvania. His second and final trip north led him to Carlisle from the west, so he had never actually traveled due north across this part of Maryland up to Carlisle. H. S. Tanner, "A New Map of Virginia with Its Canals, Roads & Distances," *Tanner's Universal Atlas* (Philadelphia: H. S. Tanner, 1833), available online at www.n2genealogy.com/atlasmaps/1836-VA.html (accessed October 1, 2011).

221. Maryland would be about forty to fifty miles wide at this point, depending on where Williams crossed the Potomac, so he was continuing to describe a pace of about ten miles a day. He probably would have entered Pennsylvania just north of Emmitsburg, Maryland. H. S. Tanner, "A New Map of Maryland and Delaware with Their Canals, Roads & Distances," *Tanner's Universal Atlas* (Philadelphia: H. S. Tanner, 1833), available online at www.maps.n2genealogy.com/1836-MD-DE.html (accessed October 1, 2011).

222. If Williams continued to travel north about ten miles a day on the road to Carlisle, the tavern where he stopped would have been in a village whose name would one day be well-known: Gettysburg. In actuality he probably did not take this particular route on either of his escapes north and would have arrived in Carlisle from the west, not from Gettysburg to the south. H. S. Tanner, "A New Map of Pennsylvania with Its Canals, Rail-Roads & Distances," *Tanner's Universal Atlas* (Philadelphia: H. S. Tanner, 1833), available online at www.n2genealogy.com/atlasmaps/1836-PA.html (accessed October 1, 2011).

223. Emmor Kimber wrote Lewis Tappan, stating "that James had arrived at Carlisle on the 9th December," which would be three days after he bought dinner at the tavern. Carlisle is about thirty miles north of Gettysburg, so Williams was still describing a steady pace of ten miles a day. He may actually have approached Carlisle from Chambersburg, about the same distance to the southwest, on his way from Cincinnati. Birney and Tappan, "Alabama Beacon versus James Williams."

224. An ostler, or hostler, was "the person who has the care of horses at an inn." Noah Webster, *An American Dictionary of the English Language* (New York: S. Converse, 1830), 419. Nowhere in the narrative until now did Williams hint that he was experienced as a coachman, but he had in fact been the "former carriage driver" of Mrs. Janey in Virginia, according to George Larimer.

225. Williams may have realized that once he arrived in Carlisle, he had been passed from person to person directly to New York and thus needed to make everything he said in New York consistent with what had actually happened since then. The abolitionists in New York learned from Emmor Kimber that in Carlisle Williams "had there received friendly assistance, and had been enabled to reach the house of Daniel Gibbons on the 15th, where he had to remain several days on account of his feet which had become sore; that on the 20th Joseph Gibbons conveyed him to Lindley Coates' where he staid two nights; that on the 22d he reached John Vicker's, where he again rested till the 25th when he came on to Kimberton," where Emmor Kimber lived.

The journey covered about a hundred miles, ending about thirty miles northwest of Philadelphia at Kimberton. Despite it being a major Underground Railroad route across eastern Pennsylvania, abolitionists described it openly, giving names of each of the conductors, in their publications such as the *Emancipator.* John G. Whittier even published a version of his poem "Stanzas for the Times," taunting the enemies of abolitionists to "storm Lindley Coates's poultry-yard."

Although the federal Fugitive Slave Act of 1793 was nominally still on the books, it had been undercut by state laws and lack of enforcement in areas with antislavery sentiment. The Fugitive Slave Law of 1850 increased enforcement, forcing Underground Railroad conductors to do their work in more secrecy. Daniel Gibbons, who had been keeping a book with information on each slave he assisted, burned the book after the new Fugitive Slave Law was passed.

The term *friends* had several overtones besides the simple meaning that they would be friendly. Quakers would refer to each other as "friends," and "friends of the slave" was a common phrase used by abolitionists to refer to their allies.

William Sloane Kennedy, *John G. Whittier, the Poet of Freedom* (New York: Funk & Wagnalls, 1892), 124–25; Michael C. Cohen, "Cultures of Poetry in Late Nineteenth-Century America" (Ph.D. diss., New York University, 2007), 113–18; R. C. Smedley, *History of the Underground Railroad in Chester and the Neighboring Counties of Pennsylvania* (Lancaster, Pa.: Office of the Journal, 1883), 57.

226. The man was obviously telling Williams how to recognize a Quaker. In fact, Quakers helped him across Pennsylvania, and he was currently dictating his words to one.

227. It is possible the man was James Mott of Philadelphia, mentioned by Whittier in the preface on p. 13. On that page the names listed before Mott were Pennsylvania Underground Railroad members, while the names after his were connected with the American Anti-Slavery Society in New York, implying the men may be listed approximately in the order that Williams interacted with them. The Kimbers in general and Abby Kimber, Emmor's daughter, in particular were friends of the Motts, and James Mott's daughter Elizabeth attended Emmor Kimber's school.

Unbeknownst to the abolitionists, this ruse, posing as the servant of his white companion, was not new to Williams; he and James B. White had used it to travel from Alabama to Baltimore a year earlier. Joan M. Jensen, *Loosening the Bonds: Mid-Atlantic Farm Women, 1750–1850* (New Haven: Yale University Press, 1988), 177.

228. "On his arrival [in New York City], James received the hospitality of John W. Hill, at whose house, with the exception of two or three nights passed at the houses of others friendly to him, he remained about three weeks (all the time he was in New York)," according to abolitionists Birney and Tappan. Hill was a woodturner who lived at 604 Water Street and took in boarders, including Whittier. For more information, see the editor's introduction.

Birney and Tappan, "Alabama Beacon versus James Williams"; A.S.W. Rosenbach, *A Catalogue of the Books and Manuscripts of Harry Elkins Widener* (Philadelphia, 1918), 2:273; *Longworth's American Almanac, New-York Register and City Directory* (New York: Thomas Longworth, 1837), 314; *The New York City Directory for 1842–1843* (New York: John Doggett, 1842), 158.

229. Although Whittier would not have known this, Williams was describing his own misfortune. When he escaped from Alabama with abolitionist James B. White, this was exactly what had happened when he reached Maryland, the final slave state before freedom in Pennsylvania. After Williams spent a long journey of swindling and (as he thought) betrayal with White, the abolitionists he met in Pennsylvania and New York during his second escape must have seemed different.

230. Williams may indeed have heard stories in Alabama about abolitionists. The newspapers around Tate's plantation regularly reported on their activities, even mentioning by name Arthur Tappan, the president and founder of the American Anti-Slavery Society and Lewis Tappan's brother.

Two weeks before Williams's final escape, the *Selma Free Press* published a statement by a local preacher who had been accused of leaving a copy of the *Emancipator* on the counter of a store in Greensborough, about forty-five miles away. Published by the American Anti-Slavery Society, it was the same newspaper whose editor, Theodore Dwight Weld, Williams would meet two and a half years later and which would be advertising his book. The preacher denied the accusation and published his "sentiments in relation to the Abolitionists of the North, of whom A. Tappan is a prominent actor." He thought of them like "any banditti who might league together against my country's dearest rights."

Tappan's name also appeared several times in the newspaper that summer, in jokes, accusations, and editorial items. More relevant to Williams's personal situation, however, the *Selma Free Press* printed in August 1835 a long excerpt from Virgil A. Stewart's newly written exposé of John Murrell's gang, telling how Murrell and his men would entice away enslaved people: "Well, Clitto, would you like to be free, and have plenty of money to buy land, and horses, and everything you want? . . . If I will steal you, and carry you off, and sell you four or five times, and give you half of the money, and then leave you in a free state, will you go?"

The excerpt omitted the actual fate of enslaved men who believed such false abolitionists, so Alabama slave owners may have made up their own ending, telling slaves that they would be sold at last where they could not escape and held in jail for their masters to reclaim them. In fact, the full book described a worse fate: Murrell's gang shot slaves once they were done reselling them. Williams may have been aware of such stories when he heard the same promise from James B. White a few weeks later but nonetheless took the risk of trusting him.

Local slave owners did not rely only on convincing slaves to distrust abolitionists to keep them home. The month before Williams's final escape, Caleb Tate had attended a meeting in Selma to adopt "measures to check the attempts of certain Abolitionists to excite an insurrectionary spirit amongst the colored population." Tate was named to the committee to monitor slave patrol duty—unsuccessfully, apparently, since Williams managed to escape from his plantation a few weeks later.

Rev. J. A. Butler, qtd. in *Selma Free Press,* October 3, 1835; P. K. Foley, "Whittier and the 'Narrative of James Williams,'" *Nation,* April 29, 1897, 321; "Murel the Land Pirate—The Mississippi Conspiracy," *Selma Free Press,* August 29, 1835; H. R. Howard, comp., *The History of Virgil A. Stewart and His Adventure* (New York: Harper & Brothers, 1836), 51–52, 65–66; "Public Meeting," *Selma Free Press,* September 5, 1835.

NOTE BY THE EDITOR

[JOHN GREENLEAF WHITTIER]

The reader may perhaps feel a curiosity to know something further of James Williams, and whether he has found a place of security from the hunters of human chattels at the South. He came to New York on the 1st of the 1st mo., 1838. He was taken to the house of a true friend of the oppressed, where he was received and entertained with much sympathy and kindness.[1] While in this city he was visited by a large number of gentlemen, who were deeply interested in his narrative.[2] An accurate and striking sketch of his face was made by an eminent artist,[3] the engraving of which, by PATRICK REASON, a colored young gentleman of this city, is prefixed to this volume.[4] He had, however, been in his asylum but a few days, when information was received that two white men were in pursuit of him, accompanied by a colored man, who knew James, and would be able at once to recognise him. The informant stated that they had been as far as Boston, and had just returned to this city.[5] After consultation, his friends came to the conclusion that he would not be safe in any part of the United States, and that, in the present unsettled state of the Canadas,[6] it would be best to send him to England. He accordingly sailed for Liverpool, with the best wishes and sympathies of all who had an opportunity of hearing his story.[7]

It is with deep humiliation and sorrow that we are thus compelled to proclaim to the world, that even the nominally free states of America afford no protection to the man of color, escaping from a land of slavery. Even the soil which is yet greener for the blood of the revolutionary sacrifice—the plains of Lexington and Saratoga—may not be trodden in safety by the scarred and toil-worn fugitive from Southern Slavery. Rome had her temples where the slave could flee and be secure, for the master dared not violate his sanctuary. But America has no place too sacred for the profaning presence of slavery. It pervades the whole land,—an active and almost omnipresent despotism. The weary stranger may be plucked away from the domestic fireside, or dragged from the very horns of the altars of religion. The whole constabulary and municipal force of the country, the entire civil and military authority, are pledged, by the constitution itself, to aid the master in recovering his runaway slaves. Judges, sheriffs, constables, and citizens of the free states, are bound by the constitutional law of the land to hunt men like wild beasts, for no other crime than that of preferring freedom to bondage. Better would it be to forego, at once, this mockery of freedom, and wear the acknowledged chains of slavery ourselves, than thus to stand ready at the beck of our masters to howl in the track of the fugitive, in concert with the trained bloodhounds of the South.[8]

NOTES TO THE 2013 EDITION

1. As mentioned on p. 129, this was the home of John W. Hill at 604 Water Street.

2. James G. Birney and Lewis Tappan wrote: "Whilst James was here, he was visited by many of the friends of the slave; among them we now remember the Rev. Charles Follen, Theodore D. Weld, John G. Whittier, Elizur Wright Jr., Rev. E. F. Hatfield, the editor of this paper, and the undersigned. To them he rehearsed his adventures—corresponding with remarkable consistency with the account that had been received in Emmor Kimber's letter, without any knowledge, on his part, so far as is known, that this had been transmitted to any of his hearers."

Rev. Charles Follen (1796–1840) and John Greenleaf Whittier were both boarding at the house where Williams stayed. German-born Follen was a refugee in the United States, due to his attempts at political agitation in Europe, and had just been forced from a professorship at Harvard University for his antislavery views and outspoken opinions. He received the title "reverend" in 1836 and had preached occasionally as a Unitarian minister. He was a member of the executive committee of the American Anti-Slavery Society.

Theodore Dwight Weld (1803–95) was editor of the *Emancipator* and other publications of the American Anti-Slavery Society. Elizur Wright Jr. (1804–85) edited several of the American Anti-Slavery Society's publications and was a secretary of the organization. Rev. Edwin Francis Hatfield (1807–83), a Presbyterian minister, was the least committed to the antislavery cause among the group, but he was acquainted with members of the society. They would ask him to compile a collection of antislavery hymns, *Freedom's Lyre*, published in 1840.

"The editor of this paper" (the *Emancipator*) would probably be Weld again. "The undersigned" would be James G. Birney, also a secretary of the society, and Lewis Tappan, brother of the society's president, Arthur Tappan. Most of the men had been involved in the founding of the society as well and had held various positions within it.

James G. Birney and Lewis Tappan, "Alabama Beacon versus James Williams," *Emancipator*, August 30, 1838, reprinted in *Friend of Man*, September 19, 1838;
John Greenleaf Whittier and Elizabeth Hussey Whittier, *The Writings of John Greenleaf Whittier* (Boston: Houghton Mifflin, 1888), 29–30.

3. Whittier recalled: "Prof. Follen of Harvard University and a friend of his, an Italian patriot

refugee were with me. I remember the latter drew the slave's portrait." Whittier to T. Y. Holbrown, June 31, 1886, qtd. in A.S.W. Rosenbach, *A Catalogue of the Books and Manuscripts of Harry Elkins Widener* (Philadelphia, 1918), 2:273.

4. Patrick Henry Reason, about twenty-one years old at the time, was an engraver at 35 Thompson Street, New York City, five blocks west of Broadway. He had gained recognition at a young age as a talented engraver and supporter of the abolitionist cause. P. H. Reason, 1840 United States Federal Census, New York Ward 8, New York, image 263; *Longworth's American Almanac, New-York Register and City Directory for 1839* (New York: Thomas Longworth, 1839), 544.

5. Birney and Tappan described the same circumstances in "Alabama Beacon versus James Williams": "Three or four days after he came to New York intelligence was received that two men in chase had overrun his track—had gone on as far as Boston and had returned to this city, having found out their error. It seemed to strike new dread into his soul; his slumbers became unquiet, and in his sleep he would cry out in alarm of the man-hunter."

6. Armed rebellion had broken out in both Upper and Lower Canada the previous year and still continued.

7. Birney and Tappan described the specifics:

> James sailed . . . a few days afterward, for England. He was befriended by John Cropper, jr., of the house of Cropper, Benson, & Co., of Liverpool, whose brother-in-law, Joseph Sturge, in a letter to Lewis Tappan, dated April 30, says, "his (J. Cropper's) acquaintance with him (James Williams) fully confirmed your favorable account."
>
> This is the last authentic intelligence that we have received of James, except that he was soon to sail from England for some one of the British colonies. If we could have satisfactory assurance that he would be safe as a freeman in New York from the claims of the slave-holder, the Executive committee ought to proceed to make inquiry for the place of his residence, that he might be brought back and subjected to the most rigid cross-examination that those who dispute his story could impose.

Williams probably left sometime after January 24, 1838, the date on Whittier's introduction to the completed narrative, and before early April, in time for Sturge to meet him and pen a letter, though Birney and Tappan implied he had sailed soon after dictating the narrative, around the end of January. The voyage, lasting about three weeks, would have been entirely by sail; the first transatlantic steam vessels did not begin running until later that year.

Several ships were sailing at the time, so Williams may have been on any of them. According to the *Southern Literary Messenger*, "In the months of December, 1837, and January and February, 1838, fifteen packets, and about as many transient vessels, sailed for Liverpool" from New York. The most unfortunate was the *Archimedes* under Captain Foque. Another New York–Liverpool ship, the *Duncan*, came upon it on February 14 "burnt to the water's edge and sinking," as reported in the *New-Yorker* newspaper. "The crew and passengers were taken on board the Duncan and landed at Liverpool."

The cost of Williams's passage was probably a hundred dollars or less. One writer mentioned steerage fare from New York to Liverpool as eighteen dollars on one ship and fourteen dollars on another in 1834. The *New-York State Register* for 1843 mentioned fixed prices of one hundred dollars for cabin passage.

Wealthy philanthropist and Quaker John Cropper (1797–1876), whose father, James, had earned the family fortune in the firm Cropper, Benson & Co., was a natural choice for the abolitionists. The *Jr.* was surely an error, given that his young son, John Jr., was only a boy, but they may have mistakenly made him a "Jr." to distinguish him from his older and equally well-known father.

The Croppers and Robert Benson dissolved their partnership January 31, 1838, while Benson was embroiled in a controversial resignation from the Quaker society, but the Croppers' charitable work continued. James Cropper had long been connected with the London and Liverpool Anti-Slavery Societies, and his son was equally dedicated to the antislavery cause, corresponding regularly with abolitionists in the United States.

Joseph Sturge (1793–1859), also a Quaker and husband of Eliza Cropper, John's sister, shared the Croppers' dedication to the antislavery cause. He had taken a special interest in the abolition of slavery in Jamaica and the similar apprenticeship system there. The previous year, on a trip to Jamaica, he had purchased the freedom of a young man and brought him to England. The young man dictated his story of abuse under the Jamaican apprenticeship system, and it was published in June 1837 as another narrative by a "James Williams," *Narrative of Events since the First of August 1834*.

The identical names were coincidental. The former Shadrach Wilkins had used his new name during his escape from Alabama, and it appeared as his alias on depositions in 1836, long before Sturge met the other James Williams in Jamaica on February 24, 1837. By the time Sturge met the American James Williams, the Jamaican James Williams had had a falling out with Sturge and had returned to Jamaica.

Unfortunately, there is no available evidence indicating to which British colony Williams planned to sail. He seemed to slip almost immediately from the abolitionists' minds; after all, they had already taken their trophy—his narrative. Sturge attended a breakfast in Birmingham, England, on August 1, 1838, celebrating the end of the apprenticeship system in Jamaica, which he had worked so hard to accomplish. His narrative by the Jamaican James Williams received much of the credit, but one of the speakers noted that "perhaps the meeting was not aware that there were two James Williams—one of whom was an American; and he held in his hand the narrative of the latter, as taken from his lips."

Sturge, who spoke next, "begged to say a word or two . . . in reference to the American, James Williams." Although he had helped send Williams to some colony only a few months earlier, he used the opportunity to say nothing about the man himself and instead crowed about the narrative, which had not yet been discredited. The reporter at the meeting recorded Sturge's words in the third person: "[James Williams] had undergone a most searching inquiry as to the truth of his narrative, and so satisfied were the Committee of the American Anti-Slavery Society of its faithfulness and accuracy in every particular, that they had printed and circulated no less than ninety thousand copies of the book. He gave so appalling an account of the horrors of the cotton plantations in the Southern States, that his mind was deeply impressed with the conviction that they should unite in refusing to use slave-grown cotton." In his retelling the reporter shifted from *he*, meaning James Williams, to *he*, meaning Joseph Sturge. Sturge continued to talk about himself, the situation in Jamaica, and the efforts of another man at the meeting, Dr. Archibald Leighton Palmer, without referring to Williams again.

Birney and Tappan, "Alabama Beacon versus James Williams"; "Direct Trade with the South," *Southern Literary Messenger* (January 1839): 7; Thomas Baines, *History of the Commerce and Town of Liverpool* (London: Longman, Brown, Green & Longman, 1852), 654; William O'Bryan, *A Narrative of Travels in the United States of America* (London: Published for the author, 1836), 298; O. L. Holley, ed., *The New-York State Register for 1843* (Albany: J. Disturnell, 1843), 213; "Summary," *New-Yorker*, April 21, 1838, 74; David Brion Davis, "James Cropper and the British Anti-Slavery Movement," *From Homicide to Slavery: Studies in American Culture* (New York: Oxford University Press, 1988), 258; "Summary of a Narrative of Events since the First of August, 1834, by James Williams, an Apprentice Labourer in Jamaica," *Documenting the American South*, http://docsouth.unc.edu/neh/williamsjames/summary.html (accessed October 3, 2011); Joseph Sturge and Thomas Harvey, *The West Indies in 1837* (London: Hamilton, Adams & Co., 1838), 195; *Report of the Birmingham Anti-Slavery Committee, Presented at the Annual Meeting, Held in the Town-Hall, Birmingham, August 1, 1838: and Also the Proceedings at Birmingham, on the 1st and 2nd of August, in Commemoration of the Abolition of Negro Apprenticeship in the British Colonies* (Birmingham, Eng.: Birmingham Anti-Slavery Society, 1838), 59.

8. Under the Fugitive Slave Act of 1793 the owner of a fugitive slave, or the owner's agent, was permitted to cross state lines and "seize or arrest such fugitive from labor." The fine for obstructing a slave catcher, rescuing a slave from him, or concealing an escaped slave was five hundred dollars. While legislators in some states attempted to pass laws to weaken the federal law, the situation would get worse before it got better, due in part to the passage of the Fugitive Slave Act of 1850. Finally, the Thirteenth Constitutional Amendment, ratified in 1865, abolished slavery in all states, superseding Article 4, section 2, of the Constitution—the basis of the Fugitive Slave Acts—and ending all fugitive slave acts connected with it.

APPENDIX

[ORIGINAL EDITION]

In our prefatory remarks we adduced only the testimony of inveterate and determined advocates of slavery. In corroboration of the facts stated by James Williams, we offer now the testimony of several gentlemen, who are natives of the South, or have been residents in that section of the country.

DISCUSSION IN LANE SEMINARY, 2D MO., 1834.[1]

A member from Alabama, speaking of the cruelties practiced upon the slaves, said—"At our house it is so common to hear their screams from a neighboring plantation, that we think nothing of it. The overseer of this plantation told me one day he laid a young woman over a log, and beat her so severely that she was soon after delivered of a dead child.[2] A bricklayer, a neighbor of ours, owned a very smart young negro man, who ran away, but was caught. When his master got him home, he stripped him naked, tied him up by his hands, in plain sight and hearing of the academy and the public green, so high that his feet could not touch the ground; then tied them together, and put a long board between his legs to keep him steady. After preparing him in this way, he took a paddle, bored it full of holes, and commenced beating him with it. He continued it leisurely all day. At night his flesh was literally pounded to a jelly. It was two weeks before he was able to walk. No one took any notice of it; no one thought any wrong was done."[3]

TESTIMONY OF JOHN RANKIN,[4]

A native of Tennessee, educated there, and for a number of years a preacher in slave states—now pastor of a church in Ripley, Ohio.

In some parts of Alabama, you may see slaves in the Cotton fields without so much as even a *single rag* upon them, shivering before the chilling blasts of mid-winter. Indeed, in every slave-holding State *many slaves suffer extremely,* both while they labor and while they sleep, *for want of clothing* to keep them warm. Often they are driven through frost and snow without either stocking or shoe, until the path they tread is dyed with the blood that issues from their frost-worn limbs! And when they return to their miserable huts at night, they find not there the means of comfortable rest; but *on the cold ground they must lie without covering, and shiver while they slumber.*

In connection with their extreme sufferings, occasioned by want of clothing, I shall notice those which arise from want of food. As the making of grain is the main object of their mancipation, masters will sacrifice as little as possible in giving them food. It happens that what will *barely keep them alive* is all that a cruel avarice will allow them. Hence, in some instances, their allowance has been reduced to a *single pint of corn each* during the day and night; and some have no better allowance than a small portion of cotton seed!! And in some places the best allowance is a peck of corn each during the week, while perhaps they are not permitted to taste meat so much as once in the course of seven years, except what little they may be able to steal! *Thousands of them are pressed with the gnawings of cruel hunger during their whole lives.*

Many poor slaves are stripped naked, stretched and tied across barrels or large bags, and *tortured with the lash during hours, and even whole days, until their flesh is mangled to the very bones.* Others are stripped and hung up by their arms, their feet are tied together, and the end of a heavy piece of timber is put between their legs in order to stretch their bodies, and so prepare them for the torturing lash—and in this situation they are often whipped until their bodies are covered *with blood and mangled flesh,* and in order to add the greatest keenness to their sufferings, their wounds are washed with *liquid salt!*[5] And some of the miserable creatures are permitted to hang in that position until they actually *expire;* some die under the lash, others linger about for a time, and at length die of their wounds, and many survive, and endure again similar torture. These bloody scenes are *constantly exhibiting in every slave-holding country—thousands of whips are every day stained with African blood!* Even the poor *females* are not permitted to escape these shocking cruelties. —*Rankin's Letters, pages 57, 58.*

TESTIMONY OF ASA A. STONE,[6]

A Theological Student, who resided near Natchez, Mississippi, when he published the following statement, dated 24th 5th mo., 1835.

No one here thinks that the slaves are seldom over-driven and under-fed. Every body knows it to be one of the most *common occurrences.* No planter of intelligence and candor denies that slaves are very generally badly treated in this country. *I wish to be understood now at the commencement, that, intending as I do that my statements shall be relied on, and knowing that, should you see fit to publish this communication, they will come to this country, where their correctness may be tested by comparison with real life, I make them with the utmost care and precaution.* But those which I do make are made without the least apprehension of their being controverted . . . In the first place, with respect to labor. The *time* of labor is first to be noticed. It is a general rule on all regular plantations that the slaves rise in season in the morning to *be in the field as soon as it is light enough for them to see to work,* and remain there until it is *so dark that they cannot see.* This is the case at all seasons of the year; so that during the summer they are in the field at least *fifteen hours.* This does not include the time spent in going and returning; that must be done while it is too dark to suffer them to work, even if the field, as is frequently the case, is a mile distant. It is literally true, what one of them remarked to me the other day, that "they never know what it is to sleep till daylight."

. . . Their suppers they have to prepare and eat after they return home, which, at this season of the year, takes them until nine o'clock: so that, without leaving a *moment* of time for any other purpose, they can have but seven hours' sleep before four in the morning, when they are called . . . On almost every plantation, the hands suffer more or less from hunger at some seasons of almost every year. On the majority of plantations, the feeding supplies the demands of nature tolerably well, except in the winter, and at some other occasional times. There is always a *good deal of suffering* on them from hunger in the course of the year. On many plantations, and particularly in Louisiana and among the French planters, the slaves are in a condition of *almost utter famishment* during a great portion of the year. Let a man pass through the plantations where they *fare the best,* and see fifty or sixty hands, men and women, sitting down on the furrows where their food-cart happens to overtake them, and making their meal of a bit of corn-bread and water, and he will think it is rather hard fare. This is not unfrequently the case on plantations where they are considered well fed . . .

I will now say a few words about treatment and condition in general. That floggings are very common and severe, appears from what has already been said. I must now say that flogging for all offences, including deficiencies in work, are *frightfully common,* and *most terribly severe.*

Rubbing with salt and red pepper is very common after a severe whipping.[7] The object, they say, is primarily to *make it smart;* but add, that it is the best thing that can be done to prevent mortification and make the *gashes* heal.

TESTIMONY OF THE PRESBYTERIAN SYNOD OF KENTUCKY,[8]

A large majority of whom are or have been slave-holders.

This system licenses and produces *great cruelty.*

Mangling, imprisonment, starvation, every species of torture, may be inflicted upon him (the slave,) and he has no redress.

There are now in our whole land two millions of human beings, exposed, defenceless, to every insult, and every injury short of maiming or death, which their fellow-men may choose to inflict. *They suffer* all that can be inflicted by wanton caprice, by grasping avarice, by brutal lust, by malignant spite, and by insane anger. Their happiness is the sport of every whim and the prey of every passion that may occasionally or habitually infest the master's bosom. If we could calculate the amount of wo[e] endured by the ill-treated slaves, it would overwhelm every compassionate heart—it would move even the obdurate to sympathy. There is also a vast sum of suffering inflicted upon the slave by humane masters, as a punishment for that idleness and misconduct which slavery naturally produces. * * *

Brutal stripes, and all the varied kinds of personal indignities, are not the only species of cruelty which slavery licenses. * * * Brothers and sisters, parents and children, husbands and wives, are torn asunder, and permitted to see each other no more. These acts are daily occurring in the midst of us. The shrieks and agony often witnessed on such occasions proclaim with a trumpet tongue the iniquity and cruelty of our system. * * * *There is not a neighborhood* where these hear-rending scenes are not displayed. *There is not a village or road* that does not behold the sad procession of manacled outcasts, whose chains and mournful countenances tell that they are exiled by force from all that their hearts hold dear. —*See Address of Synod to Churches, in* 1835, page 12.[9]

TESTIMONY OF THE MARYVILLE (TENNESSEE) INTELLIGENCER, OF THE 4TH OF 10TH MO., 1835.[10]

The Editor, in speaking of the sufferings of the slaves which are taken by the internal trade to the Southwest, says:

"Place yourself in imagination, for a moment, in their condition: with *heavy galling chains* riveted upon your person; *half-naked, half-starved;* your back *lacerated* with the 'knotted whip'; travelling to a region where your *condition through time will be second only to the wretched creatures in Hell.*

"This depiction is not visionary. Would to God that it was."

TESTIMONY OF COLONEL WILLIAM KEYES,[11]

A native of Rockbridge County, Virginia, where he resided about thirty years—now well known and greatly respected in southern Ohio.

In that part of Virginia where I resided (the valley,) so far as relates to food, clothing, and labor, slaves may be said to be well used, when compared with the *barbarity* of their treatment farther south, or wherever they are held in large numbers; yet, even where I lived, though few slaves comparatively were held, *many* acts of *atrocious cruelty* were perpetrated. I have seen *aged, gray-headed slaves stripped, tied up, and whipped with a cowhide,* forty or fifty lashes, for no fault but absence for a few minutes too long when wanted. Such things I call cruelty, but they pass among slave-holders *for nothing.*

Dated Hillsborough, Ohio, 1st of 1st mo., 1835.

NOTES TO THE 2013 EDITION

1. Lane Theological Seminary in Cincinnati, Ohio, hosted a series of debates on slavery in February 1834, a date that Whittier wrote in the Quaker style, "2D Mo.," for "2nd month." Theodore Dwight Weld (p. 132) was a student there at the time and promoted the debates. Although James G. Birney was present, the "member from Alabama" quoted here was probably

James M. Allan, formerly of Huntsville, Alabama, where Birney also used to live. See nn. 2–3 for more information. Asa A. Stone (p. 138) also attended. Arthur Tappan had contributed to the school's funding and spurred on the debates. Henry B. Stanton, *Random Recollections* (New York: Macgowan & Slipper, 1886), 30; Hermann Richard Muelder, *Fighters for Freedom* (New York: Columbia University Press, 1959), 91; Ann Hagedorn, *Beyond the River: The Untold Story of the Heroes of the Underground Railroad* (New York: Simon & Schuster, 2004), 66–68.

2. Rev. William T. Allan, James's brother, described the incident in more detail:

> There was one plantation just opposite my father's house in the suburbs of Huntsville, belonging to Judge Smith, formerly a Senator in Congress from South Carolina, now of Huntsville. The name of his overseer was Tune. I have often seen him flogging the slaves in the field, and have often heard their cries . . . Tune was so severe in his treatment, that his employer dismissed him after two or three years, lest, it was said, he should kill off all his slaves. But he was immediately employed by another planter in the neighborhood. The following fact was stated to me by my brother, James M. Allan . . . Tune became so displeased with one of the women who was pregnant, he made her lay down over a log, with her face towards the ground, and beat her so unmercifully that she was soon after delivered of a *dead child.*

Williams related a similar event that resulted in the death of an unborn child on p. 51. Rev. William T. Allan, qtd. in Theodore Dwight Weld, *American Slavery as It Is: Testimony of a Thousand Witnesses* (New York: American Anti-Slavery Society, 1839), 45–46.

3. William Allan reported this story in more detail as well:

> My brother also stated to me the following, which occurred near my father's house, and within sight and hearing of the academy and public garden. Charles, a fine active negro, who belonged to a bricklayer in Huntsville, exchanged the burning sun of the brickyard to enjoy for a season the pleasant shade of an adjacent mountain. When his master got him back, he tied him by his hands so that his feet could just touch the ground—stripped off his clothes, took a paddle, bored full of holes, and paddled him leisurely all day long. It was two weeks before they could tell whether he would live or die. Neither of these cases attracted any particular notice in Huntsville.
> —Rev. William T. Allan, qtd. in Weld, *American Slavery as It Is*, 46.

4. John Rankin wrote a series of letters to his slave-owning brother, Thomas, who lived in Middlebrook, Virginia. Published first in the Ripley, Ohio, newspaper the *Castigator*, they appeared in book form, printed by various publishers, starting in 1825. As noted at the end, this excerpt is from these letters. The first two paragraphs are from pp. 36–37 of the book version, with light editing, while the rest is from pp. 57–58. Jeff Biggers, *The United States of Appalachia: How Southern Mountaineers Brought Independence, Culture and Enlightenment to America* (Berkeley, Calif.: Counterpoint Press, 2006), 98–99; John Rankin, *Letters on American Slavery* (Boston: Garrison & Knapp, 1833).

5. See p. 54 for Huckstep's use of the salt wash.

6. Asa A. Stone (1810–35) was a student at Lane Theological Seminary in Cincinnati along with Theodore Dwight Weld and the Allan brothers (see p. 137). This excerpt is edited down from a "Letter to the Editor" that Stone wrote to Dr. Joshua Leavitt, editor of the antislavery *New York Evangelist.* It was dated "Natchez, May 24, 1835," three months before he died, on August 23. After leaving Lane Seminary, he returned to Natchez, Mississippi, to teach for eight months, then died suddenly of a fever after returning to Cincinnati in early August.

Dr. Leavitt, who published the letters, was a member of the American Anti-Slavery Society's executive committee and would take over editorship of the *Emancipator* from Theodore Weld in 1840. Paul Finkelman, *Slave Rebels, Abolitionists, and Southern Courts: The Pamphlet Literature* (1988; repr., Clark, N.J.: Lawbook Exchange, 2007), 265, 282–84.

7. See p. 54 for mention of this procedure by Williams.

8. This was an excerpt from a report, published in 1836 as a thirty-six-page pamphlet entitled *Address of the Presbyterians of Kentucky Proposing a Plan for the Instruction and Emancipation of Their Slave.* The report was created by a committee of ten members and elders, appointed for that purpose in 1835. Committee members were Chairman John Brown, Esq., Thomas P. Smith, Esq., Charles Cunningham, Esq., James K. Burch, Nathan J. Hall, John Green, Esq., J. R. Alexander, Esq., Rev. Wm. L. Breckenbridge, Robert Stewart, and John C. Young, who served as secretary.

Although the committee presented the strongly antislavery report to the synod, it spurred no action, according to Horace Greeley:

> The Synod met at Danville, in the Autumn of 1835, and appointed a Committee of ten—five ministers and five elders—who were instructed to "digest and prepare a plan for the moral and religious instruction of our slaves, and for their future emancipation," etc. The Committee did its duty faithfully, and the report in due time appeared . . . The result was duly submitted to the Synod at its next meeting, at Bardstown, in 1836; but no action was taken thereon, beyond noting on the Synod's records the reception of the report, which had meantime been printed, and had excited some feeling among the slave-holders.

Committee of the Synod of Kentucky, *Address of the Presbyterians of Kentucky Proposing a Plan for the Instruction and Emancipation of Their Slaves* (Newburyport, Mass.: Charles Whipple, 1836); Horace Greeley, *The American Conflict: A History of the Great Rebellion* (Hartford: O. D. Case & Co., 1864), 1:631.

9. Asterisks are in the original and indicate where the testimony was elided. The original text is from pp. 12–14 of the pamphlet. The date of 1835 was a mistake for 1836, unless it was meant to reference the year the committee was appointed rather than the year it presented the report.

10. This quote, originally published on October 4, 1835, was not written by a native southerner, despite the fact that it appeared in a southern newspaper. Rev. Darius Hoyt (1804–37), a Presbyterian minister and the editor of the *Maryville Intelligencer,* was born in Danbury, Conn. His father, Ard Hoyt, moved the family from Connecticut when he became pastor of a church in Wilkes-Barre, Pennsylvania, then transplanted them farther south when he served as a mis-

sionary among the Cherokees at the Brainerd Mission in Tennessee, on the Georgia border, from 1818 to 1824.

Darius Hoyt remained in Tennessee and founded the *Intelligencer* in Maryville in 1832. He served as its editor for three years, at the same time that he was professor of languages at the Southern and Western Theological Seminary in the same town. He also published the *Temperance Banner*, using both it and the *Intelligencer* to promote the causes of temperance and antislavery.

His obituary, published on August 18, 1837, in the newspaper he founded, said, "Mr. Hoyt was the slaves friend, although he did not feel safe in sanctioning the ultra measures of some friends of the cause of universal liberty, he never laid aside his golden rule in directing his course on the subject." He supported colonization, rather than encouraging emancipated slaves to live in the United States.

Robert Sparks Walker, *Torchlights to the Cherokees* (1931; repr., Johnson City, Tenn.: Overmountain Press, 1993), 43; *Maryville Intelligencer*, August 19, 1837, Glenn Teffeteller, Blount County TN Archives News, http://files.usgwarchives.net/tn/blount/newspapers/miscella5gnw.txt (accessed October 4, 2011).

11. Colonel William Keyes (1778–1864), or Keys, was born at Timber Ridge, Rockbridge County, Virginia. He moved to Hillsboro, Highland County, Ohio, in September 1805 "with a strong team, large wagon, and a heavy load . . . Our company consisted of two family connections, each of which was subdivided into one or two smaller families . . . number twenty-three persons in all, eight of whom were full grown men." The journey took eight weeks, traveling over "the most difficult wagon ways conceivable."

He was "the first auditor of the county, commander of a regiment in the war of 1812 [where he gained the title colonel], and a devout Presbyterian elder and radical abolitionist, [and] lived by cabinet making," according to a county history. Among his many abolitionist activities, he attended the Ohio Anti-Slavery Convention held in Putnam in April 1835, where he met James G. Birney, James Rankin, Elizur Wright, and other influential abolitionists.

Rev. J. W. Klise, *The County of Highland* (Madison, Wis.: Northwestern Historical Association, 1902), 104–5, 222; *Proceedings of the Ohio Anti-Slavery Convention* (Putnam, Ohio: Beaumont & Wallace, 1835); *Person: William Keys*, www.werelate.org/wiki/Person:William_Keys_(9) (accessed October 6, 2011).

APPENDIXES TO THE ANNOTATED EDITION

APPENDIX A

George Larimer's Letter

George T. F. Larimer, the son-in-law of Williams's Virginia owner, wrote the following letter to John B. Rittenhouse, editor of the Greensborough *Alabama Beacon*, in response to an inquiry from Rittenhouse, who was trying to discover if the person in Williams's narrative called George Larrimore actually existed. Rittenhouse printed the letter in the *Beacon*, and it was reprinted in an article by James G. Birney and Lewis Tappan, "Alabama Beacon versus James Williams," in the *Emancipator*, August 30, 1838. The same article including the letter was reprinted in the *Friend of Man*, September 19, 1838, from which the version here was taken. Changes from the *Emancipator* version are noted. The letter is the most accurate overall summary of Williams's life, written by one of his contemporaries.

Bowlers, June 22, 1838.

Dear Sir,—Your letter under date of the 8th of April, has been received, and I should have answered it ere this, had not my absence from home prevented me from doing so, so soon as I could have wished. But before proceeding to respond to your enquiries, I must express my surprise at being selected by the abolitionists as one of the objects of their slanders, and that I should have been represented as being so wealthy, is equally a matter of surprise. I do not know that I have the pleasure of Mr. Williams' acquaintance, though I infer from several circumstances alluded to in your letter, that he was formerly the slave of Mrs. Janey (my mother-in-law,) and her former carriage-driver, who called himself Shadrach Wilkins, and who was sold by her in consequence of his having been detected, in connection with others, in attempting to poison Dr. Roy and his family; his accomplices were tried for the offence above alluded to, one of whom was transported, and the other was sentenced to be hanged, and afterwards reprieved, and likewise transported. Had Shadrach been tried, there is scarcely a doubt, but that he would have been hanged, as it appears from the testimony in the case, after he was sold, that he was the principal one ["principal mover" in the *Emancipator*] in the business. He was sold to a Mr. Tate of South Alabama, and as well as my recollection now serves me, he lived in Greene county, and his Post Office was a little place called Selma. Some one or two years after Shadrach was sold, he made his escape from Alabama in company with an abolitionist, and got as far as Baltimore where he was through mistake sold by the abolitionist to a trader, who as soon as he had purchased him, put him in jail, when Shadrach confessed every thing, believing that he was betrayed by his friend the abolitionist,—and among other things he stated that the abolitionist had sold him frequently between Alabama and Baltimore, and that he had always been very particular in selling him to farmers, so as to be enabled to steal him again. Mr. Hays, the high constable of Baltimore, told me that Mr. Tate went on to Baltimore, and that he sold Shadrach to a trader who carried him on to New Orleans, and there sold him, since which time I have been informed that he has written to his sister, who belongs to a Mr. Hundly of this county, informing her that he went to the Mississippi river in a steamboat, and succeeded in getting to Cincinnati, where he remained a short time, and from thence he went on to New York, where I suppose he now is. Having said thus much of the supposed Mr. Williams, I will answer your questions in the order in which they occur.—My father's name was James T. Larimer. He married a Miss Catherine Fauntleroy, a daughter of Samuel Fauntleroy, deceased in the county of King and Queen. He had three children, James H.T., William E.L. and myself.—He had two sisters, one of whom died single, and without ever having been married; a Mr. Thomas Fauntleroy married the other. There was never any family connection between my father's family and the Lcotto [*sic* Scotts], or Brookenborough's, that I know of. My father owned between 80 and 90 slaves, and all of them except two or three were sent to Florida. I never was at the University of Virginia, in Paris or in Europe. I never was in New Orleans; my father went many years since, say about 1804, as far south as Milledgeville, Georgia, and he carried with him a servant named James Brown, who has since died (say about 2 years ago.) But he never called at Mr. M'Duffie's that I ever heard of, nor do I believe he ever saw Mr. M'D.—My mother died in 1836; my father and Wm. E.L. my youngest brother died in 1827. A family of Brooks' lived near my father's but they never had any thing to do with the guardianship of myself, or any one else, that I know of; in fact I never had a guardian. My father never owned a native born African to my knowledge, nor did he ever own a negro by the name of Meespeck [Meshech], nor do I know any thing of the negro belonging to Mr. Griggs, and sold to Mr. Scott of Fredericksburg; nor do I know any thing of the one belonging to Mr. Smith of King and Queen. I never at any period of my life taught, or attempted to teach, any of my father's slaves to read or write. I did not know this Mr. Williams, as he styles himself, until the fall of 1832, nor was he ever owned by my father, nor did I ever have the management of him in any way. My father's residence was called Thackersville in the county of Middlesex, at which place he was raised, and there lived until he died. He was never acquainted with Mr. Neal to my knowledge, and having died before the setting of the Virginia Convention, could not have had the quarrel before alluded to. He never resided in Richmond nor did he ever own any property in that place. He never purchased any slaves of the gentleman alluded to in the county of Caroline, nor did he ever purchase any slaves of any person to my knowledge except of Mr. Fauntleroy, and they were a portion of the slaves belonging to the estate of his father. This James Williams alias Shadrach Wilkins took as a wife a mulatto girl by the name of Harriet, belonging to Mrs. Janey, who sold her likewise to Mr. Tate rather than separate her from her husband.—I was the only overseer of my father. I never knew Huckstep, Crop, Flincher, Stiulivant (Sturtivant) nor any of the concern. There was but one mulatto on my father's estate ["and he was about his age," appeared here in the *Emancipator*], and he never owned any land, nor did he ever live in Powhattan county. I am the only male by the name of Larimer in Virginia that I know of; there was not a mulatto child born on my father's estate from 1804 till 1830; when the slaves were sent to Florida. I disposed of my portion of the slaves to Mr. Craig of Florida after having hired them out until the 1st of January, 1834, and I never owned any land in any state of the Union except in Virginia, nor did I ever cultivate a crop in any part of the United States except in Virginia. John Dillard, Esq., of your county lived in Florida a part of the time my negroes were there, and he knows that the above statement in reference to land, &c. is true.

In conclusion, I must express my astonishment that the citizens of your state should suffer papers of the kind alluded to in your letter to be circulated among them; and will further add, that the whole story is a base fabrication ["and falsehood" appeared here in the *Emancipator*] from the beginning to the end.

I have endeavored to answer all your queries, and have added what seemed to be important; but should you find it necessary to address me again on the subject it, shall be promptly attended to.

Respectfully your friend,

GEO. T. F. LARIMER.

APPENDIX B

Poisoning Trial Transcript

James Williams, under his original name Shadrach Wilkins, and three other enslaved people, Warner, Tabby, and Mary Jr., were brought to court in Essex County, Virginia, on August 18, 1834, in connection with the attempted murder of a neighboring couple, Dr. Augustus Gustavus Dunbar Roy and his wife, Lucy Carter Garnett Roy. Warner and Tabby were tried and found guilty, while the attorney for the commonwealth declined to prosecute Williams and Mary Jr. (a male, also recorded as Merry Jr. or possibly Merry Jo in Joseph Janey's estate inventory).

The governor reprieved both Warner and Tabby and ordered them to be sold and transported instead. On October 27, 1834, John McMurry purchased them, with John B. Williamson also posting bond, and McMurry agreed to "carry out of the United States all and every of the said slaves so purchased by him." Dr. A.G.D. Roy received reimbursement of $1,050, the court-ordered value of the slaves. (Auditor of Public Accounts, Condemned Blacks Executed and Transported, Miscellaneous Reel 2549, October 28, 1834, and Condemned Slaves, Court Orders and Valuations 1833–45, Miscellaneous, Reel 2553, pp. 0160–0161, Library of Virginia, Richmond.)

A transcript of the legal proceedings on August 18, 1834, is reprinted here, from Essex County Court Orders, no. 48, 1833–36, Reel 97, Library of Virginia, Richmond.

At a Court of Oyer and Terminer called and held for Essex County at the Courthouse in Tappahannock on the 18th day of August 1834 for the trial of Warner and Tabby negro slaves the property of A.G.D. Roy charged with plotting and conspiring to murder the said A.G.D. Roy and Lucy his wife.

Present

Austin Brockenbrough	Laurence Roane	Gentlemen Justices
Warner Lewis	and	
James Semple	Larkin Hundley	

The prisoners are led to the bar in custody of the Keeper of the common jail of this County, whereupon the Court doth assign, Wm B. B. Seward counsel to the prisoners, and the prisoners being arraigned upon their arraignment plead "Not Guilty," and divers Witnesses being sworn and examined and the arguments of Counsel as well in behalf of the Commonwealth as the prisoners being heard, it is the unanimous opinion of the Court are guilty of the criminal offence aforesaid, with which they stand charged and doth accordingly adjudge and order that the prisoners be hanged by their necks at the public gallows on Friday the nineteenth day of September next until they be dead, and that execution of this judgment be done by the Sheriff of this County between the hours of Nine O'Clock in the morning and 4 O'Clock in the evening of the same day. And it is further Ordered to be entered of record that a Majority of the Court recommend the prisoner Tabby to the clemency of the Executive of this Commonwealth, and it is Ordered to be certified to the executive that the negro slave Warner is worth six hundred and fifty dollars and that the negro slave Tabby is worth four hundred Dollars.

The deposition of Harriet a negro woman slave the property of A.G.D. Roy, being first charged and sworn according to law, Deposeth and saith that she was lying down, in the kitchen of her master Dr. A.G.D. Roy on thursday the 7th Instant, in the evening immediately after dinner. Warner (the prisoner) came into the kitchen and inquired of her (the Witness) if she had a phial, she told him she had none, that she had given hers to Tabby (the prisoner), the witness told Warner if he wanted a phial, for any particular use, she the Witness would loan it to him, he replied he wanted it for a very particular use, the phial was on the kitchen shelf and she gave it to him. Warner took the phial & went up stairs. Tabby (the prisoner) came in and asked what was that which had been mentioned of a phial, she the Witness told Tabby that she had loaned Warner the phial that she had given her[,] the prisoner, then Tabby remarked is that the way you do, you give away a thing to one person, and then take it away and give it to some other person, the Witness told Tabby she had not given it to Warner, but only loaned it to him, and when he was done with it, he should return it to Tabby again. Warner remarked that after he was done with it, it would never be fit for any thing again. After he said that he held the phial down, he standing on the steps, that went up the kitchen loft, that when he held the phial down he asked the Witness and Tabby, if they knew what kind of root that was in the phial, she the Witness told him she did not know but that she expected it was a dose for Mr. Newbill who had apprehended Warner in the morning of that Day, he having been runaway, he the prisoner remarked that it was a dose to fix them, that wanted to kill him, the Witness asked him, who it was, he the prisoner replied her pretty Mistress and Master, that the prisoner Tabby when Warner held the phial down and asked if they knew what it was, said that it would take twenty four hours to steep it, and Warner replied that it would take a longer time. Tabby asked Warner how he intended to give it, he asked Tabby when she intended boil rice, she answered and said she did not know when she should boil rice, that he had better put it in the milk, which was in the spring, she Tabby further said if the poison was put in the milk, it would certainly kill, and also that there was more ways to kill a dog besides hanging him. Tabby further remarked to Warner, that he knew where his master and Mistress visited that if he would go and lay the poison at the door it would take away the use of their Master and Mistresses limbs, and that [they] would no longer be able to injure them the prisoners neither could they be of any service to themselves. The Witness told Warner she would tell. Tabby then remarked to Warner that she had cautioned him before, about talking before the Witness and that he had as well have gone in the house and told his Master and Mistress himself, and that he (Warner) ought to give the Witness sufficient warning before she left the kitchen. Warner said to the Witness if she told he would fix her too, that by Wednesday following, he would have all three going out of the gate, just as the people were carried to the burying ground in Richmond, that the Witness informed her Mistress of what had occurred as herein before detailed, on Sunday night after it happened, that on Monday morning her Master sent the Witness to look for the phial she had loaned Warner, that she went up the kitchen stairs and found the phial and two separate papers of powders in a bag lying on the logs of which the kitchen is built, that the vial had a liquid and a root in it, that she gave the vial and papers of powders to her Master, that Warner told the Witness it was *Hug* root, the Witness further states that the phial now shown her is the same found by her in the kitchen as aforesaid. And further this deponent saith not.

The Deposition of A.G.D. Roy he being first duly sworn deposes and says,

That on the information of Harriet, a servant girl belonging to him, he apprehended Warner the prisoner on Monday the 11th of the present month Augt., that on taking him up the deponent showed him a phial with a root and some liquid in it also a paper containing some Cobalt. He, the prisoner, immediately acknowledged having put the root in the phial with the liquid and said that it was prepared by Mrs. Adelaide Janeys Shadrack and that prisoner called it *Hug* root and stated he was informed it would carry him straight and make persons like him, the prisoner said he obtained the root on Mrs. Janey's farm, near the house of a negro woman named Betsy belonging to Mrs. Janey that in consequence of this information on the part of the prisoner Mr. Geo. T. Lorimer, the son in law of Mrs. Janey searched and found near the house aforesaid where several roots had been dug, some of which he brought to the Witness and that upon an examination he the Witness believed it to be hemlock, the Witness thinks the papers spoken of in the deposition of Harriet contained Cobalt which may be mixed with some other white powder that he the Witness has not tried them by any chemical tests. The Witness is a Doctor of Medicine, and that the phial and papers produced to the Court are the same that were given him by the servant Harriet. And further this deponent saith not.

The deposition of Thomas Matthews he being first duly sworn deposeth and saith, That on the night the prisoner Warner was brought to Jail, he the Witness was at the Jail door, when Mr. Crewdson who was present remarked to the prisoner Warner that from what he Mr. Crewdson had heard he the prisoner would be hanged, that Mr. Crewdson at this same time asked the prisoner if it were possible he meant to poison his master, the prisoner answered, Yes. Mr. Crewdson asked what could induce him to wish to destroy his Master, the prisoner answered that his master had whipped him. Mr. Crewdson asked him again, if he would destroy his master merely because he whipped him, he replied Yes. That the Witness heard the said prisoner make the same confessions two days afterwards to Mr. Croxton a Justice who was examining the prisoner Warner to ascertain whether there was evidence sufficient against Tabby to commit her for trial that all the confessions were made without any threats promises or persuasions from anyone, that Tabby the prisoner has always declared her innocence, but that she acknowledged that there was a conversation held by her and Warner in relation to the phial, that she saw the phial, but that she did not know what it contained. And further this deponent saith not.

The deposition of Geo. T. F. Lorimer he being first duly sworn deposes and says—That the prisoner Warner informed the Witness, that he got the root stated to be in the phial spoken of in the previous depositions from the woods near the house of a negro woman named Betsy belonging to his (the Witness's) mother in law Mrs. Janey, that the Witness suspected the root to be hemlock and knowing that there was a small piece of swamp near the woods that he went and examined and found several stalks of weeds dug up with their roots cut off which he believes to be hemlock. And further the deponent saith not.

And thereupon this Court is adjourned without day.

(Signed) Austin Brockenbrough.

At a Court of Oyer and Terminer called and held for Essex County at the Courthouse in Tappahannock on the 18th day of August 1834 for the trial of Shadrack and Mary Jr, negro men slaves the property of Mrs. Adelaide Janey charged with plotting and conspiring to murder Dr. A.G.D. Roy and Lucy his wife.

Present

Austin Brockenbrough	Laurence Roane	Gentlemen Justices
Warner Lewis	and	
James Semple	Larkin Hundley	

The prisoners are led to the bar in custody of the Keeper of the common Jail of the County, Whereupon the Attorney for the Commonwealth with the assent of the Court declares that he will not prosecute further for the commonwealth in this behalf. It is therefore ordered and adjudged that they be hence discharged from this prosecution. And thereupon this Court is adjourned without day [*sic*].

(Signed) Austin Brockenbrough

Ordered that the Court be adjourned till to morrow morning 10 O'Clock.

(Signed) Austin Brockenbrough

APPENDIX C

Runaway Ads

Williams attempted to run away from Caleb Tate's plantation in Alabama at least three times. Tate advertised for him in the closest newspaper, the *Selma Free Press,* as well as other surrounding papers, the *Huntsville Advocate,* the *Mobile Advertiser,* the *Montgomery Journal,* and the *Tuscaloosa Intelligencer and State Rights Expositor.* Williams did pass near both Montgomery and Selma on his final escape, according to his description in the narrative.

There are two known ads. The first appeared August 29, 1835, and ran through October 17, 1835. The one presented here is taken from the August 29 *Alabama Intelligencer and State Rights Expositor:*

FIFTY DOLLARS REWARD. Absconded from the subscriber on Sunday night the 23d inst *four Negroes,* of the following description, viz:

SHADRICK, a yellow complected, likely fellow bold and impudent look, about 5 feet 10 inches high 26 years old, wears his hair roached, eyes of a yellowish cast, and wore a white hat.

HARRIET, the wife of Shadrick, a bright mulatto, low in statue [*sic*] and heavy built, wears her hair long and about 22 years old. They took with them their child, a boy named BEN, about 15 months old. They absconded previously, and Shadrick assumed the name of Ben Jonson and Harriet that of Eliza.

MACK about the same height of Shadrick, yellowish complected, about 19 years of age, and quick spoken.

The clothing of said negroes cannot be described as they had some not known to the owner. They may have been supplied with forged free papers or stolen by some white person, as our county is litterally [*sic*] filled up with persons of suspicious character.

I will give the above reward for the confinement of said negroes in some jail so I can recover them, or for their delivery to me, residing in Dallas county, eight miles from Selma.

CALEB TATE.

The second ad ran from October 24, 1835, through at least December 5, 1835. The following example is taken from the October 24, 1835, *Selma Free Press:*

40 DOLLARS REWARD.—Ranaway from the subscriber, residing near Valley Creek Academy, Dallas county, Ala. on the night of the 16th Oct. inst. two Negroes of the following description, viz:

William, a very black man, about 5 feet 4 inches high, has a blemish in his right eye, has a scar on his shoulder occasioned by a burn, and aged 25 years.

Shadrick, a yellow complected, likely fellow, bold and impudent look, about 5 feet 10 inches high, 26 years old, wears his hair roached, eyes of rather a yellowish cast, and wore a white hat.

Ten dollars will be paid for the commitment of each of the above negroes within the State, or twenty dollars each if committed out of the State, so I may get them.

CALEB TATE.

Oct. 17, 1835.—tf11
The Montgomery Journal, the Mobile Advertiser, the Tuscaloosa Intelligencer, and the Huntsville Advocate will give the above three insertions and forward bills to this office.

APPENDIX D

Recapture in Baltimore

The following court records relate to Williams's capture and sale in Baltimore, after he escaped from Caleb Tate on October 16, 1835. The records are found in Alabama Governor (1835–37: Clay), Extraditions and Requisitions File, SG24782, Reel 11, Alabama Department of Archives and History, Montgomery.

Caleb Tate
Affidavit
"John Smith"

The State of Alabama
Montgomery County

Personally appeared before me Benajah S. Bibb judge of the County Court in and for the County and State aforesaid, Caleb Tate who being duly sworn deposeth and saith that he residing in Dallas County, State aforesaid, and that John Smith, now confined in prison, in Baltimore, Maryland, is guilty of stealing from his possession in the County of his residence aforesaid, his negro man, ~~James~~ Shadrach.

Caleb Tate

Sworn to & subscribed before me this 1st June 1836.

Benajah S Bibb
J.C.C.M.C. [Judge County Court Montgomery County]

State of Maryland Baltimore City to wit:

Be this remembered that on this 18th day of May 1836 James F. Purvis appeared before me and shew before me, the original of a certificate of a certain John ^Smith describing the qualities and ^character of a certain negro, James whom he had just sold to said Purvis, stated that he had been raised with said negro and knew him well, and that the foregoing instrument of writing is a true and verbatim copy of said original paper. Certifyed and given under my hand this 18th day of May 1836.

Joseph Shane (seal)

State of Maryland Baltimore County
I hereby certify that Joseph Shane gentleman by whom the above and [illegible] certificates were given and before whom the annexed deposition were made and who hath thereto subscribed his name even at the time of so doing a Justice of the Peace of the State of Maryland in and for the City of Baltimore duly commissioned and sworn.

In testimony whereof I have hereto set
my name and affixed the seal of
Baltimore County Court this eighteenth
day of May Eighteen hundred and
thirty six

Thos Kell Clk [clerk]

State of Maryland Baltimore City to wit.—on this Seventeenth day of May Eighteen hundred thirty-six, before me the subscriber a Justice of the Peace, in and for the City aforesaid, personally appeared, Simeon Hays, Police officer, and being duly sworn on the Holy Evangely of the Almighty God, deposeth and saith, that on the 13th day of April 1836 he arrested John Smith alias James B. White in the City of Baltimore, and that on his person were found a considerable number of papers, when the said J. Smith alias J. B. White stated that he knew what his fate was to be and he might as well confess the whole matter, and then commenced stating ^that on this paper, with some other, showing that money was subscribed, for the purpose of going on to the south, with the view of liberating slaves, and taking them on to Buffalow ^and Canada where he had already taken a number, he had applyed to the abolitionists in New York for money and papers, but that they had not entire confidence in him, and did not succeed there, but that in Philadelphia he obtain[d] subscribtions [*sic*] in money, for that purpose, and that he obtained papers at different places from different persons with the view of furthering his objects—the disclosure he made freely, deponent stated to him at the time, that he had gotten himself into a bad situation and that he had nothing to hope for short of the penitentiary, and said Smith alias White further stated to deponant, that he was on his way to Alabama for the purpose of liberating said James alias Shadrick's wife and children to take them likewise to Buffalow, which belonged to Caleb Tate of said State and that he was regularly engaged on behalf of the Abolitionist in getting slaves to go to Buffalow & Canada and further deponant saith not.

sworn before
Joseph Shane

State of Maryland, Baltimore city to wit:
On the 18th day of May 1836 before me the subscriber a Justice of the Peace, in and for the City aforesaid, personally appeared James F. Purvis, and being duly sworn on the Holy Evangely of Almighty God deposeth and saith, that a certain man, then calling himself by the name of John Smith, did on the 12th day of April 1836 sell to him a negro man calling him at that time James, for which the said Purvis paid the said Smith the sum of $700 and took his bill of sale for said Negro, subsequently ascertained the said Negro was a runaway slave from the state of Alabama belonging to Mr. Caleb Tate.

sworn before Joseph Shane

APPENDIX E
Slatter v. Holton

When Caleb Tate sold Williams to slave trader Hope H. Slatter in Baltimore, Slatter transferred him to his brother, Shadrach F. Slatter, a trader in New Orleans. Shadrach Slatter sold him to Charles Armstrong, from whom Williams soon escaped in January 1837 by stowing away on the steamboat *Henry Clay*. The *Henry Clay* took him as far as the mouth of the Cumberland River, where he transferred to another steamboat, the *Wave*. The captain of the *Wave* let him work for his passage from the mouth of the Cumberland to a few miles above Flint Island on the Ohio River, where Williams disappeared and was not recovered.

Shadrach Slatter returned Armstrong's purchase price of sixteen hundred dollars and successfully sued the captain of the *Henry Clay*, John A. Holton, in the Parish Court of New Orleans to recover the money, claiming that Holton had vouched for Williams to the captain of the *Wave*. Holton appealed to the Louisiana Supreme Court, claiming the plaintiff's lawyers had offered no proof that Williams belonged to Shadrach Slatter, was ever in New Orleans, or had boarded his boat there. In *Slatter v. Holton* the state supreme court upheld the lower court's ruling and also refused a later request for a rehearing, closing the case finally on July 5, 1841, over three years after Williams had already published his narrative and left for England. There is no evidence that any of the people involved in the suit ever realized their runaway was the author of the narrative.

The following statements come from the testimony assembled for the state supreme court. Also included are the decision of the lower court, the statements on behalf of the plaintiff and defendant to the supreme court, and the supreme court's decision. The witnesses called Williams either by his birth name, Shadrach, or a variation of that name (which was coincidentally the first name of his new owner), or by the alias he was using then, Jim Thornton.

The testimony comes from *Slatter v. Holton*, Docket no. 2894, Eastern District, June 1841, Supreme Court of Louisiana 19 LA 39, Earl K. Long

Library, University of New Orleans, http://libweb.uno.edu/jspui/handle/123456789/12613 (accessed October 23, 2011).

Statement of William Holton, first mate of the *Henry Clay* and brother of the defendant, April 3, 1837:

> Also the deposition of Wm Holton who deposes & says that he was on board the steamboat Henry Clay on her trip from New Orleans to Louisville commencing about the 10th of Jany last acting in the character of first mate, and he is confident that the negro Shadrack claimed by the plaintiff in this cause was not on board the Henry Clay when she left New Orleans or at any other time during the trip. There was no chance of his being there without deponent's knowing it unless he came on board during the time the boat lay at Cumberland bar and departed before the boat got under way from that place.
>
> There were no coloured persons on board during the trip from Louisville to New Orleans & back to Louisville except the servant of Capt Slade and the stewart of the St Lawrence except those who belonged to the boat. Deponent is brother to the defendant Capt Holton.

Additional statement of William Holton, December 22, 1837:

> First William Holton being of lawfull age and first duly sworn deposeth and saith that he was on board of the Henry Clay steamboat in January last in character of first mate, that he was been on board of said boat whilst running for about five years he descended the Ohio river from Louisville upon her to New Orleans in December last and returned upon her leaving New Orleans about the 9th or 10th of January last. It was a part of his duty to see and know what persons were upon board of said boat upon her ascending trip and he took much pains to ascertain who was on board and particularly if there were any run away negroes—the deck passengers on the trip were frequently mustered for the purpose of seeing that no person was improperly on board, and he is satisfied that there was not on board of said boat in Louisiana the Negro Shadrack claimed by the plaintiff in this cause. The steamboat

Henry Clay left New Orleans in January on the 9th or 10th of the month as well as he recollects about the same time the Mississippi[,] Daniel Webster, and Rocky Mountain left New Orleans bound up the river.

The Clay was stopped by low water at Cumberland bar where she remained a considerable time. The Webster & Mississippi, were laid up at the bar near the Clay, and the Rocky Mountain and other boats were lying at the town of Smithland about 2 miles off when the steamboat Wave came along side of the Clay remained there all night and next day took passengers from the Clay, and other boats lying near.

There was ready communication from the Clay to the land and to the other boats and many persons then came on board and passed through the Clay. The passengers of the Clay were taken on board the Wave together with a mulatto man named Bob who came down in December preceding as second Cook in the boat and as a free man, and who is now in this City. He is about 25 or 30 years of age and going from appearance about 6 feet high handsome well formed man—and also a man by the name of Sanders a coloured man who came on board the Clay from the St. Lawrence near the mouth of White river—and also a servant (a coloured man of Mr. Slade one of the passengers) who was a black man.

There was no man on board the boat by the name of Shadrack or Jim Thornton or any other who did not then belong to the boat except the servant of Captain Slade and Sanders of the steamboat St. Lawrence.

He is satisfied that if there had been on board the Clay the man Shadrack or Jim Thornton he would have known it and he is confident he was not on board of her passing up the river—he might have passed through her whilst she lay at Cumberland bar and this deponent have known nothing of it.

Witness is brother of the defendant & had before been examined in the former cause.

Statement of William M'Bride, pilot of the *Wave*, filed January 11, 1839:

William M'Bride produced by Pltf [plaintiff] deposes that in January last he was pilot of the steamboat Wave Capt. Spalding about 60 or 65 miles above the mouth of the Ohio they fell in with the steamboat Henry Clay which was unable to proceed—they took from her a number of passengers who were to be carried to Louisville amongst these was a coloured man who passed by the name of Jim Thornton rather tall he thinks about 5 feet 9 or 10 of a copper color wore his hair well combed back from his face & was remarked on board the Wave for his neatness & activity in acting as a Waiter. Deponent is clear that he was received from on board the Henry Clay he remarked him as being very active in bringing the baggage from the Henry Clay to the Wave—did not see him employed in any other manner tho he saw him in the cabin of the Henry Clay.

They afterwards overtook the steamboat Tuscarora from which they took other passengers among others was a gentleman called Peterson. This gentleman pointed out Jim Thornton to Mr. Plastridge Clerk of the boat as a slave & belonging to some person of his acquaintance whose name deponent does not recollect. In fact he did not pay particular attention to it as he was the only pilot & a good deal exhausted by loss of sleep & exposure to the cold.

The boat was stopped lying about 90 miles below Louisville when the said Jim Thornton left the boat & deponent has never seen him since[.] The Wave had been lying alongside the Clay about half an hour before he saw the Boy called Jim Thornton.

Upon being cross examined says he had no interest in the Wave further than receiving wages as a pilot. The Wave received passengers whilst lying alongside the Clay from the Mississippi or a boat commanded by Capt. Burch. He knows of no other coloured persons who came on board the Wave from the Clay except the one he has mentioned.

Ex^{m} in chief resumed[.] They took the passengers from the H Clay before they went along side the Mississippi which was lying some 50 or 100 yards above. They received as well as he recollects only two passengers who came alongside the H-C in her small boat.

Cr[oss]. Examined—Does not know the persons who came from Mississippi to the Wave—they arrived on Wave the morning after the landing near the Clay. The Clay & Mississippi were both made fast to land whether their planks were out does not know.

Statement of Walter Cox, passenger on the *Wave*, filed March 26, 1839:

Walter Cox a witness for Pltf [plaintiff] deposes that about the middle of January last he arrived at Paducah on his way to Louisville on the steamboat Mississippi—where he changed to the Tuscarora in company with a Mr. Henry F. Peterson—after proceeding about an hundred miles they got aground, when they were taken off by the steamboat Wave which boat saw on board the passengers of the Henry Clay which latter had arrived at Paducah the day after they had left it—on board the Wave Mr. Peterson pointed out to deponent a mulatto or griffe man who he said he knew perfectly well as belonging to a friend of his—said griffe was a man about six feet high & every way well proportioned & said he should require the Capt of the Wave to have him arrested whether he did so or not Deponent only knew by the Statement of Peterson. When they got within about 70 miles from Louisville the ice stopped them & each one had to get on as he could, the boy in question left the Boat before either deponent or Peterson & he has no further knowledge of what became of him.

The defendant objects to the conversations between witness & Peterson as evidence herein or any other matter of hearsay.

Upon being cross interrogated he says He does not recollect the name of the griffe he is under the impression he has since seen him in Louisville Kentucky the said man was about 30 to 35 years of age. This Deponent has no personal knowledge whether the Wave had passengers of the Clay or other boats, the Clay having arrived at Paducah after he left as he was informed she was not there when he passed.

When he left Paducah the Mississippi steamboat was lying there bound from New Orleans to Louisville and there were several other boats lying not very remote from her.

Ex^{m} in chief resumed[.] Deponent is certain the boy in question was not amongst the passengers of the Mississippi he himself having been one. The other boats lying near Paducah were small boats which appeared to be laying up out of the way of them & Deponent should judge had no passengers.

Statement given August 3, 1837, by Henry F. Peterson, passenger on the *Wave,* who recognized Williams as a runaway:

First. To the first Interrogatory on behalf of the Plaintiff to him propounded, this deponent answereth and saith:—That he does know the parties plaintiff and defendant in this cause, that he has known the Plaintiff two or three years; and the defendant a longer time.

Second. To the Second Interrogatory this Deponent saith—That he first saw the Boy Shadrack referred to in this Interrogatory, about the month of May Eighteen hundred and Thirty Six, in the Jail of Baltimore County; a day or two afterwards this Deponent saw the said boy at the house of the Plaintiff's brother Mr. H. H. Slatter, in the City of Baltimore; that this deponent saw the said boy frequently afterwards in the possession of Mr. H. H. Slatter; that some time about the first part of October last, this Deponent accompanied Mr. H. H. Slatter to the City of Alexandria in the District of Columbia, said Slatter having with him several slaves, and among them the Boy Shadrack above referred to, for the purpose of shipping them to said Slatter's brother, the plaintiff, in New Orleans; that the said slaves and this boy also were put on board a Brig at Alexandria, bound for that place.

Third. To the third Interrogatory this deponent saith, that he was on the Ohio River in the month of January last returning from Vicksburg to Wheeling; that he came into the Ohio River in the steamboat Mississippi; that the said boy Shadrack was not on board this boat as Deponent saw.

Fourth. To the fourth interrogatory this Deponent saith; that he left the steamboat Mississippi at the mouth of Tennessee River and went on board the steamboat Tuscarora; this Deponent thinks the name of the Captain of the Tuscarora was Smith; that he proceeded up the Ohio River in the Tuscarora about twenty four hours, when the Boat ran aground, and this Deponent was taken on board the steamboat Wave commanded by Captain Spalding. That this Deponent immediately on going on board the steamboat Wave, saw the boy Shadrack referred to in the second interrogatory, spoke to him, and knew him well, and this Deponent is perfectly satisfied that he is the same boy that was shipped by Mr. H. H. Holton, [*sic* Slatter] at Alexandria to his brother, the plaintiff, at New Orleans.

Fifth. To the Fifth Interrogatory this Deponent saith, that immediately on recognizing the Boy Shadrack, as stated in the answer to the fourth

Interrogatory, this Deponent spoke to Captain Spalding and *told him that the boy belonged to Mr. S. F. Slatter of New Orleans;* that this deponent was of opinion he had run away, and that Capt Spalding ought to have him arrested:—

That Capt Spalding replied to this Deponent, that the boy was put on board his boat by Captain Holton of the steamboat Henry Clay; and that he did not believe that Captain Holton would have put him on board his boat, if he had not authority to do so; and that as Captain Holton was responsible for the boy in case he should be a slave, he thought he would not arrest him. The boy told this deponent that his name was Jim Thornton; he passed by this name on board the boat[.] [O]n the arrival of the boat at Flint Island on the Ohio River in Indiana State, the river was blocked up by the ice. Having arrived there in the evening, the boat lay there all night, and the next morning the boy was missing. This Deponent never saw the boy afterward.

Sixth. To the Sixth Interrogatory this Deponent saith; that he doth not know any other matter or thing beneficial to the Plaintiff in this cause . . .

To the first cross Interrogatory to this deponent propounded—he answereth and saith; That he is not in any manner interested in this suit; nor is he in any manner related to either of the parties.

Second. To the second cross interrogatory this deponent saith; That he did not, at any time, see the boy referred to on board the Henry Clay, not having been on board that boat at the time spoken of in the third and Fourth direct Interrogatives.

Third. To the third cross Interrogatory this deponent saith; *that he was present when Mr. H. H. Slatter bargained for the boy Shadrack* referred to in the direct interrogatory, with Mr. Tate in the City of Baltimore;—and he afterwards saw the boy put on board the Brig at Alexandria by Mr. H. H. Slatter, and this Deponent knows of no other boys paid for by the Plaintiff, at this time but the one above referred to.

Fourth. To the fourth cross Interrogatory, this Deponent saith;—That he does not know that he ever did [see a negro traveling as a passenger or hand aboard Captain Holton's boat without the authority of a white man].

Fifth. To the Fifth cross Interrogatory this Deponent saith; that he never did point out the slave, referred to in this Interrogatory; to Capt Holton on board his boat or elsewhere.
Sixth. To the Sixth cross Interrogatory this deponent saith; that he has known Capt Holton for more than three years, and has sailed with him two or three times; and that as far as this deponent knows, he has no reason to doubt his watchfulness, carefulness, or honesty as master of a boat.
Seventh. To the Seventh cross Interrogatory this Deponent saith; that he knows of no other matter or thing of benefit to the Defendant in this cause.

Statement of Erasmus D. Plastridge, clerk of the *Wave*, November 30, 1837:

When the Wave first went along side the Henry Clay Deponent saw Jim Thornton waiting on the passengers who were at Supper in the cabin, & afterwards aiding to carry the passengers baggage on board the Wave from the Henry; Capt Holton was at this time on board the Henry Clay walking about & sometimes on the guard where they were passing out the baggage—at Flint island the boat was stopping by ice & all the passengers left her & Jim Thornton left her in company with the other three boys since when deponent has never seen him.

Cross Examined by Defendant

Deponent is not connected with either of the parties to the suit[.] He is clerk on the river, at the time when the Wave dropped down to take passengers as above stated, the Henry Clay was lying about three miles below the mouth of Cumberland river. There were two other steamboats lying at the same place the Mississippi and the Daniel Webster. These steamboats were lying close to each other, there was no gang way from one to the other. Communication was very easy from one boat to the other, each boat having a gang way from itself to the shore.

The Wave lay all night by the side of the Henry Clay. The Wave took two passengers from the steamer Mississippi, witness cannot say positively that the Wave took on other passengers from the other boats, but to the best of his recollection she did not when the four negroes mentioned above came on board the Wave the witness did not see Capt Holton point out or identify them as those servants which he had requested the Capt of the Wave to transport to Louisville and never heard Capt Holton state this Boy Jim Thornton was under his charge or was one of the servants or crew of the Henry. Deponent only knew from Capt Spalding that Jim Thornton was one of the Boys desired to be carried to Louisville by Capt Holton, and he learned, this only from the remark of Capt. Spalding.

Given in the direct examination—witness was not part owner of the Wave. He does not recollect of seeing boy Jim Thornton in presence of Holton nor does he recollect of having heard any orders given to him by Holton or any of the officers of the Clay. The Daniel Webster was bound up the Cumberland & the two persons taken from the Mississippi were her capt & clerk, her passengers having left her previously. Did not know other negroes that came on board the Wave had not seen any of them before this time—two of the negroes paid their passage, and deponent gave the passage to the other two on account of their services. The boy Jim Thornton being one of them. Witness was not present nor did he hear conversation between Capt Spalding & Capt Holton.

Statement of Ulysses Spalding, captain of the *Wave*, June 15, 1838:

Answer to first interrogatory of the Plaintiff
Ulisses Spalding age Forty one merchant not acquainted with the plaintiff do not recollect of seeing the defendant but once that was on board of steamboat Henry Clay.
Answer to Second Interrogatory

I was on board the steamboat Wave in Jany 1837 she was trading from Nashville to Smithland on the Cumberland River, met with the S[t] Boat Henry Clay between three and four miles below Smithland at the port of the Cumberland Island she was from New Orleans bound to Louisville.
Answer to 3 Interrogation

She did receive passengers from on board of the Henry Clay and there was a coloured boy that passed by the name of Jim Thornton from steamboat Henry Clay together with some others of his cabin boys who captain Holton requested me to let such as I should need work their passage the rest pay, this Jim Thornton being very active about the table and my Steward being sick at the time I let him work his passage above Flint Island where I discharged him, I had no conversation with Capt Holton respecting the boy no more than the balance of the boys that came on board of the Wave, I see him on the Henry Clay waiting on the table did not learn from Capt Holton whether he was in his employ or not but supposed he was[.]

Answer of Fourth Interrogatory

Mr. Paterson came on board of the Wave a few miles below Shawnitown or Golconda [Illinois] I think from S[t] Boat Tuscarora[.] Paterson did recognize Jim he pointed him out as a slave I should suppose him to be between twenty two and twenty five very active and went ashore together with the other passengers a few miles above Flint Island that is the last I knew of him.

Answer to Fifth Interrogation

I know of nothing further to the advantage of Plaintiff.

Answer to the first interrogatory by the defendant[.] I have no interest in this controversy.

[. . .]

Ninth Interrogatory

The passengers from S[t] Boat Henry Clay came on board of the Wave soon after coming long side and made inquiries about their passage two or three times and not all at the same time[.] Capt Holton came with some of them on board.

Tenth Interrogatory

I saw Jim Thornton on the Henry Clay waiting on the table and he was present among those that Capt Holton mention had money to pay in case I did not need his services.

Eleventh Interrogatory

I have no farther knowledge of any thing material to the defendant.

Statement of Nicolas C. Snethen, second clerk of the *Henry Clay*, given April 3, 1837:

First Nicolas C Snethen being duly sworn deposeth and saith that he has been acting as second clerk on board the steamboat Henry Clay since December last and that he was on board of her when she left New Orleans about the 10th of January last and continued on board of her untill her arrival at Louisville. That it was his particular duty to know who was on board the boat at the time of her departure and during her trip that he caused the deck passengers to be mustered several times during the trip it was his duty which he faithfully performed to examine the boat that there might be no run away slaves on board—that he has no recollection of the boy Shadrack being on board, he feels confident he was not as the deponent never saw him or even heard of him untill the commencement of this suit and his duty and opportunities of knowing it were such as he should have known it had he been on board.

The steamboat Daniel Webster left New Orleans on the same day that the Henry Clay did in January and they both arrived at Cumberland bar the Webster arriving first. The Webster, Clay, the steamboat Mississippi and Independence were lying at the bar for 10 or 12 days, all bound up the river the Mississippi had left N Orleans before the Clay & the Independence after it. During their stay at Cumberland bar there was a very free communication kept up amongst the passengers &c of the respective boats, hands, passengers and others passing from one boat to the other and also from the shore—that whilst the Clay was lying at Cumberland bar the steamboat Wave came alongside the clay and took on board some of the passengers among others a tall man by the name of Bob who had made the trip from Louisville to New Orleans in Decr last and he was the only coloured person who left the Clay and went on board the Wave. The Wave also stopped along side the Mississippi and took from on board many of her passengers, when this Deponent does not know. He states that there was no negro or coloured passengers on board the boat during the trip that did not belong to the boat except a servant of capt Slade of Mobile who was a cabin passenger and a man who got on board the Clay near the mouth of White River & who was the stewart of St. Lawrence named Sanders.

Statement of Thomas D. Cox, second mate of the *Henry Clay*, given April 3, 1837:

> Also Thomas D. Cox, who deposes & says he was second mate of the Henry Clay from Louisville in Decr last and her return in January which commenced about the 10th that he is confident there was no slave on board the Boat whilst she was under way during the entire trip except those who belonged to the boat and had made the downward trip on her except the servant of Capt Slade and the Steward of the St Lawrence the first got on board at New Orleans in the cabin & left at Cumberland bar the other got on board at near White River & left at Cumberland bar as well as he recollects.

Judgment signed May 10, 1839, by Judge Charles Maurian, in case of *Slatter v. Holton*, State of Louisiana Parish Court for the Parish and City of New Orleans:

> The Court after carefully examining the evidence and weighing the arguments of Counsel considering:
> 1st That the testimony produced by the plaintiff clearly establishes the fact that the Pltf's slave was on board the Henry Clay, the defendant's boat waiting at table, which fact cannot be considered as contradicted by the defendant's witnesses by their stating that they did not see him.
> 2^d That it is moreover in evidence that the Plaintiffs slave on getting from the Henry Clay on board the steamer Wave was recommended by the defendant to the Captain of the Wave.
> 3^d That these facts being brought home to the defendant impose upon him the obligation of showing how the Pltfs slave happened to be on board of his boat, and that on failing so to do, the conclusion must be that the boy was carried off from New Orleans by the Henry Clay commanded by the defendant.
> 4th That from the above, and other particulars made out by the evidence the Court is satisfied that the Pltf has fully made out his case, and established the claim presented by his petition
>
> It is therefore ordered, adjudged and decreed that Judgment be entered in favor of the Pltf against the defendant for Sixteen hundred Dollars and the cost of suit, with priviledges on the steamboat Henry Clay provisionally seized in this case.

Statement of George Strawbridge, attorney for the plaintiff, in the supreme court case *Slatter v. Holton* 19 LA 39:

This suit brought to recover the price of a slave carried out of the state by pltfs turns on matters of fact & these the Judge of the Parish court decided to have been proved as charged in petition.

I confess there was a time when the strong negative proof of the mate staggered my beliefs. The diligence of the pltfs however has supplied testimony which destroys his statement.

The boy Shadrach disappeared from his master about the 10 Jany. The def shows the Henry Clay s[team]b[oat] left here the 9th or 10th. About the middle of the month she arrived at Cumberland bar where she was stopped. While lying there a s[team]boat called the Wave passing from the Cumberland bound up the Ohio came along side & took off the passengers of the Henry Clay, amongst whom was undoubtedly the boy Shadrach passing then by the name of Jim Thornton. He was waiting on table. He assisted in passing the baggage from the Henry Clay to the Wave & he was put on board the latter as one of the servants of the H. Clay. On the same day some distance further up the Ohio, they fell in with the steamb[oat]. Tuscarora from whom they took some other passengers & amongst the number a Mr. Peterson who strangely enough happened to be the man who bought the boy for Slatter who saw him shipped for New Orleans & who recognized him at once as Slatter's property. The captain of the Wave however relying more on the defs statement refused to have him arrested & he escaped. I hope these facts to be indubitably proved.—& in reply there is an absence of any proof of consent by his owner, or of any person thus required before taking a coloured person out of the state. see 1 M Dig 676 7 & 8 &ct.

The act of 1835/152 gives the owner in such case a recourse against the master personally & also a lien & privilege on the boat which has been sequestered & bonded. I pray the court to affirm the Judgment of the Parish Court with 10 per Cent damages for a frivolous appeal.

Statement of Richard H. Chinn, attorney for the defendant in the supreme court case:

This suit is brought to recover the value of a slave alleged to belong to the plaintiff and to have been carried out of the State of Louisiana by the defendant. The cause was submitted by the Parish Court and a Judgment was rendered in favor of the plaintiff for 1600 [*sic*] & costs.

It would tax credulity to aver, but it is nevertheless true and was strangely overlooked by the court.

1st There is not a particle of testimony in the cause going to show that either Armstrong or Slatter ever owned any slave whatever.
2nd There is not a particle of testimony in the cause that the man Shadrach complained of was ever at any time within the limits of the State of Louisiana, and without the establishment of right to the slave in the plaintiff and the abuse of that right by the defendant removing him out of the state of Louisiana there can be no recovery.

The first we hear of the slave Shadrach is from the Witness Peterson who says he saw him about the month of May 1836 in the jail of Baltimore County in the State of Maryland, and a few days afterwards he saw him at the house of H. H. Slatter the plaintiffs brother in Baltimore, he saw him frequently in his possession that in October 1836, he with others was put on board a brig at Alexandria bound for New Orleans, to be shipped to the plaintiff. The next time he is heard of was at Cumberland bar near the mouth of the Cumberland river. Whether the brig ever sailed from Alexandria, or whether the slaves was on board at the time she sailed—what was her fate—whether she ever reached her destination does not appear. If any title is shown by the proof (sufficient to maintain such an action as this) to be in any person then it is shown to be in H. H. Slatter whose rights would not be carried by the judgment in this cause. Neither of the plaintiffs appear to have ever been even possessed of the slave with or without title.

In the entire absense of any proof of right in the plaintiff,—or of possession *in Louisiana* I can scarcely deem it necessary to investigate the facts whether the defendant carried this slave out of Louisiana as charged by the plaintiffs. But it is not an arduous task to prove the defendant to be not guilty.

It is shown by the witnesses in the cause that Holton is a gentleman whose fame in his line is equal to the name which his boat bears. Indeed it may be said near to be a part of the history of the River Miss:—Clear & satisfactory witness should be had of his guilt before he should be condemned.

He proves by competent, reputable, and credible witnesses that

Shadrach or Jim Thornton was not upon the Henry Clay during her voyage from New Orleans to Louisville.

If it can be proved that one was not on board of a boat it is so proved in this case.

The steamboats Daniel Webster, Rocky Mountain, & Mississippi left N. O. about the same time and all reached Cumberland bar about the same time—where many other boats were lying—free intercourse existing among them for many days and the Wave came along side of Henry Clay and the plaintiffs witnesses say that the negro Shadrach or Jim Thornton got on board the Wave from the Clay and the Captain of the Wave who was responsible for not arresting the negro when informed that he was a runaway endeavors to acquit himself by stating that Holton had placed the negro under his charge. In this he was mistaken. The negro may have been on the Clay, he may have waited upon the passengers with Baggage &c. But it must have been without the knowledge of Holton or they were mistaken from the resemblance to another who was on the Clay.

If the negro was in N. O. may he not have ascended the river on some boat other than the Clay. A fair interpretation of the testimony would authorize that conclusion. If it were a case of doubt Holton should have been acquitted. $1600 for a runaway negro the inmate of Baltimore prison for crime or otherwise would seem to be an exhorbitant estimate. And there is no proof to authorize that. Altho it is admitted on the trial that Slatter had refunded that sum to Armstrong, but that was not evidence of value.

Judgment in *Slatter v. Holton*, Supreme Court of Louisiana 19 LA 39, issued June 1841 by Judge Alonzo Morphy:

> Plaintiff seeks to recover the value of a slave named Shadrack who, he alleges, was carried out of the State without his knowledge and consent on board of the steamboat Henry Clay whereof the defendant was master on or about the 10th of January 1837. The answer denies the facts set forth in the petition and sets up a reconventional demand of $2000 damages for the unlawful and unjust detention of the boat in this suit; and for the expenses and trouble imposed on defendant in causing him

to be released from former proceedings instituted by plaintiff against him but afterwards discontinued. There was a Judgment below in favor of Plaintiff from which defendant prosecutes the present appeal.

This case presents no question of law, and the matters of fact which it involves have been determined in favor of Plaintiff. An attentive examination of the evidence does not enable us to say that there is error in the Judgment complained of. However strong may appear the negative proof resulting from the declaration of several witnesses that they did not see the plaintiff's boy on board of the Henry Clay during her voyage from New Orleans to Louisville, it cannot destroy the positive testimony in the record showing that during the trip the boy was acting on board as one of the servants of the boat under the name of Jim Thornton. This testimony shows that the Henry Clay left New Orleans on or about the 10th of January 1837 for Louisville; that while she was lying below the Cumberland bar where she was stopped by the low stage of the waters, a steamboat called the *Wave,* which was passing from the river Cumberland into the Ohio, came alongside of the Henry Clay to take off her passengers, that Plaintiff's boy was seen waiting at the supper table in the cabin of the latter boat and aided in carrying the baggage of the passengers from the Henry Clay on board of the Wave; that besides the passengers, the boy Jim Thornton together with three other servants were received on board the Wave at the instance of defendant who requested the captain of this boat to allow such of these cabin boys as might be wanted to work their passage, adding that the others would pay but expressing a wish that he should be moderate in his charges, that the boy Shadrack or Jim Thornton being remarkably active about the table was permitted to work his passage above Flint Island when he was discharged and was never afterwards heard of; that at some distance further up in the Ohio, the Wave fell in with the steamboat Tuscarora from which other passengers were taken, and among them a Mr. Peterson who instantly recognized Jim Thornton as being the boy belonging to the Plaintiff, under the name of Shadrack; being perfectly satisfied of the identity of the slave, this witness urged the captain of the Wave to arrest him as a runaway, but the latter declined to do it, saying that the boy had been put on board of his boat by defendant who would not have done it without authority, and that moreover defendant was responsible for the boy in case he should be a slave; but it is said that there is not a particle of testimony going to show that either Slatter or Armstrong, his vendee, who brought this suit for his use, ever had any title to the slave or that the boy Shadrack was ever at any time within the limits of this State. It was admitted on the trial of the cause "*that Slatter had returned to Armstrong the purchase money ($1600) of the slave mentioned in the plaintiff's petition.*" With such an admission, the Plaintiff's counsel did not perhaps suppose that either the title to, or the possession of the slave would be disputed nor do these points appear to have been made below. Although no evidence was taken or particularly directed to these facts, we found in the record testimony, admitted without objection, which satisfies us of the ownership and possession of plaintiff in Louisiana. Peterson declares that he told the captain of the Wave that the boy passing by the name of Jim Thornton belonged to S. F. Slatter, of New Orleans; that he had been present when H. H. Slatter, the pltf's brother bargained for the boy Shadrick with Mr. Tate in the City of Baltimore; that he afterward saw him put on board of a brig at Alexandria (District of Columbia) to be sent to the Plaintiff at New Orleans. From the circumstances that other boats were lying near the Henry Clay at the mouth of the Cumberland River, it has been contended that Plaintiff's boy may have been taken up the river by any one of these boats & that he may have got on board of the Henry Clay at that place, as there was a free intercourse between these boats for several days. This bare possibility cannot avail the defendant, when the proof is abundant that the Defendant knew of the boy, being on his boat as a servant and recommended him to the Captain of the Wave. The good character and excellent reputation which the testimony establishes for the defendant, and which he is no doubt deserving, entirely acquits him of any improper motives; but cannot relieve him from the consequences of his neglect to comply with the formality required by our laws in relation to persons of color; 1 Bullard & Curry's Digest: 253 sec 1&2. Session acts of 1835 p 152.

It is therefore ordered that the Judgment of the Parish Court be affirmed with costs.

INDEX